Praise for *Indigenomics*

Indigenomics is the anti-thesis of Adam Smith's 1776 *The Wealth of Nations*, which has been the dominant economic theology of free-market capitalism and the codex of colonization. Carol Anne Hilton has authored one of the most important books of our economic era providing a new yet ancient Indigenous framework for building economies of well-being. *Indigenomics* represents a pragmatic framework for decision making, policy development, monetary policy, and budgeting that places collective economic well-being, relationships, and Indigenous laws at the heart of wise governance. *Indigenomics* reflects how Canada (Kanata), meaning "sacred or pure land," was intended to be prior to colonization. Like *The Wealth of Nations*, I feel that Hilton's work will shape global economics for many generations.

> — Mark Anielski, economist and author,
> *The Economics of Happiness: Building Genuine Wealth* and
> *An Economy of Well-Being: Common-sense Tools
> for Building Genuine Wealth and Happiness*

This book is well overdue. Hilton is a visionary who situates how and why Indigenous worldviews are important to enhancing the modern economy. *Indigenomics* provides an anti-colonial lens to reframe narratives about Indi genous entrepreneurship, business leadership, health, and well-being.

> — Dr. Jacqueline Quinless, Adjunct Professor of Sociology,
> University of Victoria

Indigenomics is the concept the world has been waiting for. As the failure of old fashioned linear economic models becomes increasingly evident, Carol Anne Hilton showcases regenerative models based on Indigenous wisdom, both social and spiritual—the "economy of consciousness"—that represent pathways of possibility that are essential if humanity is to survive.

> — Amanda Ellis, Director, Global Partnerships, Julie Ann Wrigley
> Global Futures Laboratory, Arizona State University

A deep bow for Carol Anne Hilton and all the other Indigenous angels of our time! What an inspiring source of wisdom for how to be in the world in the fullness of our humanity. What a powerful guide to building an inclusive economy and serving a new balance between the souls of all living creatures, economics, and nature.

> — Ivo Valkenburg, co-founder New Financial Activators

Carol Anne Hilton's writing tells an intergenerational narrative, from an Indigenous economy, to the rise of Wiindigo Economics, and to the resurgence of Indigenous. Her analysis illustrating the foundational differences between Industrial and Indigenous economics is insightful and clear, allowing a reader to contemplate what are more than surface differences. Hilton's work reaffirms the significance of relationship economics, AKA to be just and fair to all the relatives, and the centrality of Indigenous thinking to the next economy, the one we must restore and create—the green path—as opposed to the scorched path. Her words clearly illustrate that Indigenomics is the path for the future. As we move through the portal of this time, knowing that pandemics change our world, let's walk through to a path of restorative economics, founded on land, spirit, and the reality of Mother Earth's wealth, which is our responsibility to acknowledge and respect. Her book is essential core material for the next class of economists. The time of Keynesian economic analysis has passed, along with the empire. The time of cooperation is here.

— Winona LaDuke, executive director, Honor the Earth

Immense gratitude for *Indigenomics*. With our world in crisis, Carol Anne Hilton shows us how to view economic and social values through an Indigenous lens. For thousands of years First Nations people have held the knowledge of the ancestors and the great laws of nature, which govern all life. With this deep understanding and masterful rigor, Carol Anne takes us step by step across a bridge to the future, where economics, productivity, and prosperity are guided by the innate and universal values of our humanity, which is one with all creation.

— Tracey Anne Cooper, creator and producer,
Beyond Crisis Webinar Series

In the tradition of an "economic philosopher" Ms. Hilton has read the times in which we live in and is reframing the dialogue on nation building with Indigenous Peoples' place at the economic table—advancing Indigenous worldviews, human values, and relationships as new constructs for change. Now it is our collective responsibility to advance meaningful employment and economic inclusion strategies, and outcomes.

— Kelly J Lendsay, President and CEO, Indigenous Works

INDIGENOMICS

INDIGENOMICS

TAKING A SEAT AT THE ECONOMIC TABLE

CAROL ANNE HILTON, MBA

new society
PUBLISHERS

Cover design by Diane McIntosh.
Cover image: © iStock.

Printed in Canada. Third printing, January 2022.

Inquiries regarding requests to reprint all or part of *Indigenomics* should be
addressed to New Society Publishers at the address below.
To order directly from the publishers, please call toll-free (North America) 1-800-
567-6772, or order online at www.newsociety.com

Any other inquiries can be directed by mail to:

New Society Publishers
P.O. Box 189, Gabriola Island, BC V0R 1X0, Canada
(250) 247-9737

LIBRARY AND ARCHIVES CANADA CATALOGUING IN PUBLICATION

Title: Indigenomics : taking a seat at the economic table / Carol Anne Hilton, MBA.

Names: Hilton, Carol Anne, 1975– author.

Description: Includes bibliographical references and index.

Identifiers: Canadiana (print) 20200398083 | Canadiana (ebook) 20200399098 |
ISBN 9780865719408 (softcover) | ISBN 9781550927337 (PDF) |
ISBN 9781771423298 (EPUB)

Subjects: LCSH: Indigenous peoples—Canada—Economic conditions. |
CSH: Indigenous business enterprises—Canada. |
CSH: Indigenous businesspeople—Canada.

Classification: LCC E98.B87 H55 2021 | DDC 338.7089/97071—dc23

Funded by the Government of Canada   Financé par le gouvernement du Canada

New Society Publishers' mission is to publish books that contribute
in fundamental ways to building an ecologically sustainable
and just society, and to do so with the least possible impact on
the environment, in a manner that models this vision.

new society
PUBLISHERS

Certified (B) Corporation

FSC
www.fsc.org

MIX
Paper from
responsible sources
FSC® C016245

Contents

Acknowledgments

I bring to this space special acknowledgments and gratitude. For my daughter, Cecelia Ambrose, the light of my life, thank you for helping me to change the story. We did it together. For my late mother, you are everything. For my Grams, Dolores Bayne, thank you for always telling the stories of the old ways. They help me to remember. Thank you to my Uncle Joe Tom; thank you for your wisdom, teachings, and the beautiful skill of always focusing on the human and spiritual side. This travels with me wherever I go in this world. To my mentor and friend, the late Richard Wagamese, for helping me to understand my own ability to create, for teaching me how to "stay in the zone," to release the doubt, and to stay curious. God speed.

Thank you to Don Richardson of Shared Value Solutions, for answering the call and helping to validate Indigenomics on social media as a space to play in and invite into a new narrative. Thank you to Carmen Thompson for all that you do and for who you are! Thank you to the late Ainjil Hunt for always expecting more from me. And to Nicole Chaland for the leadership, and the foresight in making space for Indigenomics within Simon Fraser University and within local community economic development. Your leadership is exceptional.

Thank you to Bill Gallagher, JP Gladu, Dara Kelly, Shannin Metatawabin, and Clint Davis for your insight into Indigenomics—we truly are experiencing an Indigenous global power shift. Thank you for your leadership in it. To each one of you, I hold up my hands to you in the highest respect and gratitude.

And a special thank you to the Banff Centre for offering a Fleck Fellowship to write *Indigenomics* in a beautiful studio in the mountains. Thank you for an experience that was so much more: for a space where I dared, where I grew, and where I became alongside *Indigenomics: Taking A Seat at the Economic Table*. And lastly, to the East West Center in Honolulu at the University of Hawaii for offering a space filled with Aloha to continue writing *Indigenomics*.

Forever grateful and inspired.

Kleco, Kleco—with gratitude and respect
Carol Anne Hilton, W'aa?katuush

Foreword

I am not sure Canadians are ready for the wisdom and insights of Carol Anne Hilton. But they had best adjust. She has emerged as one of the most articulate and creative commentators on Indigenous business and economic development in Canada and is widely respected for her forward-thinking analysis on the role of Indigenous Peoples in the Canadian economy.

This country marginalized and isolated First Nations for generations. Carol Anne reminds us that Indigenous Peoples have long commercial histories, producing impressive surpluses, trading with other Indigenous nations, and quickly coming to terms with the arrival of Europeans and the advent of the commercial fur trade. Successive new economies—fishing, forestry, mining, agriculture, and industry—initially made space for Indigenous folks but over time pushed them aside for immigrant labor. But the core lessons of commerce and hard work were not forgotten, even when the advance of the Canadian welfare state sucked the vitality out of Indigenous communities.

Indigenomics is a convincing and exceptionally promising book. Carol Anne rejects the negativism that surrounds so much commentary on Indigenous economic development. She does so from a position of deep understanding of Indigenous cultures. She understands that poverty, racism, and discrimination are big parts of contemporary realities. She also understands the skills, determination, entrepreneurial spirit, and cultural strengths that underlie Indigenous commitment to economic development.

Carol Anne Hilton's work deviates from standard commentaries on Indigenous business in two important ways. First, she knows that Indigenous engagement is based on cultural and social values and that Indigenous worldview concepts and practice shape their business activity. Carol Anne asserts Indigenous business is not "regular" business done on Indigenous land. She understands that Indigenous Peoples are engaged in business so that they can break away from dependency on government and so they can revitalize their languages and cultures. Profit and good business practices are priorities, but the primary goal is to strengthen Indigenous Peoples.

Secondly, Carol Anne Hilton has a vision of a remarkably different future for this country. She recognizes the growing legal and political authority of Indigenous Peoples, appreciates the intensification of Indigenous business activities, and sees these as promising developments in Canadian economic history. She is convinced that Indigenous economic growth will continue to outstrip the Canadian average, that engagement with the resource sector will grow, and that Indigenous communities and their development corporations will convert treaty settlements and court rulings into valuable investments. Where almost all Canadian commentators are obsessed with Indigenous poverty, Carol Anne Hilton sees entrepreneurial success, Indigenous innovation, resilience, and community determination. She sees Indigenous Peoples and governments having to manage prosperity, not be swamped by poverty.

Indigenomics provides a portrait of the country's economic future and an Indigenous revitalization that Canadians need to embrace. Carol Anne offers a challenging portrait that rises above the study of business as an assessment of profit, loss, and return on investment. She knows that Indigenous business is culturally unique and brings a new long-term and community-based approach to investment and commercial engagement. Most importantly, she understands that Indigenous economies are key parts of Canada's economic present and future.

More than anything, Carol Anne Hilton provides an introduction to a revolution in progress. She describes the strength, commitment, and passion that is producing widespread Indigenous commercial success and that is rewriting the rules of Canadian business. Her work deserves careful attention as one of the most important books ever written in the integration of Indigenous culture and contemporary business.

—KEN COATES, Canada Research Chair in Regional Innovation,
Johnson-Shoyama Graduate School of Public Policy,
University of Saskatchewan

Introduction

As I am writing this on the beautiful Stoney Nakoda territory in Banff, Alberta, the sun is hitting the majestic mountains around me. If you listen carefully, you can hear the ancient ones' songs echoing off the mountains, reminders of the ceremonies of here, steeped in the ancient teachings of existence and reality. Reaching deep into this existence, I acknowledge the ancestors of this place, the original songs of this place, the dances, the traditional names of here, the language of here, the teachings of here, all creating the energy field of this place translated to mean Sacred Buffalo Guardian Mountain.

This book sets out to examine the significance of the Indigenous presence in today's modern economy and within the emerging economy here in Canada and beyond. This book is a contribution to a new world of thinking—where economics, productivity, development, progress, and prosperity are aligned with human values from an Indigenous perspective.

In authoring this book, it is important to locate my sphere of influence as an Indigenous person being deeply impacted through the establishment of Canada and through the development of the mainstream economy of today. I am most influenced by being a Hesquiaht woman. I am of Nuu chah nulth descent from the west coast of Vancouver Island—a name that describes the location and identity meaning "all along the mountains" and serves to center me in this world. They call me W'aa?katuush, which refers to Big Sister, a name that means I come from a line of the oldest women. I am from the house of Mam'aayutch, a Chiefs' house, that means "on the edge." My roots stretch from Ahousaht, Ehattesaht, and as far as the Makah people in Washington State. I am the first generation out of residential school system. I am the fifth generation since the existence of the Indian Act. I come from over 10,000 years of the potlatch tradition of giving and demonstration of wealth, connection, and relationship. My parents went to residential school, my grandparents went to residential school. Being the first generation out of residential school, I am deeply connected to focusing on building a collective reality that centers Indigenous Peoples in social and cultural well-being and economic empowerment today.

It is time. It is time to increase the presence, visibility, and role of the emerging modern Indigenous economy. It is time to bring to light and realize the increasing role and responsibility of Indigenous Peoples both within Canada and globally. This is the highest intention of Indigenomics.

As the founder of the Indigenomics Institute, my work specifically brings focus and attention to the economic empowerment of Indigenous Nations to design our own future as Indigenous Peoples. The Indigenomics Institute focuses on modern, constructive, generative economic design to fully realize the growing potential of the emerging Indigenous economy today and into the future.

This book is centered within the United Nations Declaration on the Rights of Indigenous Peoples (UNDRIP), which is an international human rights instrument adopted by the United Nations General Assembly. UNDRIP emerged from over 20 years of negotiations by Indigenous Peoples worldwide. The Declaration establishes the minimum standard for the treatment of Indigenous Peoples. The rights outlined within the Declaration establishes the minimum standards for the continued survival, dignity, and well-being of the Indigenous Peoples of the world. The articles serve to affirm the distinction of Indigenous rights from human rights and describes Indigenous Peoples having the right to self-determination and, by virtue of this right, to freely determine political status and pursue economic, social, and cultural development. The Declaration is an international call for a new model of development; one that advances Indigenous self-determination and the right to an economy. Indigenomics connects to the UNDRIP framework that calls for the self-determination of our continued reality and rights as Indigenous Peoples globally both now and into the future.

Indigenomics serves as a tool to facilitate increased understanding of an Indigenous worldview of economy and works to facilitate the creation of space for a collective response based on economic inclusion within the emerging modern Indigenous economy using Canada as a context.

Indigenomics directs our attention to the power center of the evolving Indigenous economic reality today that ties the future of Canada to the economic success of Indigenous Peoples. It brings into focus the historical context of Indigenous economic distortion, the emerging power shift, and the rise of Indigenous economic empowerment. As a platform for modern Indigenous economic design, Indigenomics brings to the forefront an Indigenous economic development model that moves away from a narrative of "happened to us" toward a new "designed by us" approach. It acknowledges the unfolding story shaping Canada through the law courts that is testing the very foundation of the Crown relationship with Indigenous Peoples and the historical formation of Canada itself. It brings focus to the media narrative regarding Indigenous Peoples that feeds the collective national and global consciousness. It highlights the thinking behind the archaic response to now and the invitation to a new evolved response based on recognition. Indigenomics facilitates a new narrative: Indigenous Peoples are economic powerhouses.

Indigenomics is a platform to facilitate leadership of the economic convergence upon the emerging economy of now. It describes the unfolding power play is expressed within the legal system and the establishment of the new emerging economic space of Indigenous Peoples. This is the global power shift—the convergence of human values and the economic system. It's time to take our place at the economic table.

Indigenomics is a platform to design economic empowerment, inclusion, and economic reconciliation. Economic reconciliation is the space between the lived realities of Indigenous Peoples, the need to build understanding of the importance of the Indigenous relationship, and the requirement for progressive actions for economic inclusion. It is through economic reconciliation that Indigenous Peoples are creating a seat at the modern economic table.

This book sets out to address the uncomfortable space. This uncomfortable space is the emergence of Indigenous recognition in the story of Canada's formation, the evolution of rights and title, and the new requirement for making space for Indigenous Peoples at the economic table. This is the foundation of economic reconciliation.

The well-known concept of the *seventh generation* is founded in Iroquois philosophy that outlines the need to ensure that the decisions we make today result in a sustainable world seven generations into the future. Indigenomics is the seventh-generation economy. It is the economy behind the economy. This is the relational economy. This is economic future pacing.

Indigenomic's future paces and facilitates the insertion of the dual concepts that there is an alternative Indigenous reality at play within our experience of the modern economy as well as within the development of the Indigenous economy. To future pace is to insert, imagine, and design the future reality of Indigenous economy. Future pacing establishes the scenarios or the pathways of possibility. Indigenomics is both the light on the pathway and the focus on the leadership and tools for modern Indigenous economic design.

This book is set against the backdrop of the Canadian media narrative; it points to the language structures of the evolving Indigenous economic relationship in this country as told within the influence of media. This book draws heavily on the current media narrative to respond to the pervading myths of this country in regard to Indigenous Peoples who are too often perceived as a burden on the fiscal system of this country. This book retains a Canadian focus and at times draws on parallel international Indigenous experience and insight.

In authoring this book, I interchange the terms Indigenous, First Nation, and Aboriginal. I use "Indigenous" most frequently as it is politically neutral, inclusive, and most current and consistent with government language usage. Some quote sources utilize the terms "First Nation" or "Aboriginal." The term "Indigenous" as used here is intended to be inclusive of Métis peoples and Inuit as distinct cultural groups.

Indigenomics works to escape the boundaries of methodology and instead follows the pathway of an Indigenous worldview as expressed through economy and the lived realities of Indigenous Peoples today. Indigenomics is not pedagogy, it is not epistemology, scientific theory, or philosophy. Indigenomics is grounded in Indigenous worldview, focusing on the values and belief systems that have allowed a foundation for Indigenous success through the continuation as people for thousands of years. At the heart of Indigenomics is the creation of space for Indigenous economic modernity. It outlines the foundation of a distinct Indigenous worldview that is embedded in both physical and spiritual relativity.

Moving away from the standard format of academic-focused referencing of previous external work or thought, this book instead draws from living examples of current leadership in relation to the growth of the Indigenous economy. This book calls upon the leadership and the insight of key business leadership, both Indigenous and non-Indigenous, who are bringing awareness to the growing Indigenous economy here in Canada. I interviewed the following six key business leaders, all exceptional in their field. Each leader is a living example of Indigenous business thought leadership, and each is actively participating in the increased visibility and growth of the Indigenous economy today.

Bill Gallagher, author of *Resource Rulers* and *Resource Reckoning*, is a lawyer and strategist in the area of Indigenous, government, and corporate relations and is a leading authority on the rise of native empowerment in the Canadian resources sector. *Resource Rulers* tracks the rise of native empowerment and the remarkable legal winning streak in the Canadian resource sector. Gallagher's work is instrumental in building understanding of the growth Indigenous legal and economic empowerment.

Don Richardson is a partner in Shared Value Solutions. Don brings over 25 years of experience as a skilled facilitator supporting project implementation, impact assessments, and building agreements between energy, infrastructure, and resource management project proponents; community/nongovernmental organizations; government agencies; and rural/Indigenous communities. Richardson works to foster constructive engagement to create *shared value* between communities and infrastructure proponents. He currently manages stakeholder and government relations on several large-scale environmental and infrastructure development projects.

Dara Kelly is an assistant professor at the Beedie School of Business at Simon Fraser University, teaching in the Executive Master of Business Administration program in Indigenous Business and Leadership. In 2017, she received her PhD in commerce from the

University of Auckland Business School in Aotearoa, New Zealand. Kelly's doctoral thesis, "Feed the People and You Will Never Go Hungry: Illuminating Coast Salish Economy of Affection," focuses on Indigenous knowledge systems as a way to inform approaches for economic development grounded in Indigenous notions of freedom, wealth, and interconnectedness. Kelly is from the Leq'á:mel First Nation of the Coast Salish people and is an advisor to the Indigenomics Institute.

JP Gladu, past president and CEO of the Canadian Council for Aboriginal Business, is Anishinaabe from Thunder Bay and is a member of Bingwi Neyaashi Anishinaabek Nation located on the eastern shores of Lake Nipigon, Ontario. Gladu completed a forestry technician diploma in 1993, obtained an undergraduate degree in forestry from Northern Arizona University in 2000, and holds an Executive MBA from Queen's University. Gladu has over two decades of experience in the natural resource sector. His career path includes work with Indigenous communities and organizations, environmental nongovernment organizations, industry, and governments from across Canada and internationally. At the Canadian Council for Aboriginal Business, Gladu led the mandate of working to grow and improve opportunities for Aboriginal businesses across Canada.

Shannin Metatawabin, the CEO of the National Aboriginal Capital Corporations Association, is Cree/Inninow from Fort Albany First Nation of the Mushkegowuk Nation. He holds a Bachelor of Arts degree in political science from Carleton University and an Aboriginal Economic Development certificate from the University of Waterloo. Metatawabin has over 15 years of industry and economic development experience, primarily focused on Aboriginal development. He is an entrepreneur, commercial lender, business and community developer, and management consultant with proficiency in remedial management, optimization, and business planning.

Clint Davis, an Inuk from Labrador, is the Partner and Managing Director of Acasta Capital Indigenous, an Indigenous-owned subsidiary company of Acasta Capital that works with Indigenous governments and economic development corporations to achieve growth and value creation by assisting in the maximization of their inherent competitive advantage. Prior to the creation of this company, Davis served as the Vice President of Indigenous Banking at TD. Davis is the Chair of the Board of Directors for the Nunatsiavut Group of Companies, which is the economic arm of Nunatsiavut Government, a self-governing entity that represents the political, social, and economic interests of the Inuit of Labrador. Under Davis's leadership, the Nunatsiavut Group of Companies has grown to owning and partnering in fourteen operating companies with general revenue of over $35 million annually. Clint is an advisor to the Indigenomics Institute.

Each of these leaders brings a key voice and insight into the developing Indigenous economy, and all are actively contributing to its development, visibility, and growth in their own way.

The Indigenomics Manifestation

Indigenomics is a new word. It is intended to serve as a tool to insert into national and global consciousness the importance of building understanding of the Indigenous economic and legal relationship and its role within the modern economy today. Indigenomics welcomes you to an Indigenous worldview. It is a place to wonder, a means to converge on the ancient and the modern and on the potential of an Indigenous economy today. Indigenomics is bringing focus to the pathway forward. It is about building on the previous work of the ones who came before us. It is a light on the pathway that establishes what it can mean to have a "right to an economy" as confirmed within the United Nations Declaration on the Rights of Indigenous Peoples. Indigenomics is about honoring the powerful thinking of Indigenous wisdom and facilitating that into economic outcomes today.

Indigenomics calls into visibility the relevance of an Indigenous worldview in today's modern economy. It is the conscious claim to and the creation of space for the advancement of today's emerging Indigenous economy. Indigenomics is a statement of claim of Indigenous space in modern existence. It is a callout or invitation into an Indigenous worldview and its application into the concept and experience of "development" and "progress."

Indigenomics is the economy behind the economy—the values that spin the relationship between nature and human kind—the life force of intention. Indigenomics is the seventh-generation economy.

It is the spiritual reality behind the modern economy. It is the spiritual dimension that connects our humanity and worldview as Indigenous Peoples across time.

Indigenomics is about honoring the powerful thinking of Indigenous wisdom of economy, relationships, and human values. Indigenomics works to bring to the forefront human values and to increase Indigenous visibility and insight into modern Indigenous economic presence. It is bringing into visibility the practice of economic inclusion, and the building of a modern response to now, a response built from the too common rhetoric "We were never taught this in school!" Indigenomics converges upon today's modern economic context—the evolving, shifting, growing influence of Indigenous Peoples across time and inviting the leadership in shaping the new narrative—we are a powerful people.

Indigenomics invites dialogue and thought-provoking insight into the possibility of the Indigenous economic relationship both in Canada and beyond. The time is now. The opportunity is here to influence and participate in the emerging reality and contrast of the new economy.

Indigenomics is Indigenous intelligence in motion. It is the practice of bringing an Indigenous perspective into economic and social development. It works to connect community economic development practices and principles for building an inclusive local economy. Indigenomics is the slow realization of the application of Indigenous values into local economy. It is an inception into economic theory that allows for another worldview.

Indigenomics is an Indigenous approach to the global economic and financial crisis. It questions the reality of current economic thinking while examining the pathway of humanity to bring into focus where we have collectively come from and where we are going. It examines the characteristics of accountability, reciprocity, and responsibility as expressed as fundamental to the Indigenous economy.

Indigenomics is the modern expression of Indigenous existence. It is how we pay attention and create a collective response to the emerging Indigenous economy today. Indigenomics is the return to human values within our economic relationships. It is the economy of consciousness.

Indigenomics is an expression and acknowledgment of the historical and current devaluing of an Indigenous way of life and worldview. It is a way to frame the creation of value and the destruction of value from both an Indigenous and mainstream worldview. It is an expression of modern indigeneity and the evolution of our economic well-being. Indigenomics is a response to hundreds of years of colonization. It is a response to the economic degradation, distortion, and regression experienced across time by Indigenous Peoples globally through the process of decolonization.

It is the social field for economic reconciliation. It is an invitation to build a modern response to the Indigenous relationship. Indigenomics is about influence. It is a platform for the deconstruction of the experience of systemic Indigenous economic exclusion. It is an explanation of a belief of the relevance of an Indigenous worldview to the modern economy. It is a collaborative framework that calls the economic system toward Indigenous values. It is a social media platform to share Indigenous business success, excellence, and struggles.

It is a way to frame the understanding of who has been left out of the economy and who is included in the emerging economy. It is about connecting the current economy with the growing number of Indigenous businesses and entrepreneurs and recognizing the growing value of Indigenous economies through strategic focused actions and collective design. Indigenomics is a platform to facilitate the Indigenous relationship of this country to collectively re-imagine the future we want and redesign the systems to get us there.

Indigenomics is a process of claiming our Indigenous place at the economic table. Indigenomics speaks to the uncomfortable space from which the truths of the experience of Indigenous Peoples are built. It shapes the pathway forward and works to establish the requirement for inclusion, for visibility, and the collective actions for facilitating the emergence of today's Indigenous economy.

An Indigenous worldview allows us the ability to express what is most important to us as Indigenous Peoples. Indigenomics examines how we see the world in such a way that we can act to ensure the continuance of who we are as Indigenous Peoples across time.

It is time to pay attention to this evolving, emerging Indigenous economy and the quality of the Indigenous economic relationship. This emergence is happening now, and it is happening globally. This is the global power shift. It is time.

Why Indigenomics? Because the Indigenous economy is growing. Because new thinking is required today to evolve the Indigenous relationship. Because new language will get us there. Because an Indigenous worldview is required in our future, and not just the past. Because there are increasing land and resource pressures. Because Indigenous continuity to our ways of life are threatened. Because there is a convergence upon the current limitations of the state of the global economic system.

Why Indigenomics? Because we still have Canadians saying "Why don't you just get over it?" Because we are still confronting the Aboriginal Question today. Because Canada is in a treaty relationship and because we have over 150 years of broken treaties and still need a pathway for treaty implementation. Because the "right to an economy" has yet to be defined. Because 76% of Indigenous children live in poverty in some areas of Canada today. Because there are still Nations without running water in this country or access to the internet.

Why Indigenomics? Because Indigenomics is about the strength of the Indigenous relationship that is at the heart of shaping the future of our country. Because this country is in a legal and an economic relationship with Indigenous Peoples. Because the global economy is slowing. These are the truths of our time. Because it is time to build from the truth—we are a powerful people.

Through the Lens
of Worldview

Culture is the backbone of the existence of our people.
Our culture is a way of life.
—ELDER TOM CRANE BEAR, Blackfoot Nation

A worldview is described as a philosophy or a way of life as expressed through individuals and groups such as family, communities, or societies. It is a collective set of beliefs and values that make up a way of life, a way of seeing the world, and a specific way of experiencing reality. A worldview is passed on through our children, grandchildren, and across generations and works to ensure continuity through time. Indigenous Peoples hold a distinct worldview with distinct differences from a mainstream or Western worldview. The intent of this chapter is to highlight these distinctions for the purpose of framing economics from within an Indigenous worldview.

Humanity's worldview is the channel through which we interpret reality as we see it and experience it. Our worldview directly influences every aspect of our lives from what and how we think to how we act, our emotional responses, and how we form, maintain, and uphold our beliefs, values, and goals. Our worldview encompasses our assumptions about the world and how we see it, how we see ourselves and others, and how we experience reality. Our worldview includes what influences us, what motivates us, how we see the world in a particular way, what we experience as "good," what we identify as "right," and also what we see and define as "truth." Every single human being has a worldview, and each has a story about how we perceive reality. Worldview defines our cultural and personal beliefs, our assumptions, attitudes, values, and ideas that form the maps or model of our lived reality, perception, and experience of our humanity.

A worldview is the centralized system that serves to structure the perception of reality from which stems the human values system. The highly esteemed educator and author Leroy Little Bear writes extensively on Indigenous worldview. Little Bear describes values as "an abstract, generalized principle of behaviour to which the members of a group feel a strong, emotionally toned positive commitment and which provides a standard for judging specific acts and goals."[1] Values can provide the organizing principles for the integration of individual, family, and community or societies' collective goals.

An Indigenous worldview is centered within the relationship to the land. As Little Bear states in *Aboriginal Paradigms*, "Worldview is important because it is the filter system behind the beliefs, behavior, and actions of our people. It is the implied infrastructure people use for their beliefs, behavior, and relationships."[2]

An Indigenous worldview is what allows us as Indigenous Peoples to be able to express what we value most and how we experience reality through the physical and spiritual domains. An Indigenous worldview focuses on the experience of holism—an embedded understanding of the concept of the connection of the "whole" that has supported the continuity of Indigenous existence, culture, success, and survival across time. It is this continuity of thousands of years that reaffirms and upholds our modern existence, resilience, and relevance.

An Indigenous worldview helps to frame the questions: What are the teachings that have sustained us for thousands of years? How do we see the world in such a way that we can ensure the continuance of who we are as people, but that we can also look at what new thinking is required today? How do we interact with our environment today? How do we want to interact with our environment in the future? What decisions will we make today that will impact the seventh generation? The answers to these questions form insight into an Indigenous worldview and, through answering, begin to demonstrate distinct differences from a Western or mainstream worldview.

The Indigenous economy is a source for our well-being, a platform for our worldview. It acts as the center of the interconnection between social, spiritual, and our livelihood or economy. Indigenomics works to center Indigenous ways of knowing and an Indigenous worldview to support modern economic development.

A worldview, both consciously and unconsciously, serves to construct a conceptual framework that provides a way to systematically organize the beliefs and values about who we are, about the world we live in, and about our experience and perception of ourselves and of others. This process of organization shapes the very basis of our reality and lived experience. These maps or models help to explain how we view the world and gives explanation or meaning as to why we act or believe the ways that we do. Language is an invisible line to our past and is a primary tool of this transmission of worldview. A worldview brings rationality and organization and helps to form both meaning and structure in our lives.

The inherent characteristics of an Indigenous worldview can be observed and expressed both within the culture and through the relationship to land. As demonstrated in the words of Frantz Fanon in *The Wretched of the Earth*, "For a colonized people, the most essential value, the most concrete, is first and foremost the land: the land which will bring bread and, above all, dignity."[3] Bigger than the sum of its parts, the interconnection between worldview, land, values, and beliefs forms the basis of the concept and structure of Indigenous reality.

Over 150 years into the reality of what we call Canada today, the essential Indigenous relationship remains to the land. The Indigenous worldview prevails across the crisis of colonialism and exists as an alternative to a world in an economic crisis stemming from its own worldview and as a parallel reality to the global marketplace of today. As described by Little Bear, "The relationship to and use of the land manifests itself through a complex inter-relational network with all of creation—one that sees humans as simply part of creation, not above it and has balance and harmony as the goal."[4]

The work of Dara Kelly, a leading Indigenous academic who is of Coast Salish descent, is centered on understanding the underlying fundamental values that are embedded in our traditional Indigenous knowledge systems and how these can inform our world today. In my interview with her, she describes an Indigenous worldview:

There are different levels of philosophies. There are values and philosophies that are embedded into our own interpretations across our tribes and nations. There are philosophies that operate in terms of protocol that are common across our tribes, and then there are values and philosophies that are at the highest level which are unchangeable. These are the things that are universal within a Coast Salish Indigenous worldview.[5]

As further articulated by Oren Lyons, the spiritual leader from the Haudenosaunee of the Six Nations Iroquois Confederacy, who sums up an Indigenous worldview as being in sharp contrast with the modern economic paradigm in *Changing the Narrative* as follows: "You've been trying to instruct the Indians to be capitalists ever since you got here. But we don't value what you value."[6] A simple statement demonstrating a clear divergence in worldviews: "We don't value what you value."

Building from these pointed words of Lyons, it is important to identify some of the key distinctions between an Indigenous and mainstream Western or European worldview. Each has a distinct approach that centers reality and shapes experience. These differences can be seen in the expression of knowledge systems of science, law, religion/spirituality, commerce, and economy and how these knowledge systems are transmitted across time. The following demonstrates a comparison of broad features of these distinctions between a Western/mainstream worldview and an Indigenous worldview.

Each of these distinctions, while only providing the briefest of insight, identifies an expression of differences in worldview that has played out across time. As the world-renowned environmentalist and activist David Suzuki articulates:

The way we see the world shapes the way we treat it. If a mountain is a deity, not a pile of ore; if a river is one of the veins of the land, not potential irrigation water; if the forest is a sacred grove, not timber; if other species are biological kin, not resources; or if the planet is our mother, not an opportunity—then we will treat each other with greater respect. Thus, the challenge is to look at the world from a different perspective.[7]

Indigenous Worldview	Western/Mainstream Worldview
Disctinction 1: Spirituality	
Four central operating domains: physical, spiritual, mental, and emotional	Science based
Spiritually oriented experience of reality	Is based on "skeptical thinking" or critiquing
Based on belief in the natural world as a knowledge system	Requires proof as a basis of belief
Economy must be spiritually based and about connection	Truth is formed through empirical evidence and methodology
Relationship is everything	Truth must establish proof and be replicable
Cosmos-centered approach shapes an expansive perspective	
Spirituality informs experience of reality	
Disctinction 2: Spirit	
One's spirit and the function of business must be directly connected	Devoid of spirit
Spirit is everywhere—everything has spirit	Evidence is found in tangible numbers and metrics
It is all spiritual	Spirit is not measurable; therefore, irrelevant to economy
Economy is spiritual: a way of being in relationship or having right relationships	
Disctinction 3: Nature of Reality	
Truth is multidimensional	Only one truth based on science of empirical evidence
There can be more than one reality— only limited by our internal state to understand multiple realities or dimensions	Can be seen in legal system
Reality is a unified force	Singular or compartmentalized knowledge systems

Indigenous Worldview	Western/Mainstream Worldview
Disctinction 4: Connectivity	
Community operates within a state of relatedness of connectedness	Compartmentalized society
"All my relations" is expansive connectivity of the whole	Disconnected, silos, isolation
Is inclusive, expansive, universal	Based on hierarchy and order
Connected to the cosmos	
Systems reinforce connectedness, and identity stems from connectedness	
Disctinction 5: Concept of Responsibility/Liability/Risk	
Land is sacred, and the inherent role of stewardship is directly connected to identity	The land and resources should be available for "development" and extraction
Risk is managed through responsibility	Value is not created until it reaches the "marketplace"
Liability is found in carelessness and lack of connectivity or relationship	Risk/liability is to be managed
Responsibility is passed across generations and directly connected to governance and personal self-management	Risk/liability can be paid for/bought
Responsibility is between worlds: physical and spiritual realities. The spiritual domain must be taken into account in decision-making	Risk is externalized to others (governance regulations or legal system)
Risk takes the form of "taking caring"—care for our ancestors/offsprings' needs, and they will care for our needs	Responsibility is to the "owners" or "shareholders"
The marketplace is the cosmos; risk can be found in lack of care of relationships	
Seen within concepts of justice and law	

Indigenous Worldview	Western/Mainstream Worldview
Disctinction 6: Concept of Time	
Time is cyclical	Time has linear structure
Non-linear	Framework of time reinforces industrial structure of productivity
Can be multidimensional	Growth and time are connected
Generational	Time is connected to quarterly/ annual profit-based performance (time is money)
Decision-making related to natural cycles	
Future paced	
Disctinction 7: Concept of Wealth	
Wealth is based on accumulation and distribution that supports good of community	Amassing wealth is for individual gain
Wealth is connected to the quality of relationships	Wealth represents status. Wealth is disconnected from community
Wealth can be symbolic and will not always take "monetary" form	Wealth needs to be structured, measured and is intended to multiply
Status is earned by the ability to "give"	Wealth accumulation is a measure of success
Wealth is framed in the system of distribution and relationship	Competitive in nature
Generosity forms basis for success	
Wealth is connected to family (having many grandchildren is an expression of wealth)	
Collaborative in nature	

Indigenous Worldview	Western/Mainstream Worldview
Disctinction 8: Concept of Ownership	
Ownership can be collective	Individual, rights based
Rights extends across generations and is connected to stewardship	Fee simple
Rights means responsibility not ownership	Linear
Ownership is not singular; everyone has a vested interest	Contract based
Connected to all living things	Polorized concept of ownership
	Based on "authority"
	Responsibility is externalized within law
Disctinction 9: Knowledge and Power	
Knowledge is based on traditional teachings	Scientific process, replicated
Knowledge is formed and shaped from Traditional ecological knowledge systems (TEK)	Ego based
Connected to environment: environment is source of knowledge	Critical
Generational: to be transmitted across time and is a responsibility	Short-term
Distribution of power available in the cosmos, universal thinking	Humans hold distribution of power in the universe. Distribution of power concentrated on the wealthy and decision makers
Decision-making must be universal	Power originates in authority
Power originates from alignment between physical and spiritual realm	Knowledge is based in science of knowing
Knowledge is reflected in our environment and allow us to continue over time	

Indigenous Worldview	Western/Mainstream Worldview
Disctinction 10: Economy	
Spiritually based	Gold rush extraction-based mentality: get it out of ground as fast as you can
Relationship focused	Short-term thinking
Abundance stems from nature and connectivity	Growth focused
Prosperity is demonstrated in distribution	Short-term measurements
Gift giving is a demonstration of wealth and long-term value	Wealth is collected
Economy is ceremonially based	Mechanized
Is circular in nature: wealth returns and is demonstrated as an action and not a collection of wealth	Performance based
Ceremony focused	Comparative in nature
"Resources" and responsibility are intertwined	Competition is a necessity
"Resources" are our relatives	
Economy is a way to express the spiritual truths of reality	
Cooperation is essential	
Disctinction 11: Cause and Effect	
Connectivity: what you do to environment you do to yourself	To cause to grow or to diminish
Separation is a symptom	Seen as separate from the environment
Spiritually rooted	Cumulative effects are to be measured and risk mitigated

This concept of "The way we see the world shapes the way we treat it" centers an Indigenous worldview in a direct collision with the Western or mainstream worldview. At times bumping into each other, at times a full collision, the long history of power struggles shaped through a dominating Western worldview tells a story of Indigenous relations and the power structures in the development of this country. The ongoing power struggle as it plays out in the court system calls into question the validity of one worldview over another through the constant stream of Indigenous-based legal challenges within this country. It is here the emerging power shift can be observed, led by Indigenous Peoples and operating from within an Indigenous worldview. The origins of this power struggle can be found in the early language of the formation of this country.

The Indian Problem

In the early development of Canada, Duncan Campbell Scott, deputy superintendent of the Department of Indian Affairs in 1913 exclaimed:

> I want to get rid of the Indian problem. I do not think as a matter of fact, that the country ought to continuously protect a class of people who are able to stand alone. Our objective is to continue until there is not an Indian that has not been absorbed into the body politic, and there is no Indian question, and no Indian Department.[8]

These words demonstrate a clear power struggle embedded within differing worldviews that would shape the development of Canada from infancy to well beyond its first century. Through the lens of assumption viewed through another worldview, the Indians were viewed as a problem to be solved. The Indians were viewed as a problem to be solved. It is this thinking that has shaped the systemic dis-invitation of Indigenous Peoples to the economic table of this country. It is this thinking that has shaped policy, law, budgets, and regulations since the formation of this country. Indigenomics is future pacing the language construct of Indigenous economic inclusion. It is time for new thinking.

The underlying construct of the "Indian Problem" in Canada across time can be seen in questions such as "Why can't they just be like us?" or "Why don't they just get over it?" These questions are manifestations of expectation and assumptions embedded within the particular dominating worldview across time. It is this thinking that has formed and shaped the structures of this country and the very basis for a collision of distinct worldviews, and the cause of both the economic displacement and the socio-economic gap experienced by Indigenous Peoples in Canada.

Indigenous Economic Displacement and Marginalization

There is a direct causal relationship between historical economic displacement and the marginalization of Indigenous Peoples today. Economic displacement is the systemic removal of Indigenous Peoples from cultural ways and relationships to lands and resources. This can be demonstrated in the widening socio-economic gaps experienced by Indigenous Peoples and communities. This deficit narrative continuously reinforces a perception that Indigenous Peoples are falling behind. Marginalization is the over-representation of one worldview. It is from the margins that the root cause of the commonly told negative statistics of today's Indigenous Peoples' experience of colonization, poverty, and social challenges can be found. Marginalization is the systemic absence from the economic table stemming from the systemic disruption of an Indigenous worldview, sense of responsibility, and inherited rights. Indigenous Peoples are viewed through the lens of negative social statistics—such as the highest levels of suicide, education, jail, and poverty or ill health—and often viewed from these limitations. These negative statistics, often described as the "socio-economic gap," can also be described as the over-representation of one worldview. The experience of poverty in Indigenous reality is a testament of the economic displacement from lands. Furthermore, measuring the socio-economic gap also facilitates a false narrative of the fiscal burden of Indigenous Peoples.

A 2018 Auditor General report, *Socio-economic Gaps on First Nations Reserves*, by Indigenous Services Canada, succinctly focuses on the state of the marginalization of Indigenous Peoples. The report identifies the government's inability in improving the lives of Indigenous Peoples in Canada as an "incomprehensible failure" through failing to track the country's progress in closing socio-economic gaps between on-reserve First Nations and the rest of Canada. The report highlights inadequate collection of data about the well-being of First Nations living on reserve.[9]

After the report was tabled, Auditor General Michael Ferguson said, "There are too many discussions about the need to close the socio-economic gaps between Indigenous Peoples and other Canadians in this country and yet we don't see those gaps closing."[10] This is an old story still being lived out—the socio-economic gap, a story still reflecting the Indian as a problem to be solved. The social/economic gap is the effect—the cause is rooted firmly in worldview and the structures of economic displacement. It's time for a new story—of economic empowerment, inclusion, and of Indigenous Peoples taking our seats at the economic table of this country. "Closing the socio-economic gap" of Indigenous Peoples is a story that serves the invisibility of the economic distortion of the Indigenous economic and legal relationship across time. It is time for modern, constructive, generative, Indigenous economic design.

Indigenous Worldview and Responsibility

Across time, across socio-economic gaps, across margins, across high rates of poverty, across systemic economic exclusion and yet firmly embedded in an Indigenous worldview is a deeply engrained sense of responsibility. Within an Indigenous worldview, the sense of identity and responsibility are deeply intertwined. The formation of expectations and assumptions stemming from differing worldviews is the starting point for conflict. Conflict has its origin in worldview, stemming from difference in values, beliefs, assumptions, and expectations. Responsibility is the inherent life force of an Indigenous worldview.

It is this divergence in worldviews around responsibility that has played out in the unfoldment of Indigenous legal and economic conflict as further demonstrated in the following chapters. It is this distinction from the dominant worldview that has systematically allowed Indigenous Peoples to be uninvited to the economic table of this country from its establishment. It is this collision of worldviews that sets the stage for beginning to understand Indigenous conflict.

It is from this divergence that the emerging rise of Indigenous economic empowerment can begin to be seen. It is by design that Indigenous Peoples have begun to establish space at the economic table of this country.

The following examples serve to further demonstrate this distinction in worldviews as a way to draw comparisons between Western mainstream and Indigenous worldview's expression of responsibility and risk.

Clayoquot Sound: The Understanding of Liability

The first example draws from direct experience and demonstrates the culturally embedded sense of Indigenous "responsibility." I worked on a local Clayoquot Sound Climate Change Adaption project near Tofino on Vancouver Island, B.C., a number of years back. Our team worked with our Elders and scientists to learn about how the local First Nations peoples experienced climate change in our own territories over time. As a project team, we looked at how certain factors were culturally remembered, such as storm intensity, salmon levels, and water sources, and compared that to how it is done now through scientific measurements and how these have changed over time. The project identified localized decision-making tools and adaptive responses to the changing climate situation to develop adaptive strategies. In the big picture, *we* needed to confirm factors such as access to clean water was ensured over time, that water sources were protected. The project worked to incorporate an Indigenous worldview into resource management and localized decision-making. As an Indigenous-led project, we posited, "We are responsible for this place. We must make decisions for future generations."

Later, I joined a climate change task force for a local municipality that was a similar project but in a different area. Here, the first order of business was to hire a risk management lawyer. The lawyer presented an analysis report that outlined the mitigation of "risk" by identifying who was not responsible, who didn't have to pay, where liability occurred, and how to minimize it. This was the opposite of localized responsible decision-making. That was culture shock for me of comparing a mainstream concept of risk and responsibility and Indigenous concepts of managing both risk and responsibility over time.

Mount Polley Mining Disaster:
The Desecration of Responsibility

A second example contrasting responsibility and risk from an Indigenous worldview is the 2014 Mount Polley mine in central B.C., the biggest environmental disaster in the province's history. When the tailing pond broke, 24 million cubic meters of mine waste and water flowed into the nearby water systems. The stories in the media demonstrated the playbook for lack of responsibility that still continues today. With the appropriate amount of finger-pointing, the government did not want to take responsibility, the engineers did not want to take responsibility, nor the company itself. An independent panel of experts concluded the cause was an inadequately designed dam that didn't account for drainage and erosion failures beneath the pond. One of the panel's geotechnical engineers described the location and design of the pond as having a loaded gun and pulling the trigger.

In response to this disaster and the ensuing lack of action, the local Indigenous people took responsibility. The First Nation brought their leadership voice to the disaster, as a *Global News* headline stated, "Neskonlith Indian Band Issues Eviction Notice to Imperial Metals." This disaster triggered a return to Indigenous responsibility. The Nation collectively voiced, "We are responsible for this area." The response was to facilitate a reclaiming and return to Indigenous responsibility and decision-making. They voiced, "As the caretakers of our land and waters, we have an obligation to protect our land for our future generations. Neskonlith Indian Band cannot permit any mining development especially in these Sacred Headwaters that will contaminate the water or destroy our salmon habitat."[11]

The article highlights the collective failure to properly protect Secwepemc land and waters. This example demonstrates the stark contrast in approach stemming from differing worldviews. The local Indigenous people posited "We are responsible" versus the response to the disaster that was based on the narrative of "Who is to blame, who doesn't have to pay, and who is not responsible" approach. These differences in worldview play out very different pathways and form very different perceptions of risk as well as conflict. This divergence in worldview around risk and responsibility plays out in the media narrative, shaping perception, opinion, and awareness.

"We have seen the desecration of responsibility in our lifetime," expressed an Elder from the local Nation. This statement indicates the Indigenous experience of the long-term systemic removal of inherent responsibility stemming from within an Indigenous worldview. Indigenous concepts and lived realities of "responsibility" have been systematically removed through the establishment of Canada's policies and regulations. It is the sense of responsibility and managing of risk that is at the very center of Indigenous existence and reality. The effects of marginalization are experienced through the continuous removal of Indigenous responsibility expressed through the stewardship of place. Indigenous Peoples have experienced the desecration of responsibility across lifetimes. Indigenomics is a return to Indigenous responsibility. The return to the Indigenous role of responsibility and stewardship is Indigenomics in motion.

Idle No More: The Igniting of a Collective Response

A third example of the contrast between an Indigenous and mainstream worldview and the concept of responsibility is the Idle No More movement of 2015 in Canada. The movement, which gained unprecedented national and global attention on Indigenous rights, was formed from the basis of a collective Indigenous worldview of taking responsibility that was led by a core of Indigenous women.

The movement was initially ignited based on the protection of water bodies in response to the Conservative government's introduction of Bill C-45, which derogated responsibility of entire water systems across Canada, 164 water bodies in total. This caused an unprecedented Indigenous uprising of gigantic proportions; a response so swift, so strong, and grounded in Indigenous values and responsibility that it was unmeasurable. The government was unable to form a quick enough response to the Indigenous movement steeped in inherent Indigenous responsibility. This is the perfect showcase demonstrating the collision with Indigenous worldview.

The movement mobilized Indigenous leadership for the protection of a healthy water supply for all, not just Indigenous Peoples. It was ignited as a movement of Indigenous voices saying "We are responsible" but expanded into an expression of injustice, marginalization, and socio-economic gaps in Indigenous communities. It was a grassroots movement of epic proportions for Indigenous sovereignty,

Indigenous rights, and respect for the numbered treaties that shaped Canada itself. The goals of the movement included addressing environmental degradation and socio-economic inequality. This movement, while complex in nature, was essentially a pushback against the government demoting responsibility of protection of water systems and a shift toward a return to Indigenous responsibility.

The continued degradation of Indigenous responsibility is experienced through the parallel process of imposed externalized government authority as well as systems of land regulation and policies for resource management. As articulated by Eriel Deranger, a member of the Athabasca Chipewyan First Nation in Alberta, "Our people and our Mother Earth can no longer afford to be economic hostages in the race to industrialize our homelands. It's time for our people to rise up and take back our role as caretakers and stewards of the land. We are economic hostages in our own homeland."[12]

No Dakota Access Pipeline (#NODAPL): Risk Is Spiritual

A fourth example demonstrating the relationship between responsibility, Indigenous worldview, and conflict stemming from differing expectations is the No Dakota Access Pipeline (NODAPL) movement in North Dakota in the winter of 2017 in the US. The concept *Mni Wiconi* in the Lakota language means "water is life" and was the foundation of the entire movement. The Dakota Access Pipeline by Keystone XL proposed to drill beneath the Missouri River upstream from the reservation, endangering the drinking water supply. The pipeline would move half a million barrels of oil a day beneath the Missouri River, the main source of drinking water for the Standing Rock Sioux people. The Lakota people accused the government of approving the pipeline construction without consulting them, a requirement under US law.

The Lakota people believe that the pipeline correlates with a terrible Black Snake that was prophesied to enter the Lakota homeland and cause destruction. The Lakota believe that the Black Snake of the prophecies will cause unbalance and desecrate the water and render it impossible for the Lakota to use that water in their ceremonies.

The response was to set up several spiritual camps that became the largest mobilization of Indigenous Peoples in US history, rallying

Carpenter, Zoë and Tracie Williams. "Since Standing Rock, 56 Bills Have Been Introduced in 30 States to Restrict Protests," February 16, 2018; thenation.com/article/photos-since-standing-rock-56-bills-have-been -introduced-in-30-states-to-restrict-protests/

around the concept of responsibility as expressed in the concept of "water is life." This was taking a stand for Indigenous responsibility for the water which was swiftly met with extreme state-led violence. More than 200 Native American tribes pledged their support to protect the water system, in the single largest coming together of Indigenous Peoples in the history of the United States. The Lakota people argued that the project would contaminate drinking water and damage sacred burial sites.

While met with extreme state-led violence, the movement itself posited through peaceful demonstration of ceremony and dance that the pipeline would endanger the drinking water for the current and future generations. The movement was so large and so violent it caught international attention, and it brought into focus Indigenous rights and the growing sense of Indigenous responsibility for the care of water globally.

Doctrine of Discovery: Naming the Economic Distortion

This final example has had hundreds of years of impact on Indigenous sense of inherent responsibility. The Doctrine of Discovery was the singular tool in the systematic removal of Indigenous responsibility and a pillar to the colonization across the Americas.

The original Papal Bull was issued in 1452. Pope Nicholas directed King Alfonso of Spain to "capture, vanquish, and subdue the Saracens, the pagans, and other enemies of Christ and to put them into perpetual slavery and to take all their possessions and property."[13] This laid the foundation of the Doctrine of Discovery. The Doctrine served as one of the first tools that systematically derogated Indigenous responsibility and worked to override and displace an Indigenous worldview. Operating from this Doctrine, in 1492, Christopher Columbus was sent out to conquer new lands, bring gold, and subjugate the heathens.

In Canada, the origins of the application of the Doctrine stemmed from England as an upholder of the Doctrine. In 1496, the Crown granted a commission to discover countries then unknown to Christian people and to take possession of these lands in the name of the King of England. It is through this Doctrine that the continent of North America was "discovered," and it is through this "discovery" that the concept of English land title can be traced even to this day. The Doctrine described the concept of *terra nullius* as lands that were inhabited by heathens, pagans, infidels, or unbaptized persons and thus to be treated as not existing or non-human and, therefore, for the lands to be inhabitable by Christian peoples. The concept of "terra nullius" has its origins in the specific worldview that lands inhabited by non-Christians were vacant or "unoccupied lands" and, therefore, open to a right of possession by Christians. The application of the Doctrine paralleled the development of the nation of Canada. This at its core is the very essence of the colonial ego.

One of the early applications of the Doctrine in America was first seen by Judge Catron (1786–1865), in the State of Tennessee, who officially identified the Doctrine as part of the law of Christendom. Specifically, he ruled "that the principle of 'discovery' gave title to assume sovereignty over, and to govern the unconverted [non-Christian] peoples of Africa, Asia, and North and South America." The Judge declared that this principle was recognized as a part of the

Law of Nations "for nearly four centuries, and that it is now so recognized by every Christian power, in its political department and its judicial."[14]

Today, the Doctrine of Discovery remains institutionalized into law and policy on national and international levels and is the foundation of the violations of Indigenous Peoples' human rights.

> The Doctrine has resulted in centuries of virtually unlimited resource extraction from the traditional territories of Indigenous peoples, the landscapes of Indigenous worldview. This, in turn, has resulted in the dispossession and impoverishment of Indigenous peoples, and the host of problems that they face today on a daily basis."[15]

A single doctrine, embedded from the tenants of a specific worldview, thousands of miles away, and hundreds of years ago systematically removed Indigenous Peoples from their own humanity, their own worldview, and made the lands "conquerable" by virtue of being "baptized" or not. This principle of "discovery" serves the ego of the descending economy that can still be felt to this day by Indigenous Peoples worldwide. This principle built by the Americas as we know it today. This is the uncomfortable space. This formed the foundation for the systemic "dis-invitation" to the economic table for Indigenous Peoples. This is the structure of colonial shenanigans that remains in place today.

Conclusion

These examples serve to demonstrate the divergence in worldviews that is the source of conflict that reveals the distinct relationship between Indigenous worldview and responsibility. The mainstream worldview sees ownership as rights to the land, whereas Indigenous Peoples see ownership as responsibility. That is a primary source of conflict stemming from distinct worldviews.

Today's modern government and regional structures and policies continue to systematically remove Indigenous Peoples from this inherent sense of responsibility that has existed across time. The Indian Act in Canada has been and continues today to be the fundamental instrument that disconnects Indigenous Peoples from this inherent sense of responsibility.

Today, the Indigenous process of economic development struggles to maintain traditional forms of responsibility and stewardship through the web of government acts, regulations, and policies within the context of nation re-building. These external structures, systems, and processes set the foundation for a strained concept of inherent Indigenous responsibility and create conflict within the context of economic development, prosperity, and progress. These structures further serve the underdevelopment of the Indian reservation and perpetuate the perception of today's "Indian Problem."

Indigenomics is the economy of consciousness: the connection to the nature of reality, universality, cosmology, and philosophy and the development of the whole self—spiritual, mental, emotional, and physical well-being across generations. In the words of Richard Atleo, a renowned Nuu chah nulth scholar and hereditary Chief, in *Tsawalk: A Nuu-chah-nulth Worldview*, "Wholeness is not an ideology like socialism or communism but the very essence of life. It applies to all created beings."[16]

Indigenomics posits how we see the economy depends on how we see the world. Indigenous Peoples view the economy as a wholly owned subsidiary of the environment, of the Earth, of the whole, extending far out into the cosmology. Through the Indigenous lens, the world reflects back to us reality as seen through our worldview.

REFLECTION

1. Where does an Indigenous sense of responsibility stem from?

2. What are other ways to view risk? How can risk be viewed within an Indigenous lens?

3. What do you understand "relational decision-making" to mean?

4. What does the term "the underdevelopment of the Indian reservation" mean to you?

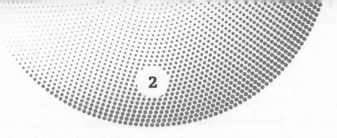

2

The Nature of Wealth

Understanding the root of the mainstream concepts of *wealth* and *economy* brings further insight into an Indigenous worldview. The origin of the word *wealth* is rooted in early 13th century England, meaning "the conditions for well-being." Today's concept of wealth stems from this original word and forms the concept of a "state of good fortune or well-being."

Today's concept of economy originates from the Greek word *oikonomia*, meaning "household management" of which the base word *oikos* means the "management of the house." Also emerging in 15th century France was the concept of *économie*, meaning the "management of material resources," which parallels the concept of economy as it is known today. The performance of economy and the acquisition of wealth form the basis of a mainstream economic worldview today. It is through this understanding of these original concepts that we can look deeper into the contrast of a distinct Indigenous worldview of economy and wealth.

From an Indigenous worldview, the concept of wealth is strikingly different. It is inherently about relationships, universal connection, continuity across generations and connects abundance to giving. Economy is both social and spiritual in nature from within an Indigenous worldview. The Indigenous economy acts as a platform for Indigenous well-being. Abundance, prosperity, and wealth are based in giving, sharing, community, ceremony, and through the quality of relationships shaped from the experience of the cosmos, to the land and to humanity, and through the recognition of life force in all things.

Drawing from my own Nuu chah nulth origin to further examine the Indigenous concept of wealth is the experience of Chief Maquinna of the Mowachant people. Maquinna was Chief during the height of the fur trade in the 1780s on the west coast of Vancouver Island. Maquinna's village of Yuqout was an important economic post in the European race for power and commerce as the era of the fur trade began. Chief Maquinna explains his Nuu chah nulth concept of wealth:

> *Once I was in Victoria, and I saw a very large house. They told me it was a bank and that the white men place their money there to be taken care of, and that by and by they got it back with interest.*
>
> *We are Indians and we have no such bank; but when we have plenty of money or blankets, we give them away to other chiefs and people, by and by they return them with interest, and our hearts feel good.*
>
> *Our way of giving is our bank.*
>
> *— Chief Maquinna*

These words of Maquinna clearly demonstrate and contrast the distinct Indigenous worldview regarding wealth, the nature of exchange, and economy. At its heart is the principle of reciprocity, of giving and receiving and relationship. "Our way of giving is our bank" establishes the basis for an Indigenous economy. This is Indigenomics.

Timeline of Money

Indigenous knowledge around time describes a concept of "since time immemorial" or "since time out of mind." As Indigenous Peoples, we go back well over 10,000 years, with some estimates going to well over 50,000 years, as verified both through Indigenous story and science. Indigenous stories tell of the time of the ice age, of the time of the beginning of light. Over 10,000 years of Indigenous reality were formed and shaped through a worldview based on relationship, reciprocity, and responsibility. Time can be told through story and through ceremony.

It has only been between the last 200 to 400 years, depending on the area, that we have had the insertion of today's concept of money on our timeline as Indigenous Peoples. This is a relatively short time frame in the experience of Indigenous reality today. This insertion of money has radically changed our cultures, our ways of life, and disrupted the center of our reality and worldview.

Indigenous systems of distribution, exchange, of giving, resource management, and distinct roles and responsibilities were all made illegal and deemed irrelevant by the dominant imposing oncoming structures. The underlying dominant policy objective was elimination, economic progress, and to "make productive" aimed at fixing the "Indian Problem."

The newly established function of the monetary system was entirely disruptive to Indigenous reality and served as a construct of Indigenomics economic displacement. This new function of money interrupted an entire way of life, of relationships, ceremony, and local economy. It brought the establishment of dependence, today's socio-economic gap, broken systems of distribution of wealth and eliminated inherent responsibility and removal of systems of inherent wealth generation, governance, and management—an intentional displacement in the timeline of our identify and a displacement from our own economic and cultural modernity and worldview. This was the early formation of the "Indian Problem."

As a Hesquiaht woman, I draw on and reflect on my own experience of the disruption of the concept of wealth over the last 150 plus years of Hesquiaht reality. In recent history, through the timeline of my own reality and that of my family and Nation, a central framing point in time was the entrance of the Christian missionary Father Brabant. He set up a mission in the Hesquiaht territory that essentially changed everything central to the Hesquiaht worldview and reality.

Hesquiaht First Nation. Source: www.hesquiaht.ca/new/getting-here

As the first contact was much later on the west coast of Canada than throughout eastern and central Canada, the Hesquiaht people identified the earliest sightings of a European ship on the coast as the Spanish corvette *Santiago*, in August 1774, and British fur traders on the coast between 1785 to 1820. Father Brabant arrived at the Hesquiaht village in 1874 to begin a mission that continued under his direction for the next three decades. In *Father Brabant and the Hesquiat of Vancouver Island*, Brabant refers to his early perception of the Hesquiaht people:

> The Hesquiaht were a loose confederacy of peoples, collectively forming from several local groups. They were tied together by economic activity, including access to resources in certain sites, by ties of kin and lineage, that were reinforced and integrated by internecine warfare and potlatching. Their concepts of the world extended to their immediate locale, and their cosmology reflected this, though a few of their myths tell of legendary heroes who entered a sky-world and an undersea world. Supernatural beings prevailed in mythology.[1]

Parallel to this timeline of the Hesquiaht peoples in this age of contact, Great Britain was establishing the Colony of Vancouver Island in 1849. Trading vessels were frequenting the coast in growing numbers, buying seal, whale, and fish oil to be used as lubricants in the sawmills that supported further resource extraction. Industry was booming and productivity, progress, and access to resources was the dominant intent. This was the age of discovery and productivity that was formative to the Industrial Age which was steeped in Indigenous economic displacement.

At this time, the smallpox epidemics of 1852 and 1862 decimated the Hesquiaht population. Further to this destruction came the transition to the monetary system and the economy of today. This was the early structure of Canada's resource economy. The Potlatch Law of 1885 served a crucial role in dismantling the distribution of wealth and the structure of the Hesquiaht economy and identity.

As maritime historian Barry Gough describes in *Father Brabant and the Hesquiaht of Vancouver Island*: "The civilization of western Europe was undergoing urbanization and industrialization in the late 19th century and it was pouring outwards to the four corners of the earth. The colonial home of Europe was rapidly establishing colonies of settlement and establishing the authority for land leases for trade and military advantage."[2] Reflecting on the work of Father Brabant, Gough notes, "He was clearly a European bringing European values and intentions to one of the world's most distant quarters.... Here were brought into conjunction two entirely different perspectives, two 'civilizations' if you will—two ideals, two concepts of eternity, two ways of life."[3]

The anthropological evidence gained through the perspective of the early explorers and missionaries of the time was insufficient to truly reflect the complexities of the actual Indigenous worldview or the expression of Indigenous economy. This was a time of dismantling and devaluing of the local Indigenous economy, ways of being and knowing and the unleashing of the full force of the descending ego of the ascending economy. With this imposing worldview came the insertion of the concept of "productivity," of "development," and of the forced divergence from the foundational structures of an Indigenous economy.

Building on this concept of the "ego of this descending economy" is understanding the distinct differences around the concept and structure of wealth, its accumulation, productivity, distribution, experience of progress, and ownership. With this divergence in worldviews, the impacts are still felt today and is in stark contrast to an Indigenous worldview where wealth stems from the ability to give, of relationship and abundance.

The Christian mandate refers to a "mission." According to Father Brabant, his mission was to bring "the worst kind of savages from the depths of ignorant pagan degradation to the heights of enlightened Christian Faith."[4] Brabant had one overarching perception of the Hesquiaht people shaped from his worldview, and upon arrival, he wrote, "The people were addicted beyond redemption to every description of pagan practices."[5] Brabant's mission was to make Indigenous Peoples "productive" and servants of God—both of these serving to displace the Indigenous economy. This Christian mission had deeply embedded within it the "ego of the descending economy" of which the impacts are felt to this day and experienced as systemic exclusion from the economic table of this country.

From Father Brabant's worldview, armed with a sense of inherent authority and a worldview stemming from the mandate of the church, he operated from a "savior" position—to make Indigenous Peoples productive and less savage. The ego of this worldview was filled with assumptions that Indigenous Peoples were not productive and had a functional relational economy. This was the ego of the oncoming descending dominating economy. Father Brabant was unable to see the distinct Indigenous worldview right in front of him and how the people were productive. He was unable to see that access to resources was based on relationships and that the economic functions of distribution, wealth generation, and productivity were further expressed and confirmed through the ceremonies of the potlatch system of recognition, relationship, and circulation of wealth. His religious and cultural worldview translated perfectly into a modern economic agenda. The overriding political and economic worldviews were formed on the belief that indigeneity itself needed breaking, savagery intercepted, souls conformed, and the land and people made to be "productive"—this is the ego of the descending economy.

Returning to the foundational construct of the Doctrine of Discovery, the removal of personhood status from all non-baptized or non-Christian people served as the primary means and "authority" to dis-invite Indigenous Peoples from the economic table. Indigenomics today is an economic platform to support the emerging space for Indigenous Peoples at the economic table of this country. Dara Kelly reflects on this concept of the "ego of descending economy."

> If we were to personify this concept of "the descending economy" as a person, that person is acting from a place of a very inflated ego and we can start to challenge the assumptions of that ego. That is the "descending economy" and is a way to describe how it has played out and how it has dominated our lives as Indigenous peoples. It is easy to demonstrate the fragility of that ego because it is a system that has built in its own justifications for its own existence. But if you present alongside that existence other systems of resilience and other ways of being and knowing then that is a threat to the existence of the descending economy itself because it is actually so fragile. It has to dominate such a big space and it has for so long that it can't afford to make space for other paradigms because the other paradigms challenge its very existence in the first place.[6]

Indigenomics is an expression and acknowledgment of the historical and current devaluing of an Indigenous way of life and worldview. It is this space that Indigenomics builds from—the revaluing of Indigenous economic worldview and economic inclusion today and in the future.

As a Hesquiaht woman, I reflect on my own personal account of the disruption of the Hesquiaht worldview and experience of economic displacement. The displacement of my people from an economy centered in a Hesquiaht worldview has been felt for many generations and continues to be felt to this day. I recollect with fond memory of my Grandmother holding me after returning home from a fragmented family torn apart from generations of the residential school system. After 16 years away in foster care, whispering in my ear "Do you know who you are?" while holding my face in her old hands as we stand in the warm sunshine of the fall afternoon. Memories. I am the fifth generation since the establishment of the Indian Act, my daughter is the sixth generation, my grandchildren will be the seventh generation. I have spent the last five years working to regain the ability to speak my traditional language. My people continue hundreds of years of economic isolation, displacement, underdevelopment, and regression under the Indian Act. The experience of the formation of Canada and of the collective historical and current underdevelopment of the "Indian Reservation" is today's motivation in establishing Indigenomics. This is the response.

Ceremony as an Expression of Wealth

The expression of Indigenous value, of value creation, and the distribution of wealth is expressed through ceremony and relationships within Indigenous reality. For thousands of years, wealth has been expressed through the giving, the transaction, the distribution through ceremony and based upon the quality of recognition of relationship and connection to each other, to our environment, and to resources with respect for life at the heart of both the economy and ceremony. This is Indigenomics.

The future value of Indigenous wealth is based on the ability to give and trust in the quality of our relationships for its return with interest over time. In a culture of giving as a demonstration of wealth, the role of receiving and exchange is important to examine in the context of prosperity. The concept of receiving can be likened to compound interest, the future value of wealth. This is Indigenous futurisms.

Seeing wealth through a cultural lens is essential to understanding an Indigenous worldview. Returning to the concept of wealth and the divergence in differing worldviews, wealth depends on how you measure it.

An example of this concept that wealth depends on how it is measured, within my own Nuu chah nulth culture, is the *?itulthla*, a ceremony for the coming of age of a young girl. Each community or family has their own specific version of this ceremony; however, this underlying concept helps to bring understanding of an Indigenous view and experience of both wealth and relationship and what is valued.

I recollect hearing a family from the neighboring village give a traditional announcement for an upcoming *?itulthla* for a young lady. Upon announcement, the host made the invitation in the traditional language for the date of the ceremony the following year. A year from then, when the ceremony is held, the host will have a give-away at the end of the ceremony where gifts are distributed to the participants. Everyone that is present receives a gift. The ceremony is not only to honor the life of the young lady becoming a woman but also to make a distinct public expression of value: that nothing that is given away, no matter how much is given, is as valuable as that young girl as a life giver. The more the host is able to give, the better the reflection of this cultural concept of wealth. It is a core premise of wealth generation and distribution within an Indigenous worldview: the more you give, the wealthier you are and the more you will receive in the future. This is the future value of wealth from an Indigenous perspective. The concept of giving is essential to an Indigenous worldview. This is Indigenous futurisms. This is Indigenomics.

The work of Dara Kelly focuses on understanding the nature of specifically the Coast Salish economy, focusing on the core questions: What is Coast Salish wealth and how do we define that? Here she reflects on her research:

> Within our culture, our children are our symbol of wealth. The reason for that and the way that can be described as "I have x number of grandchildren," and x number of great grandchildren, and therefore I am a wealthy person. This cultural notion of wealth is based on genealogy and understanding that our continuity, our resilience, and our existence relies on our ability to grow our families and communities, and so being able to have children and grandchildren is a symbol of wealth because it is a symbol of survival and continuance.[7]

Kelly highlights the importance of wealth transfer and knowledge transfer within an Indigenous economic knowledge system:

> It's not just having genealogy and lineage and just being able to have knowledge but that in fact in order to be wealthy in the truest sense you must have both. If you have knowledge and don't pass it on you are not actually wealthy and so in order to pass it on you have to have the next generation who are prepared to basically receive that knowledge and understand it. It's the combination of the two, genealogy and knowledge that constitute Coast Salish wealth.[8]

In line with this concept of cultural survival and continuance, Michi Saagiig Nishnaabeg scholar Leanne Betasamosake Simpson articulates in "Dancing the World into Being: A Conversation with Idle No More's Leanne Simpson":

> If I look at how my ancestors even 200 years ago, they didn't spend a lot of time banking capital. They didn't rely on material wealth for their well-being and economic stability. They put energy into meaningful and authentic relationships. Their food security and economic security was based on how good and how resilient their relationships were.[9]

The Economic Distortion:
Through the Lens of Wealth and Poverty

Today, with the elimination of an Indigenous economic base through the systemic removal of inherent responsibility and access to lands and resources, the nature of wealth can be viewed in the context of Indigenous poverty or the absence of wealth. Directing attention to the margins of this country, marginalization is the treatment of a person, group, or concept as insignificant or peripheral. Marginalization is the relegation to an unimportant or powerless position within a society or group. The systemic removal from the lands and resources formed the margins of this country, essentially the dis-invitation to the economic table of this country. This is the lens of economic distortion.

On further describing marginalization, Robert Moore writes in "Racist Stereotyping in the English Language":

> Many nations of the third world are described as "under-developed." These less wealthy nations are generally those that suffered under colonialism and neo-colonialism. The "developed" nations are those that exploited their resources and wealth. Therefore, rather than referring to these countries as "under developed," a more appropriate and meaningful designation might be "over exploited." Again, transpose this term next time you read about the "under developed nations" and note the different meaning that results.[10]

Questioning the construct of "underdeveloped" is at the heart of the intention of Indigenomics. A *Business in Vancouver* article, "Better Relationships Between Government and First Nations Possible," notes:

> The gap between First Nations and Canada is well documented. In recent years, Canada has ranked between sixth and eighth on the UN Human Development Index while First Nations fall between 63rd and 78th. The federal government's Community Well-Being Index shows that the gap has not changed at all since 1981.[11]

The connection between the experience of poverty and of "development" is central to understanding of the "gap." Indigenomics is an economic platform that centers the concept of a "happened to us" versus a "designed by us" approach as the economic imperative of today. We live in a Canada where over 60% of children on reserve live in poverty.[12] Further to this, over 80% of reserves have median incomes below poverty line, census data shows.[13] This is an old story—the experience of poverty and measuring the gaps—it is time for a new story.

On understanding poverty, Kelly notes:

> There are two paradigms at play when we think of wealth and poverty. This idea of "walking in two worlds" is common language within our communities. It is very tangible when communities are aware of being impoverished within a dominant paradigm and being very wealthy within an Indigenous paradigm.[14]

It is this "walking in two worlds" concept that Indigenomics converges upon: an inheritance of thousands of years' old worldview facilitated today within our modernity as Indigenous Peoples.

How can an Indigenous worldview continue to live within the experience of marginalization and abject poverty across time? It continues through the worldview expressed through ceremony, through song, through dance, through Indigenous rights, through relationships, and through traditional governance structures. As the architect of the Indian Act, Canada's first prime minister, Sir John A. MacDonald, declared to "take the Indian out of the child." However, the "Indian" could not ever truly be taken out of the Indian. All that is "Indian," the Indigenous essence, exists within the Indigenous worldview, a construct of wealth that is so deeply embedded it runs across time, across generations, and exists within the bloodstream of our indigeneity. It exists as blood memory. It is in our hair, our backbones, our eyelashes, our songs, our dances, our traditional names; it exists in our collective rights and in our inherent responsibility.

In an interview, Indigenous business leader Clint Davis describes wealth from an Indigenous perspective:

> Wealth is the way that my family places remarkable value on our connection to the land and what we do on the land. This includes our access to the land to be able to participate in certain activities: cultural, ceremonial, or spiritual. Being able to do that is wealth. Wealth from an Indigenous perspective has to accommodate the ability to do these activities over time and in the future. Wealth can be described in terms of the strength of our people and community: what we have experienced for hundreds and hundreds of years and how the strength of the community leads to greater wealth over time. Wealth doesn't necessarily have to be measured in monetary terms. To be self-sustaining, economic independence is political independence and in turn creates wealth and strength today.[15]

In direct contrast to the wording with the Department of Indian Affairs, the Indian Affairs Department Inspector Macrea of the North West said in 1886:

> The circumstance of the Indian existence prevents him from following that core of evolution which had produced from the barbarian of the past the civilized man of today. It is impossible from him to be allowed slowly to pass through the successive stages from the pastoral to an agricultural life and from an agricultural one, to one of manufacturing, commerce or trade as we have done. He has been called upon suddenly and without warning to enter upon a new existence. Without the assistance of the government, he must have failed and perished miserably and he would have died hard entailing expense and disgrace upon the country.[16]

The limitations as seen through the lens of the ego of worldview here cries out for a return to Indigenous constructs of wealth. It is this perspective that serves to transmit the structure and process of the Indian Problem across time to today.

Conclusion

Indigenomics is a new economic model that makes well-being the measure of progress grounded in thousands of years of Indigenous wisdom, excellence, traditions, and law. "Money is a creation of our imagination but is fundamentally disconnected from real assets, especially natural assets." As author, economist, and Indigenomics advisor Mark Anielski in "Why Forests Matter" notes, "Indigenomics is the emergence of Indigenous ways of knowing around wealth, and value creation."[17]

REFLECTION

1. How can we properly engage an Indigenous worldview that assesses wealth differently?

2. What insights can you gain from seeing wealth from another worldview?

3. Why is it important to also measure economic strength rather than just socio-economic gap?

3

The Landscape of
Indigenous Worldview

Indigenomics emerged as a response to the continuous thread of stories around Indigenous business success, as well as the constant state of conflict portrayed in the media around Indigenous rights, economic development, and resource development projects. Through the development of the hashtag #indigenomics, Indigenomics became a developing volume of content highlighting Indigenous business successes, challenges, and conflict. Through this distribution of media stories, some core concepts emerged. These can be viewed as the "between the lines" or the parallel story of what has not been reflected in mainstream media narrative lack of portrayal of the core elements of an Indigenous worldview.

While "Indigenous worldview" is used here in the singular form, it is essential to understand that just as there are many Indigenous Nations, there are just as many variations and expressions of Indigenous worldviews. These key themes form the following principles and are laid out only to act as conceptual markers that form the ethics or the basis of Indigenous relational decision-making or the landscape of an Indigenous worldview. These principles are neither fully inclusive nor exclusive of individual Indigenous worldviews and ways of being and knowing. The intention is to bring insight into an Indigenous frame of reference that reflects key elements of an Indigenous worldview. Here I have examined these concepts first through my own Nuu chah nulth lens and then through different Indigenous worldviews to draw from and understand similarities.

These principles are intended only as a way to highlight key aspects of an Indigenous worldview and serve to better understand and frame the source of Indigenous conflict, as well as highlight a source of business success. Each offers an initial insight into the cultural landscape of an Indigenous worldview. Each concept is best expressed within each individual Indigenous language, which is the gateway to this worldview. Each principal acts as a guidepost, or marker, reflecting the nature of reality from within an Indigenous worldview.

These principles draw attention to the distinct spiritual nature of Indigenous reality and worldview. Within an Indigenous worldview, the spiritual domain is the landscape for an Indigenous economy. As Kelly notes, specifically drawing from a Coast Salish frame of reference:

> The nature of the Coast Salish Indigenous economy is how we understand it within our ceremonies. If we think about our worldview, the nature of spiritual exchange happens between humans and the Creator and humans and the natural environment. We nurture spiritual exchanges between all three of those components. Everything that happens then within our behavior as humans is fundamentally tied to those spiritual exchanges. We nurture relationships among ourselves, within our families, across our kindship networks, with other communities. While there may be a lot of material exchange that happens to symbolize that exchange, these material exchanges are means to other ends, to nurture these spiritual exchanges. Because of the inherently spiritual nature of our worldview, if our understanding of Coast Salish economy is that if the economy is not spiritual, then it is fundamentally not a Coast Salish economy.[1]

To better understand these concepts, each can be put through a uniquely specific worldview whether it is Cree, Ojibwe, Nuu chah nulth, Māori, Hawaiian, Australian, or Mapuche from Chile. Each of the concepts outline a foundational construct of Indigenous wisdom that is used to reflect reality back to us, to reflect our humanity to each other, and our relationships or connection to the Earth.

In an Indigenous worldview, the language of economy is the language of the land. These principles are all intertwined and are of great importance in the cultural continuance as Indigenous Peoples. Indigenous languages contain knowledge systems of ways of being

and knowing and embedded within are the concepts of both responsibility and knowledge transfer.

Kelly notes:

> Traditional knowledge systems are not rigid. They are de-
> signed to be developed and grown through generations. While
> we the younger generation have a responsibility to learn and
> access these knowledge systems, we also have a responsibility
> to contribute to them and grow them even further. That is the
> metaphor that was taught to me: it is a basket of knowledge
> that we take and we contribute to.[2]

These principles form the basis of inter-generational Indigenous
wisdom that shaped economic knowledge systems, for thousands of
years. The expression of Indigenous values, while in many forms, reflect a deep cultural connection to place, to time, and to relationships.
These values are embodied in cultural traditions, expressed in song,
dance, ceremony, and language. Kelly continues: "We need to be able
to look to our Indigenous knowledge systems to be able to inform our
world today and try to understand the underlying fundamental values that are embedded in our knowledge systems."[3] It is from within
an Indigenous knowledge system that relational decision-making is
established. It is founded in a holism and forms the very basis of an
Indigenous worldview.

Principle 1: Everything Is Connected

At the heart of an Indigenous worldview, from one end of the Earth
to the other, is a central concept that expresses itself as *hish uk ish
tsa walk* in my own Nuu chah nulth language and translates into
"Everything is one and interconnected." The word *tsa walk* means
"one." The concept expresses the central operating point that all living things—humans, plants, and animals—form part of an integrated
whole brought into harmony or alignment through mutual respect
and expresses itself across the cosmos and across time.

There are thousands of different ways to express this concept in
various Indigenous cultures. It forms a central operating point, or a
core ethic, for the management of self, community, resources, and relationships and serves as a framework for intergenerational decision-
making.

In the Cree language, the concept of *mamawi wahkotowin* means "everything is one." *Mamawi* means "altogether," and *wahkotowin* means "to be related as in family and connected to all." When put together, these words form the concept "we do things in relationship." The Lakota people also express this concept as *mitakuye oyasin*.

Everything is connected. This concept serves as a focal point that acts as a platform for ecological, generational, and relational decision-making. At its heart is the tying together of life: the unifying nature of reality, life force, and relationships and through time across generations. This concept becomes a unifying force for ensuring quality of relationships and connections and decision-making throughout time and throughout the cosmos.

Through the Māori people of New Zealand, this same concept can be seen:

> The essence of the Māori worldview is based on relationships between people, the spiritual world and the natural world. "Whakapaoa" is the fundamental concept that all things are connected. These formal relationships extend from the Deities, to the wildlife and to the plant kingdom. The Māori have specific cultural values and perspectives through the continuity of this knowledge system developed over time. The "tikanga" or customs/practices are derived from this body of knowledge connected to the spiritual and natural order that guides the interaction and regulates the balance between the relationships. This worldview forms the perception of the essence of reality and the cultural perceptions to act from.[4]

In *Tsawalk: A Nuu-chah-nulth Worldview*, Nuu cha nulth scholar Richard Atleo considers the concept of "Everything is one and interconnected" to mean "It is inclusive of all reality, both physical and metaphysical."[5] He speaks to the Indigenous knowledge of nature of existence or reality. He writes, "Hii shuk ish tsawalk means more than unity of the physical universe. It denotes much more than the empirically based meaning attached to the word 'holism.'"[6] Atleo further articulates this concept as reflected through the tradition of story: "Nuu-chah-nulth origin stories indicate that the basic character of creation is a unity expressed as 'everything is one.' This is a matter of the first principles laid out in the original design of creation."[7] This concept of relativity is elevated to the design of creation itself, going to the very heart of the nature of reality. It is this concept of relationality that is the foundation of Indigenomics.

This is further seen in *Sacred Lands*, through the words of esteemed scholar Leroy Little Bear: "If everything has spirit everything is capable of relating. In the native view all of creation is interrelated."[8] In expanding this concept, he refers to this connection to land and identity:

> Land (space) is the primary context because that is where the "spider web" relational network operates within the human experience. This is the meaning of the term "all my relations... which includes but is not limited to animals, plants, inorganic matter such as rocks and the land itself. In other words, "all my relations" must also have an interest in the land, just as humans do. Relating is what maintains the continuity of all creation.[9]

Everything is connected. This is relational economics, the economic construct of relativity.

As reflected in the wise words of Elder Tom Crane Bear of the Blood Tribe:

> *We all come from the land*
> *Water sustains our lives*
> *The animals and the fish*
> *much of our body is fluid*
> *The trees purify the air we breathe*
> *The rocks purify the water we drink*
> *The trees drink the water*
> *And give us branches and leaves*
> *It's important that we look after the eco-system*
> *The undergrowth of the forest*
> *If the system breaks we all get sick*
> *"Everything is connected and doing its work"*

This is Indigenous wisdom. This is relational economics. The relational economy forms the foundation for Indigenous ways of being, a human state of being that is relational to nature, to the environment, to ourselves, to each other, to the cosmos, and to time and space itself. It forms with it a powerful insight into ecological economics and modern economic development. Everything is connected. This is Indigenomics.

The concept of interconnectedness within the Indigenous worldview pushes the boundaries of time within community development, and decision-making. As esteemed leader Wilma Mankiller of the Cherokee Nation articulates, "Our leaders are encouraged to remember seven generations in the past and seven generations in the future when making decisions that affect the people."[10] It is this relationality that forms the core operating principle from within an Indigenous reality that everything is one and interconnected.

Canada's environmental leader David Suzuki speaks to being influenced by the Haida Indigenous worldview on the Pacific Northwest region. He asks Guujaaw, the great architect of the Haida Taku case, the first Aboriginal title case brought before the Canadian courts, "Why are you fighting against logging?" Guujaaw replies, "Because when the trees are gone, we'll just be like everybody else." Suzuki acknowledges this simple statement had a profound impact on his own worldview and his work. It is saying that to be Haida means to be connected to the land in a profound way. Guujaaw continues, "We don't end at our skin or finger tips, it's the trees, and the fish, and the air, and the birds all of that is what makes the Haida who they are as Indigenous peoples."[11]

Principle 2: Story

Stories are our culture. Our culture begins with storytelling.
Stories are our culture. Stories are very important.
If they are taken seriously, they give guidance for life.
This is what the Creator wants you to see.
We have our own history—our stories tell our rights.

—ELDER TOM CRANE BEAR[12]

Elder Tom speaks of the central role of story in Indigenous reality, relaying Indigenous wisdom and worldview across time and generations. In the words of the master Ojibwe storyteller, the late Richard Wagamese, who I call a mentor and friend:

All that we are is story. From the moment we are born to the time we continue on our spirit journey, we are involved in the creation of the story of our time here. It is what we arrive with. It is all we leave behind. We are not the things we accumulate. We are not the things we deem important. We are story. All of us. What comes to matter then is the creation of the best possible story we can while we're here; you, me, us, together. When we can do that and we take the time to share those stories with each other, we get bigger inside, we see each other, we recognize our kinship—we change the world, one story at a time.[13]

The role of stories in an Indigenous worldview is a core means of transmitting teachings, history, and relationships over time. Stories relay protocol, they speak to how to conduct oneself, of consequence of action, providing alternate points of view, and of maintaining relationships. Stories transmit knowledge about reality. Stories play a fundamental role in the cross-generational transmittance of knowledge systems.

Atleo writes, "The universe is unified, interconnected, and interrelated are assumptions about both physical and metaphysical realms found in Nuu-chah-nulth origin stories."[14] Stories form the basis of explaining the nature of reality, both physical and spiritual, and serve to reflect back the truths of our humanity, of the physical; and spiritual domain and connection to all. Atleo further describes the role of story in Indigenous realities:

Story serves to transmit the knowledge of the primary protocols—respect for life, respect for others, and how to behave or conduct oneself. Stories tell of the human ethics—how to treat the great cedar and the salmon. These protocols are agreements between life forms. Their primary purpose is to ensure that life forms exercise mutual recognition, mutual responsibility and mutual respect. To fulfill this purpose, human life forms must recognize and respect their responsibility to other life forms. Non-human life forms will respond in kind. When mutual recognition, mutual responsibility and mutual respect are practiced, there is balance, harmony is achieved, and the goal of environmental and economic sustainability may be realized.[15]

Important truths about the nature of the universe are reflected in stories about the legendary teachers seen in the natural world. From the Nuu chah nulth tradition, one of the great teachers is the raven.

> It is true that in many stories Son of Raven loves to play tricks, take advantage of people, take the easy way through life and present a larger than life image to the world. But in the world-view of the Nuu-chah-nulth, Son of Raven is also much more than this. Son of Raven is also an archetype, a hero and consequently yearns to do great deeds. However, in the process of attempting these great deeds, Son of Raven, from the vantage point of earth, encounters problems, the solutions to which are naturally sought through and from the spiritual realm.[16]

The characters in these stories connect and demonstrate the truth about the nature of reality and our limited human understanding of the spiritual domain.

Blaeser notes from the Okanagan Indigenous tradition: "The spatial, temporal, and spiritual realities of Native people reflect a fluidity that disallows complete segregation between experiences of life and death, physical and spiritual, past and present, human and nonhuman. Thus, they are reflected in cycles that involve return, reconnection, and relationship."[17]

Atleo then further draws attention to the connectivity of life and the role of story:

> Nuu-chah-nulth stories and traditional way of life and experience indicate that the basic character of creation as unity expressed as hish uk ish tsawalk (everything is one). This unity of existence does not mean that individuals are denied a separate existence; on the contrary, individualism is a very strong value. Hii shuk ish tsawalk is a matter of the first principles laid out in the original design of creation. The Creator and creation are one. Within this meta-framework of existence lies the contemporary universe of quantum mechanics, superstring theory, philosophies and political ideologies, biodiversity and every expression of life known and unknown.[18]

This is Indigenous essentialism from which reality is drawn—the unifying nature of reality.

The following excerpt is drawn from the oral tradition of a Nuu chah nulth potlatch, a speech from the early 20th century.

> Hear again the stories that are old
> Traditions that our ancestors told
> The laws they made are still with us
> They are here and have not changed
> Our lands, our streams, our seas remain
> To provide for our wants, that are yours and mine.[19]

This speech upholds the role of stories in traditional governance structures, Indigenous law, and the conservation of resources and serves to reinforce the role of story within the Indigenous worldview. Further, in a talk, the Honorable Steven Point, 28th Lieutenant Governor and esteemed leader from the Sto:lo Nation also enters the role of story in Indigenous reality by reflecting:

> Our constitution is written in the land, and our stories are written by the land and territories because we have our ancestors' bones and spiritual geographies. We have ancient stories that we can still tell and that by telling these stories reinforces our belonging, and that belonging is what our constitution is all about. If you can't tell your stories, that's when you start to have problems.[20]

Principle 3: Animate Life Force

> These are not just resources.
> This is life force. A life force that we
> have relationships with.
> We don't own it.
> We don't own the rivers.
> We don't own the salmon
> We have relationships
> With these worlds and our laws are our responsibilities.[21]

Animate life force is a concept deeply embedded in Indigenous reality. Indigenous worldview has a concept of life force described as a constant yet simple truth that "life is everywhere." This recognition of life force forms a core premise of an Indigenous worldview. It shapes how we see and experience the world and is the foundation for relational decision-making. The ability to see life everywhere is the ability to call on that life force to be experienced as expansive holism. The words of a song serve to expand the Indigenous worldview of life itself and remind us that life is everywhere: "What is life? It is the flash or a firefly in the night. It is the breath of a buffalo in the wintertime. It is the little shadow that runs across the grass and loses itself in the sunset. Attributed to Crawfoot and Blackfoot tribe."

Indigenous scholar Leroy Little Bear in *Aboriginal Paradigms* brings to light that "Indigenous philosophy consists of and includes the ideas that there is a constant motion/flux, that all creation consists of energy waves, that everything is animate, that all creation is interrelated. It is this concept of flux, energy, that forms the principle of animate life force."[22]

In their recent work of holomovement in *Wholeness and the Implicate Order*, David Bohm and Alfred Whitehead describe their "discovery" of the core concept of "space is not empty." They write, "It (space) is full, a plenum as opposed to a vacuum, and is the ground for the existence of everything, including ourselves. The universe is not separate from this cosmic sea of energy."[23] This holomovement concept is a new construct that embodies a key interpretation of quantum mechanics and relationality. It brings together the holistic principle of "undivided wholeness" with the idea that everything is in a state of process or becoming: "Wholeness is not a static oneness, but a dynamic wholeness-in-motion in which everything moves together in an interconnected process."[24]

This "discovery" complex of the Western ideology as seen within the introduction of the concept of holomovement points to the understanding of animate life force that is centered within an Indigenous worldview. This new concept of holomovement as a new discovery directly reflects the ancient concept of *hii shuk ish tswalk* philosophy that everything is connected, as affirmed in Nuu chah nulth experience of reality.

Little Bear notes, "In a world in which rocks, trees, plants, animals and stars are all animate, the cosmos becomes inseparable from us. We are all part of this whole and within each of these parts is enfolded the whole. This concept of Indigenous existence, reality and worldview are so inherently intertwined that separation is not possible."[25] The concept of being intertwined adequately relays this Indigenous reality.

The Indigenous worldview easily engages this concept of animate life force.

> Everything we see is animate. In an Indigenous worldview, I don't know if there is such a notion of inanimate. If everything is animate like me, then everything must also have a spirit. Those trees, those rocks also have spirit. If everything has spirit, then everything is capable of relating. In this native view, all of creation is inter-related.[26]

It is this concept of animate life force that draws the physical and the spiritual realm together weaving Indigenous nature of reality. "To us, land, as part of creation is animate. It has spirit. Place is for the inter-relational network of all creation. When we talk of territory, we are really talking about the place where the inter-relational network occurs."[27]

It is this embedded concept of animate life force in an Indigenous worldview that draws on the ethics of Indigenous law and traditional governance systems.

> What you people call your natural resources our people call our relatives. I do not see a delegation for the Four Footed. I see no seat for the Eagles. We forget and we consider ourselves superior. But we are after all a mere part of Creation. And we must consider to understand where we are. And we stand somewhere between the mountain and the Ant. Somewhere and only there as part and parcel of the Creation.[28]

In his work, Harold Cardinal, the late esteemed Indigenous early thinker, leader in Indigenous law, and author of *The Rebirth of Canada's Indians*, highlights the words within the original treaties:

> "As long as the sun shines, the grass grows, and the river flows." These words have symbolic meaning to Indian people because the water, the grass, and the sun are all basic elements of life. In naming these elements, our people were saying that they would not give up any elements basic to their cultural practices. Our people were calling upon the sun, the water, and the grass as witnesses to the fact that they were not surrendering, by those treaties, either their sovereignty or the relationship with the Great Spirit.[29]

The deeper meaning of these words reflected within the original treaties of this land indicate a connection between commitment, promise, and a protocol between life forms signed within the treaties of this country, witnessed by the elements of life forces.

In a global context, drawing from elements of a Māori worldview is the concept of *mana* which refers to an extraordinary power, the essence or the presence of life and energy. Their worldview applies this concept to the energy and presence of the natural world. The experience of *mana* is spiritual and describes the connection to the source of life. In the Māori tradition, *mana* or energy comes from *Te Kore*—the realm beyond the world we can see—essentially an alternative reality. Within Māori reality, there are different forms of this life force. *Mana* is an energy that connects and animates all things in the physical world. The flow of *mana* is an essential element within this worldview. The recognition that *mana* flows into the world is an underpinning of Māori experience of reality.

Further, in the Hawaiian cultural landscape, nature and culture are described as one and the same; there is no division between the two. The wealth and limitations of the land and ocean resources gave birth to and shaped the Hawaiian worldview. The *äina* (land), *wai* (water), *kai* (ocean), and *lewa* (sky) are the foundation of life and the source of the spiritual relationship between people and the environment.[30]

Principle 4: Transformation

The concept of transformation is deeply embedded within an Indigenous worldview. This sacred concept is relayed within story, ceremony, dance, names, and art. Transformation is the changing of form, the recognition of the ability to shape shift and the upholding of this as sacred. Transformation serves to challenge our existing and limited understanding of reality. In Indigenous story or philosophy, shape shifting is the ability of a being to transform from its current physical form or shape into an entirely different one. This can be achieved through an inherent ability, divine intervention, or the use of magic or movement between worlds or dimensions.

Indigenous ceremony is embedded with the concept of transformation and renewal. Transformation, as a concept within the Indigenous worldview, allows insight "across worlds, across forms, across time, and is multi-dimensional. It challenges a way to look at reality."[31]

The concept of transformation can be expressed both as a process and as a being or state. A being that holds the property of transformation is referred to as a "transformer." Some transformers are legendary and known for their unique abilities, as described in Kanaka Bar's *The Memorial to Sir Wilfred Laurier*:

> When a character in an origin story modifies the world in a useful way, that character may be referred to as a transformer. Transformers take on an iconic role within Indigenous expression. "One of the most widely known transformers is Coyote, a figure often credited with making the world suitable for human habitation. Coyote is sometimes referred to as trickster because he goes about his work.
>
> Our laws and customs, what we call *yirí7 re stsq'ey's-kucw*, were given to us by Sk'elép (Coyote) as laid out in our ancient oral histories. A long time ago, maybe 5,000 years ago, the Wutémtkemc, a group of Coast Salish people sometimes called "transformers" ventured up the Fraser River. They met Sk'elép, who was sitting on a rock watching them as they approached. They tried to transform him with their powers but were able only to change his tracks into stone. Therefore, the marks of Sk'elép's feet may be seen on this rock at the present day.
>
> Sk'elép sat with his chin resting on his hand and stared at them while they were trying to transform him. When they failed, he cried out to them, "You are making the world right— so am I. Why try to punish me when I have done you no harm? This is my country. Why do you come here and interfere with my work? If I wished, I could turn you into stone, but as you have likely been sent into the world, like myself, to do good, I will allow you to pass, but you must leave this country as quickly as you can. We should be friends but must not interfere with each others work.[32]

From within an Indigenous worldview, the concept of transformation serves to provide the opportunity to challenge assumptions about physical and spiritual reality and demonstrates the limitation of human understanding and knowledge. "The assumption that underlies this dualistic aspect of all being and existence is that the world is in motion, that things are constantly undergoing processes of transformation, deformation and restoration and that the essence of life and being is movement."[33] The concept and portrayal of transformation serves to challenge our mental boundaries about the nature of reality and our conscious awareness of it.

In the Squamish reality, the visual landscape of the city of Vancouver includes the mountains called *Sch'ich'iyúy* or the "twin sisters" by the Salish people who have lived in this region for thousands of years. The story passed down through the generations tells of the twin sisters being daughters of a Squamish Chief. The tribes up and down the coast were constantly at war with each other. Through marrying twin Haida brothers and holding a feast, the sisters brought peace between the warring peoples. After they passed away, the two sisters were immortalized and transformed into the mountain peaks where they could forever keep watch over their descendants and ensure that peace was kept throughout time. The construct of transformation asks us to pay attention. The visualization and embodiment of the transformation draws our attention to the qualities of being peaceful, generous, and leadership.

Principle 5: The Teachings

Indigenous languages hold within them the teachings of how to be and how to conduct oneself and form the foundation for the relationship and responsibility to each other and to the land. Through language, story, and teachings, traditional teachings form the basis of the "original instructions" or the responsibilities and ethics at the heart of Indigenous identity. Indigenous language matches the vibrations of the land. Each is a direct reflection of the other.

Teachings are based on the whole self and reflect the spiritual dimensions of reality and of humanity. Drawing from the Anishinabe dimension that describes the Seven Grandfathers or gifts that animate life: *Nbwaakaawin* (wisdom), *Zaagidwin* (love), *Mnaadendimowin* (respect), *Aakwade"ewin* (bravery), *Dbaadendiziwin* (humility), *Gwekwaadiziwin* (honesty), and *Debwewin* (truth). The Anishinabe people understand the sacredness of these teachings as fundamental as law itself and which embodies the teachings as a way of life. Teachings form the foundation of personal and collective success: the ethics of being human, of being alive, and of being in relationship.

Drawing from the Nuu chah nulth tradition, the wrongdoing of an individual is reflected as the degree of proximity to the teachings. If one steals, it is said that person has not been taught properly. If one has lost their way, they have forgotten their teachings. The wrong doings of an individual reflect poorly on that individual's grandparents through the lack of transmission of teachings across time with the question, why have they not been taught properly? The lack of personal demonstration of these teachings are a poor reflection on the older generations, leaving space for the public perception: why has their grandchild not been taught our ways? These ways include kindness, respect, caring for each other, and helping each other.

Teachings hold the instructions for life. They act as markers, and the proximity to these teachings reflects one's quality of life and well-being. Respect is a core teaching, as reflected within the Nuu chah nulth worldview:

> Iisaak (respect) is predicated upon the notion that every life form has intrinsic value and that this should be recognized through appropriate protocols of interaction. First, what does iisaak mean in practice? It means that life forms of every kind are held in equal esteem. All life forms have intrinsic value. Humans of every race have equal value, as do the deer, the wolf, the whale, the eagle, the cedar tree. Holding life forms in equal esteem demands the balance and harmony be maintained among them by the development of protocols.[34]

There is much diversity of traditional teachings, where some are universal and some are specific to cultural groups, communities, or even families. The commonality of Indigenous teachings forms the common thread of the ethics of an Indigenous worldview. Some of these universal teachings include these concepts:

- We are all related: all beings are related and all beings are equal.
- We are spiritual beings inter-related with all other beings.
- It is essential to demonstrate respect for life in all our actions.
- We have a responsibility in our actions and decisions to each other and to the Earth: therefore, be mindful of our thoughts and actions.
- Life is based on interdependence and reciprocity. There is a reciprocal relationship between humans and the universe. This must be upheld and renewed through ceremony and protocol.

- The strength of our people is based on connection. We must maintain and uphold strong family and community connections. We demonstrate this by showing care for one another and being helpful to one another. This is the essence of community.
- We have a responsibility to nurture, educate, and develop the value of our relationships to all life forms.
- To walk on the Earth means to walk with respect, self-discipline, and to honor the connection to both the spiritual and physical domain.
- Ceremony is a reflection of both the spiritual and the physical realms.
- Showing gratitude for the Earth's abundance is to live in an abundant state.
- We are dependent on what the Earth provides. We must act like it and make decisions based on this.
- We must uphold the reciprocal nature of the relationship with the universe. This means taking what we need.

These teachings exist to tell us how to be human. They do not exist to tell us how to be Indigenous. This is an important distinction. Indigenous languages hold within them teachings for how humans can live on this land/place. The vibrations of the land are reflected within all Indigenous language and the teachings themselves. It is in our traditional languages that lies the inherent wisdom and the language of reality. This concept can be seen within contentious economic issues in project development with Indigenous communities today.

Teachings are directly connected to and expressed through ceremony, place, personal and collective responsibility, and even economy. Each is intended to be transmitted across time preserved from generation to generation through story:

> A constellation of teachings was developed to maintain and to enhance life's major purpose, namely the development of harmonious relationships between and among all life forms. These teachings applied to every dimension of life, whether within the extended family, between Nations, or between all other life forms, including those forms (such as plants and animals) that are now considered to be simply "resources."

These teachings also applied to the relationship between the physical and spiritual realms.[35]

Jeannette Armstrong is a professor of Indigenous Studies and a Canada Research Chair in Indigenous Philosophy of Syilx descent in the Okanagan region of B.C. She writes about the transmission of teachings:

> Every year, continuously, the people who are caretakers, and people who are careful of the harvest, whoever they might be, are reminded at our ceremonies and at our feasts, that *that* is what our responsibility, our intelligence and our creativity as human beings is about. That's what the gift of being human is about. If we cannot measure up to that, and we cannot live up to that, then we're not needed here, and we won't continue to be here. European cultural system evolved a view that the human is separate from, and/or dominant, and/or somehow not part of the natural world; somehow not a part of the life form of the land.[36]

Armstrong centers the elevation of Indigenous teachings as a way to permeate Indigenous consciousness through practice: "If we cannot measure up to these teachings, we cannot live up to them then we are not needed here."[37] She demonstrates the very essence of indigeneity as the proximity and the activation of these traditional teachings across time.

In expressing her indigeneity as an Indigenous woman, Armstrong continues: "On being Indigenous (Syilx), if I were to translate that word for you, contained in that world is the foundational instruction, or paradigm, that expresses the idea of being so Indigenous, and so a part of the natural word that our humanness is an expression of that natural world."[38] It is part of the natural word that our humanness expresses. This is foundational to Indigenous reality and is reflected in our worldview and economy. She continues with eloquence:

> It is speaking about the ethic of the people, the responsibility or the philosophy of the people, to continuously bind with everything that is around us: our family members, all of our

relatives on the land, and continuously maintain one unit. In other words, to be unified, to be in balance, and if we can do that, we can move forward, into the next generation as a whole. And we need to be able to accomplish that as human beings.[39]

Indigenous teachings are the ethics of indigeneity, the foundation of well-being, continuity, and resilience. Armstrong articulates the concept of teaching of connection:

To be able to move through from the idea of being individual, and the idea of being temporary in my body, and the idea being something larger than that: part of a larger being or a larger living life force, which is what we call "Tmixw." That we are all Tmixw, we are all a part of—all our thoughts, our knowledge, our understanding, and all of our feelings are a part of that. No different than all of the physical parts of that diversity, we're a part of that."[40]

Armstrong's word reinforces this concept that these teachings form a way of life and are foundational to an Indigenous worldview by highlighting the importance of living one's life in proximity to the teachings:

My elders say that it is land that holds all knowledge of life and death and is a constant teacher. It is said in the Okanagan traditions that the land constantly speaks. It is constantly communicating. Not to learn its language is to die. We survived and thrived by listening intently to its teachings—to its language—and then inventing human words to retell its stories to our succeeding generations. It is the land that speaks N'silxchn, the old land/mother spirit of our People, which surrounds me in its primal, wordless state.[41]

Separateness from the teachings means to not continue as people. The teachings are considered to be what makes us Indigenous and central to life itself. The relationship to the land and the teachings are clear within the Indigenous worldview. "We constantly rely on our teaching to guide the way that our economies and law are expressed, then some kind of a community-driven place we are able to keep pressure to ensure that our rights are recognized."[42]

Principle 6: Creation Story

Origin stories provide an orientation to the design and meaning of creation. Essentially, this design reveals that everything and every life form are of common origin. Origin stories teach that there is a natural relationship between creation and the source of creation. There is a natural relationship between that which was made and the Maker. There is a natural relationship between the spiritual and the physical.[43]

Indigenous cultures are closely connected to an origin story. Connection to origin and Creation is foundational to an Indigenous worldview and cultural landscape. Creation stories reflect the Indigenous space reality of the beginning of time to the formation of life and existence.

Within the Creation story comes a right to be in a place and belonging. Indigenous Peoples understand that the right to a place comes from the Creator and is shaped by inherent responsibility. Creation stories define relationship to place and set requirements for how to be, while demonstrating place-based values that include resource management and governance systems. Through an Indigenous worldview, the rightful place in this world is directly connected to responsibility and stewardship.

A Creation story tells you how to be, it tells you how to be human, and acts as a source of Indigenous law. A Creation story is directly related to the space/place domain of community: it connects songs, dances, and ceremony and affirms relationships. Where law and spirit or culture intersect is a source of community development.

As seen on the wall of Ktunaxa Nation Tribal Council, here is an excerpt from Ktunaxa Creation Story:

Our first ancestors are said to have descended from the sky, wrapped in clouds, before there was anything else here. These supernatural beings populated the land until, the transformer changed them into their present form as rocks, animals and features of the landscape that remain to this day. It is said that it takes 4 days to tell this story.[44]

This Creation story guides land use planning, resource management, governance framework, and Ktunaxa-based Indigenous law. There are behaviors, responsibilities, and customs that come from a Creation story. Atleo reinforces the role of origin stories in Indigenous reality:

> All aspects of formal life among the Nuu-chah-nulth, including matters related to sovereign rights over hahuulthi and its resources, together with names, prayers, chants, songs, dances and ceremony are rooted in origin stories, the truths of which have been validated by "uusumch" and subsequently translated into the various cultural expressions found in the formal ceremonies of the potlatch.[45]

Principle 7: Protocol

The beginning words of this book started with protocol:

> As I am writing this on the beautiful Stoney Nakoda territory. The sun is hitting the majestic mountains around me. If you listen carefully you can hear the ancient one's songs echoing off the mountains, reminders of the ceremonies of here, steeped in the ancient teachings of existence and reality. Reaching deep into this existence, I acknowledge the ancestors of this place, the original songs of this place, the dances, the traditional names of here, the language of here, the teachings of here, all creating the energy field of this place translated to mean Sacred Buffalo Guardian Mountain.

Protocol is the highest form of expression of recognition; it brings into focus the expression of space/place.

The Indigenous concept of protocol is central to Indigenous identity. Protocol is the responsibility of remembering, acknowledging, and witnessing. It is a means for recognition of connection, relationship, and making things right.

The concept is so closely intertwined with identity that its inclusion and practice is paramount to an Indigenous worldview. Protocol can be expressed in many ways, with the underlying intention to make right, such as the requesting of permission to enter into another's territory, the harvesting of resources, the use of lands, or the acknowledgement of the ancestors of a place. Protocol has many expressions, including through prayer and ceremony. Protocol is a recognition of all life forms. Within this concept lies the act of acknowledgment, the recognition of relationship, of right relations. Right relations form a core premise of an Indigenous worldview. Atleo speaks of protocol:

> Existence is purposeful. One of the purposes of creation is for humans to reach firm agreements. This purpose, confirmed by Nuu-chah-nulth experience, is emphasized when the terms of these agreements are broken. These agreements, as told in our origin stories, our ceremonies, our teachings are Indigenous protocol—a means to uphold and reaffirm the nature of reality.[46]

Protocol establishes a positive state of being, of having a right mind as an approach to the immediate task and to recognize life itself. Protocol is a way of being and built upon thousands of years of forming and confirming relationships. Indigenous protocol brings a perspective that is focused on right thinking, good choices, being careful, having a good mind as foundational within an Indigenous worldview. It speaks to personal responsibility, of proximity to the teachings, and is foundational to personal and collective well-being.

Principle 8: To Witness

Witnessing is the sacred responsibility of remembering—a practice that serves to validate experience events, external relationships, ownership, recognition, and ceremony across time.

Historically, because Indigenous culture was an oral society, there were no signed documents. Participants officially witnessed significant agreements and were called to the official role of witnessing. The event speaker, whose role is similar to a master of ceremonies, would call upon individuals to be the official witnesses to the agreement.

Witnesses played a very important role as the official record keepers. They could stand up at the end of a ceremony and provide their views; they could correct the discussion on the details at future meetings; and they were obliged to pass on the details of the agreement to subsequent generations. They were considered very rich because knowledge was the most valued of all possessions. Today we have formal agreements, but the practice of calling upon witnesses is still practiced to officially observe and validate the proceedings, ceremonies, meetings, and agreements.

This is the responsibility of remembering. This responsibility is sacred, and often a transaction occurs for this sacred responsibility of remembering. It is not only a responsibility of the present moment; it's about relationship and responsibility to the future. This affirms relationship as transactional across time.

For example, I was given the responsibility to remember the ceremony of my niece being given a traditional name. This was about not just the name itself but what responsibility she had been given when she was given that name. So if she is acting out and not acting in accordance to the good standards of that name, as a witness, it is my responsibility to remind her about the power of that name and what the name means and stands for.

Principle 9: To Make Visible

The concept of "to make visible" speaks to the limitations of the human understanding of reality, other dimensions, and the duality of both spiritual and physical reality.

Indigenous worldview refers to the duality of reality and allows the creation of other worlds: the supernatural, the sky world, and the sea world are all dimensions existing beyond the human mind and experience.

To make visible. It's two sides of the same coin: what is visible and what is invisible. What we experience on Earth is only a part of the whole dimension, with the opposite being spiritual. The holistic perspective is all-encompassing, even of what we can't see and experience. Much of Indigenous ceremonial design reflects this concept of as above so below.

Blaeser reflects on Armstrong's work in speaking about the complexities of Indigenous tradition of stories and the transcendence of time:

> The ability to move the audience back and forth between the present reality and the story reality relies heavily on the fluidity of time sense that the language offers. In particular, stories that are used for teaching must be inclusive of the past, present, and future as well as the current or contemporary moment and the story reality.[47]

Blaeser continues, in reference to Armstrong's work: "In the Okanagan language, perception of the way reality occurs is very different from that solicited by the English language. Reality is very much like a story: it is easily changeable and transformative with each speaker. Reality in that way becomes very potent with animation and life."[48]

The duality of life is a central tenant in the Indigenous worldview. Drawing on the work of Armstrong:

> The spatial, temporal, and spiritual realities of Native people reflect a fluidity that disallows complete segregation between the experiences of life and death, physical and spiritual, past and present, human and nonhuman. Thus, they are reflected in cycles that involve return, reconnection, and relationship.[49]

This concept of unity points to the visibility of cycles, dependancies, and connections.

Principle 10: Renewal

Renewal is the shedding of the old, of being newborn, of a new time and focused on transition from one state to another—this is both the physical and spiritual domain of an Indigenous worldview, centered in ceremony.

Scholar Little Bear articulates the concept of animate life force further: "An Indigenous society enters into relationship with the animating principles and energy flows of the cosmos and accepts its obligations for the ceremonies of renewal that must be carried out and the acts that must be performed to ensure harmony and balance."[50] It is this very concept of "animate" and "inanimate" that dances at the edges of the Western concept of civilization, drawing a line in the sand of being formidably pagan in its nature, and unapologetically Indigenous. This concept redraws the boundaries of the nature of reality and our environment and frames how we relate to it.

Indigenous ceremony is embedded with the process of renewal and reinforces our commitments, protocols, and generational relationships.

Summary of Indigenomics Principles

These principles act as markers on the cultural landscape of an Indigenous worldview, the formative ethics of Indigenous resilience, continuity, success, and cultural ethics. An ethic acts as a set of moral principles, especially ones relating to or affirming a specified group, field, or form of conduct.

The distinction of an Indigenous worldview can be observed in the nonlinear nature of relationships. As articulated by Little Bear, "The White people separate things out, even the relationship between their minds and their bodies, but especially between themselves and other people and nature...[and] spirit."[51]

Indigenous spirituality sees the interconnectedness of the elements of the Earth and the universe, animate and inanimate, whereby humans, plants and animals, land features, and even celestial bodies are considered interrelated. These relationships and the knowledge of how they are interconnected are expressed in ceremony, stories, and the perception of economy.

Conclusion

The intention here is to highlight key elements of an Indigenous worldview; this is not an exhaustive description and is best illustrated from within an individual culture. These are intended to lay a foundation from which, when these ethics are activated, each serves the continuity of an Indigenous worldview and ways of life. Further, these principles are laid out to build understanding of relational decision-making. Each shapes the cultural landscape and ethics of an Indigenous worldview.

Where do we see the emergence of ethics in mainstream economics? In 1759, in *The Theory of Moral Sentiments*, Adam Smith describes the nature of ethics as seen within people as the character of a truly virtuous person. He describes the virtue of ethics requiring people to weigh moral virtues against social norms in the context of time and place. He asserts that, as humanity, our moral ideas and actions are a product of our very nature as social beings. This book was a prelude to his foundational work *The Wealth of Nations* in 1776.

Looking to the Catholic Church, Pope Benedict XVI ties ethics and economy together:

It really seems visible today that ethics is not something exterior to the economy, which, as technical matter, could function on its own; rather, ethics is an interior principle of the economy itself, which cannot function if it does not take account of the human values of solidarity and reciprocal responsibility.[52]

REFLECTION

1. What stands out to you in developing understanding of an Indigenous worldview?

2. What is a cultural landscape and why is it important in decision-making?

3. In what ways can these principles provide insight into an Indigenous worldview?

4

"But I Was Never Taught
This in School"

*All four of my grandparents have benefited from these lands
and this place. This is the truth telling of today—
how Canadians have collectively benefited from
Indigenous lands and resources across generations.*

—SHAUN LONEY[1]

How many times have we heard this exact statement, I was never taught this in school!, followed with a look of utter surprise and dismay in regard to understanding Indigenous history? This overly common statement demonstrates the shortcomings of relaying history and makes Indigenous Peoples invisible within the long-term development of Canada. It is this invisibility upon which the legal evolution of the Aboriginal relationship has been based. This invisibility serves the absence of Indigenous Peoples at the economic table of this country.

This lack of learning forms the deficit structure that allows the continued systemic government policy and regulatory approach to Indigenous Peoples and is the elementary formation of the conflict in the Indigenous relationship. With a lack of knowledge on the formation of this country, nothing needs to change. However, with knowledge and understanding, this forms the basis for transformative relationship.

The following historical timeline shows the development of British Columbia. Adapted from an earlier version on the Union of BC Indian Chiefs website,[2] it provides a quick overview of the development of one province as an example that works to frame the history of the Aboriginal relationship in the establishment of Canada. This version has been shortened in places for the sake of brevity, with bold added for emphasis. Additions to the original timeline have been made for 2000 forward. While going through this timeline, it is important for the reader to take note of what stands out and to identify any patterns you notice across time. What serves as an early form of an economic function to the development of region and country?

A History of the Development of British Columbia

1722	British Privy Council memorandum sets out **Doctrines** of **Discovery & conquest**
1763	**Royal Proclamation** of King George III recognizes Aboriginal title and rights to land
1778	Captain Cook **charts** Nootka Sound on his third expedition to the Pacific
1792	Captain George Vancouver **charts** most of Georgia Strait
1780s	Epidemics appear on the Pacific Northwest coast

Moving from the 1700s to the 1800s, it is important to reflect upon what stands out in this century of Indigenous relations. Three major processes or structures that are found in this timeframe are the establishment of the Doctrine of Discovery, the Royal Proclamation, and the beginning of "charting" or "discovering." It is important to understand in the context of the rest of this timeline that the Doctrine of Discovery was the single most self-serving legal principle whereby Europeans claimed rights of sovereignty and ownership of regions they claimed to have "discovered." Under this doctrine, Indigenous Peoples could not claim ownership of their own lands, only the right to occupy and use the land. This Doctrine of Discovery still stands today, serving its own purpose. The Royal Proclamation sets out Indigenous relations for the next 250 plus years. Now, let's look at the 1800s.

1804	Fort Simpson **established** by Northwest Company
1805	Lewis and Clark **expedition;** first to travel overland in US from Atlantic to Pacific
1805–07	Fort St. John **established** by Northwest Company. McLeod

Lake post **established** by Simon Fraser. Fort Nelson **established** on Liard River. Hudson Hope post established at Rocky Mountain Portage. Fort St. James **established**. Fort Fraser post established by HBC at Fraser Lake

1821	**Northwest Company and Hudson's Bay Company merge, known as HBC**
1826	Fort Vancouver established by HBC on Columbia River
1834	**James Douglas becomes Chief Trader of the HBC**
1835	Coal **deposit** at Fort Rupert publicized
1838	HBC **granted** 21-year **exclusive** hunting and trading license to northwest coast
1843	Fort Victoria was established by HBC
1843	**HBC begins laying out land boundaries**
1846	Oregon Treaty establishes 49th parallel as the US-British boundary
1846	HBC's Pacific Headquarters shifts from Oregon (Columbia River) to Victoria
1849	Royal Charter **grants** Vancouver Island to the HBC
1849	Chief Factor James Douglas receives direction to **negotiate** with Vancouver Island Tribes
1849	Fort Rupert established by **HBC to supply coal** to an American steamship line
1850	Douglas concludes **treaties** in Victoria, Sooke, and Metchosin
1851	**Douglas becomes Governor but remains Chief Factor of the HBC (to 1858)**
1851	Gold found on Queen Charlotte Islands. Gunboats sent to Queen Charlotte Islands
1852	James Douglas becomes Lieutenant-Governor of the Queen Charlotte Islands
1854	Douglas concludes treaty in Nanaimo. Nanaimo coalfields purchased by HBC
1857	**Colonial proclamation claims all gold mines. Gold mining licenses introduced**
1858	*British Columbia Act.* **New Caledonia becomes Colony of British Columbia**
1858	James Douglas resigns from HBC to become Governor of the mainland Colony of BC

1858	Colonel R. C. Moody is Commissioner of Lands and Works (CLW) to 1864
1858	Royal Engineers undertake **mapping** of BC mainland
1858	**Colonial proclamation states that all land is vested in the crown**
1858	**Gunboats** sent to New Caledonia (BC)
1858	Fraser River **Gold Rush starts**
1858	Construction of Harrison-Lillooet **road** commenced
1859	*Gold Fields Act* **sets out Gold Commissioner's duties and miners' water rights**
1859	HBC trading **license** on Vancouver Island expires. James Douglas becomes Governor
1859	Douglas **appoints first Gold Commissioners** and Stipendiary Magistrates
1859	Douglas reduces price of surveyed land
1859	Peter O'Reilly (Joseph Trutch's brother-in-law) becomes Assistant Gold Commissioner
1860s	Douglas pre-Confederation reserves laid out (mostly to 1864; none after 1871)
1861	**Legislative Assembly of VI asks England for funds to extinguish Aboriginal title; denied**
1861	Gold **discovered** in the Upper Peace River region
1861	Harrison-Lillooet wagon **road completed**
1861	Proclamation consolidates laws relating to the settlement of unsurveyed crown lands
1861	**Gold Commissioners also become Assistant Commissioner of Lands**
1862	Smallpox epidemic reduces aboriginal populations
1862	Peak of the Cariboo Gold Rush
1864	Joseph Trutch is Chief Commissioner of Lands and Works (to 1871)
1864	**Douglas policy is reversed. Douglas reserve size cut back by Trutch**
1864	**Joseph Trutch is Surveyor General for BC**
1864	Queen's birthday celebration. Indians ask Governor Seymour to protect their lands
1866	New Westminster becomes capital of new colony of BC

1867	*Constitution Act s.91(24)*. **Canada responsible for Indians and lands reserved for Indians**
1867	Petition from 70 BC Indian Chiefs forwarded by Governor Seymour to England
1869	*Mineral Ordinance*
1870	Terms of Union confirms Dominion government's **responsibility for Indians**
1870	**Transfer of HBC lands to Canada**
1870	*Land Ordinance*. Crown reserves right to resume land for roads
1870	*British North America (BNA) Act* gives province control over land (s. 92)
1870	Timberlands begin to be leased
1871	Joseph Trutch is Lieutenant-Governor (to 1876)
1871	**BC enters Confederation. Indians remain the responsibility of the federal government**
1871	BC Government agents take over all non-mining duties from Gold Commissioners
1871	Exploratory surveys to determine route of CPR begun (to 1879)
1871	*Constitution Act* establishes authority of provincial departments and officials
1871	Lands and Works Department created to survey, map, and administer BC lands
1871	Peter O'Reilly works in Ominica as Gold Commissioner, tax collector, and Indian Agent
1871	Indian people not allowed to fish commercially (to 1923)
1871	Schedule of All Indian Reserves (Surveyed) in the Province of BC established
1872	First Central Registry File system called the Red Series (Eastern Canada) established
1872	The **right to vote** in BC elections withdrawn from Indian people in BC (to 1949)
1873	**Indian Superintendent granted magisterial (enforcement) powers**
1873	Metlakatla residential school established
1873	**Northwest Mounted Police formed**

1873	Bill providing for destitute Indians and half-breeds of BC
1873	Indian & Indian Lands branch set up under the Dept. of the Interior
1874	BC Gazette notice reserving 20-mile-wide strip along east coast of VI for a railway
1874	Glenora post established by HBC at Telegraph Creek
1874	St. Eugene mission established at Cranbrook
1874	Indian Board established in BC
1875	*BC Land Act* of 1874 is disallowed by Canada because it disregards Aboriginal title
1875	*Papers Connected with the Indian Land Question* published as BC Sessional Papers
1875	Canadian Geological Survey's G.M. Dawson begins explorations in BC
1875	Revised *BC Land Act* provides for Indian reserves (s. 60)
1875	*Esquimalt and Nanaimo Railway Act* (grant of lands for railway purposes to Canada)
1875	Land is available to settlers free of charge
1875	G.M. Dawson explores BC for the Canadian Geological Survey
1875	BC divided into two superintendencies, Victoria and Fraser (located in New Westminster). Superintendents report to Deputy Superintendent General of Indian Affairs in Ottawa
1876	Canadian Governor General Lord Dufferin appeals for fair treatment of Indian claims
1876	First Federal Indian Act passed; consolidates all previous legislation concerning Indians
1876	Federal proclamation excludes Indian lands and resources in BC from the Indian Act
1877	Kimsquit (Bella Coola) village destroyed by Royal Navy gunboat
1879	Burrard Inlet chosen as CPR line terminus
1880	Joseph Trutch is Dominion agent in BC on railway and Indian matters
1880	DIA is created; Superintendent General is the Minister of the Interior
1880	*An Act to further amend the Indian Act* prohibits Indians from assembling

1881	**DIA forms** six Indian agencies
1883	Province starts **granting crown lands** for railway purposes
1884	*Settlement Act* **transfers first land grant** for Esquimalt & Nanaimo Railway
1884	*Dominion Lands Act*
1884	*BC Land Act* (posted notices required for diversion of water)
1884	Motion in BC Legislature to remove Indians from valuable land. Defeated
1884	*Indian Advancement Act* introduces annual elections system
1884	Timber licenses introduced
1885	**Changes to the Indian Act prohibit potlatching (til 1951)**
1887	Nisga'a and Tsimshian delegation travels to Victoria to discuss **Indian Land Question**
1887	**Regulations** re mining on abandoned or surrendered lands in Railway Belt introduced
1887	Federal PCOC #1887 provides for **access roads** within the Railway Belt
1888	Federal policy creates Indian food fishery. Indians **not allowed to fish commercially**
1889	*Precious Metals Case* **establishes provincial jurisdiction over precious metals**
1890	Indian Reserve Commissioner O'Reilly directed not to allot fishing privileges
1891	BC railways **granted 100-foot rights-of-way** through crown lands
1892	**List of Reserves within the Railway Belt** drawn up
1893	Report on the Census of Indians (to 1895). Economic depression
1894	Dominion runs out of funds for surveys of Indian reserves in BC
1895	Indian Act amended
1895	**Department of Indian Affairs starts mandatory band elections in some parts of Canada**
1895	Boundaries of the Railway Belt are defined

This is one busy century! What do you notice in this century? What stood out for you? Structures must be established, resources identi-fied, the Indians must be "managed or handled," access to lands and resources secured, Colonial Authority established. We can see the establishment of Forts for trading purposes, expeditions, and resource deposits are "discovered." Here we see lands becoming "granted," the negotiation of early treaties. A colonial proclamation, establishing of the Crown relationship, "licensing" systems are established; structures to ensure access to gold resources. We see the "extinguishment" of Aboriginal title, we see roads and transportation systems established to move the resources, laws are being formed. Here we see smallpox devastate the Indigenous populations.

Later in the century brings water rights, the gold rush, mineral ordinances, land transfers, timber leases begin, reserves surveyed and established, the first residential school opens in BC. The rail strip is established to move resources. Here we see the beginning of the Indian Land Question, the further granting of lands to settlers, overall colonial shenanigans if you will. The continuing surveying, granting of land for settlers (Ever wonder where your land title of where you live comes from?). Here we learn of native villages destroyed by gunboat, in the way of land acquisition, to remove resistance and access to resources.

The Indian agent position was created to manage the Indians; the position is connected to both rail and Indian matters. Later in the century, we begin to see the managing of the Indian Problem: prohibiting of Indians assembling, leaving the reserves, or obtaining legal counsel, and the removal of spiritual and economic functions. Finally, we see the formation of the Department of Indian Affairs and Resources. Land is being freely distributed to settlers. And lastly, "disallowing" a commercially fish for native peoples. Provincial jurisdiction on precious metals. All actions that formed the perfect structure of economic apartheid are being formed.

Again, moving from the 18th century into the 19th century, it is important to reflect on the key themes and patterns. Notice what stands out for you. It is here we see the beginning of the structure and processes to further address the Indian Problem. Through the establishment of the reserves came confinement, limitation, and the devaluing of an Indigenous worldview and way of life.

1900 Forest sector begins to dominate BC economy
1904 *Vancouver Island Settlers' Rights Act*

1905	**Province of Alberta formed**
1906	Delegation of BC Chiefs meet with King Edward to discuss the **Indian Land Question**
1908	BC's Executive Council decides it will not make any further reserve allotments
1906	Second delegation of BC Chiefs to England
1910	**BC refuses to submit question of Aboriginal title in BC to British Privy Council**
1910	*Amendment to the **Water Act** defines the powers of the Water Commissioner*
1910	Indian Reserve Commission is dismantled
1910	Interior Chiefs sign declaration setting out their position on Aboriginal title and rights
1910	While in BC, Laurier visits Kamloops. Learning that he is in favor of larger reserves and recognition of Aboriginal Title, the Chiefs of Shuswap, Okanagan, and Thompson Tribes present *The Memorial to Sir Wilfred Laurier, Premier of the Dominion of Canada from the Chiefs of the Shuswap, Okanagan and Thompson Tribes*, condemning BC land policies and game laws and rejecting BC's takeover of their lands. Believing that the Queen's laws will guarantee their rights, they request treaties with Canada
1910	BC divided into three inspectorates: Northern, Southwestern, and Southeastern
1912	Dr. J.A.J. McKenna memo to BC premier agreeing to set aside Aboriginal title question
1913	**Approximately 500,000 acres in BC alienated for mining purposes;** 8.5 million acres in BC **alienated** for timber purposes
1914	First World War begins (ends 1918)
1914	*BC Water Act*
1919	CNR and CNPR incorporate as Canadian National Railway Company
1920	Federal legislation permits **enfranchisement** of Indians without their consent. Repealed
1920	**Duncan C. Scott makes it mandatory for Indian children (7–15 years) to attend school**
1920s	Indian population reaches lowest point

1924	The elective system is introduced to replace the hereditary leadership system

1924 **The elective system is introduced to replace the hereditary leadership system**

1926 Chief William Pierrish of Neskonlith tables statement with King of England

1927 Indian Act prohibits raising money or hiring lawyers to pursue land claims (to 1951). Canada **amends the Indian Act to make it illegal to obtain funds or legal counsel to advance Aboriginal Title cases.** This ends the Allied Tribes hope of having a case heard at the Privy Council in London, and the Allied Tribes dissolves. Indigenous resistance goes underground.

1930 *Canada–BC Natural Resources Transfer Agreement*

1931 Native Brotherhood of British Columbia formed. The Haida and Tsimshian form the Native Brotherhood of British Columbia (NBBC). NBBC organizes protests on fishing, lands, taxation, and social issues. The founding declaration is similar to the Allied Tribes' statement, but avoids mentioning Aboriginal Title. Its official mandate is to improve the socio-economic conditions of Indian people in BC. Unofficially, the NBBC seeks recognition of Aboriginal Title.

1936 Indian administration absorbed by the Department of Mines and Resources (to 1949)

1943 *British Columbia Indian Reserves Mineral Resources Act*

1943 *Schedule of Indian Reserves in the Dominion of Canada-Reserves in the Province of B.C.*

1951 **Oil and gas boom** begins in Peace River District

1952 **Nechako Reservoir Study is first archaeological impact assessment in BC**

1953 Trans Mountain Oil pipeline reaches Port Moody

1953 Northern Affairs portfolio part of Department of Northern Affairs and Natural Resources

1955 *The Indians of BC: A Survey of Social and Economic Conditions* published

1960 Secwepemc leader, George Manuel and Nisga'a leader Frank Calder present briefs to the Joint Committee for the Review of Indian Affairs Policy. Citing the 1763 Royal Proclamation, Manuel and Calder both demand recognition of and compensation for loss of Aboriginal Title. The

Committee recommends the establishment of an Indian Claims Commission to settle outstanding land claims in Canada.

1960 Federal voting rights extended to include Indian people

1961 Provincial Government purchases BC Electric Company

1962 BC Electric Co. amalgamates with BC Power Commission to create BC Hydro

1962 Bill C-19, *An Act Respecting the Canada Court of Indians* receives first reading

1962 North American Indian Brotherhood calls for legislated Indian Claims Commission

1966 Confederation of Native Indians of BC formed

1966 Department of Indian Affairs and Northern Development (DIAND) is formed

1960s High-voltage power transmission lines begin to be erected in BC

1967 Duncan dam on Columbia River completed

1967 Mica Dam-Kinbasket Lake Reservoir construction begins

1967 *Worrall Report* on mineral resources on Indian reserves in BC published

1968 Nisga'a take their land claim to court

1968 Indian Homemakers Association formed

1968 DIA establishes and administers *Indian Mining Regulations*

1969 Indian Claims Commission is established under *Inquiries Act* (Barber Commission)

1969 Trudeau government's *White Paper* asserts that Aboriginal title does not exist. Prime Minister Trudeau and his Minister of Indian Affairs, Jean Chretien, introduce a white paper on Indian policy. The policy is one of aggressive assimilation and is soon dubbed "The White Paper" by Indigenous leaders.

1969 The Union of BC Indian Chiefs (UBCIC) forms as 144 Chiefs and delegates from all over BC meet to discuss the White Paper and its effects on Indian people in BC

1969 Federal government takes direct control over Indian residential schools

1970 INAC Membership starts transferring local administration of membership to bands

1971	The Canadian Government formally withdraws the White Paper and, soon after, the UBCIC adopts its Constitution and By-laws and is incorporated under the *BC Societies Act*.
1972	UBCIC submits BC claim based on native title to the federal government. UBCIC presents a *Claim Based on Native Title to the Lands now Forming British Columbia* to Prime Minister Trudeau, demanding recognition of Aboriginal Title and compensation for its loss.
1973	Federal Indian Affairs Minister Jean Chretien introduces federal land claims policy
1973	Aboriginal rights discussed for first time in the federal House of Commons
1973	*Calder vs. A-G* recognizes land rights based on aboriginal title (SCC). Calder v. Attorney General of BC. The Supreme Court of Canada recognizes that the Nisga'a held title to their land before BC was established, however the court splits evenly on whether Nisga'a title had been extinguished since the establishment of BC. In response, Trudeau changes federal policy to allow negotiation of "Comprehensive Claims" based on Aboriginal Title and "Specific Claims" based on reserve lands.
1974	INAC establishes Office of Native Claims to receive claims submissions
1974	Nisga'a comprehensive claim accepted for negotiation by the federal government
1979	BC Chiefs and Elders make constitutional visit to England
1981	Nazko-Kluskus comprehensive claim submitted to federal government
1981	UBCIC mobilizes the Constitution Express. Trainloads of Indigenous Peoples travel from BC to Ottawa to lobby Trudeau and the Premiers to guarantee Indigenous Peoples' right to self-determination in the Canadian Constitution. In the end, Canada passes the *Canada Constitution Act*, 1982 recognizing "existing aboriginal and treaty rights" (Section 35). Three years later, after a series of unsuccessful First Ministers' Conferences, the task of defining Aboriginal Rights is left to the Canadian courts.

1981	Some McKenna-McBride cut-off lands claims are settled (into the mid-1980s)
1982	*Canada Constitution Act* recognizes existing Aboriginal and treaty rights (s. 35)
1983–84	Meares Island logging controversy
1985	Bill C-31 passes, ending discrimination against Indian women who married non-Indians
1985	Bill C-31 results in addition of many new members to BC Indian bands
1986	Canada revises its comprehensive claims policy
1986	*An Act Relating to the Establishment of Self-government for the Sechelt Indian Band*
1986	United Church of Canada first to apologize for treatment at residential schools
1988	Canadian Bar Association affirms need for claims to be submitted to an independent body
1990	The Oka standoff begins.
1990	Province abandons 119-year-old policy of refusing to acknowledge Aboriginal title
1990	BC joins the Nisga'a and Canada in the negotiation of the Nisga'a Comprehensive Claim. This is the first time BC agrees to negotiate a Comprehensive Claim. BC still refuses to acknowledge Aboriginal Title.
1990	UBCIC submits a draft *Comprehensive Framework Treaty* to Canada and BC, setting out a process for treaty negotiation in BC. The first principle is that no extinguishment of Aboriginal Title will occur with as a result of the signing of a treaty.
1991	Canada establishes a Royal Commission on Aboriginal Peoples to examine the relationship between Canada and Indigenous Peoples. The Commission visits 96 communities, holds 178 days of hearings, and completes over 350 research projects over four years.
1991	Report of the BC Claims Task Force recommends new treaty process for BC
1991	BC government formally acknowledges the Indian Land Question

1991 BC Court of Appeal rules that Aboriginal rights were extinguished before 1871

1991 Indian Specific Claims Commission created to mediate rejected specific claims

1992 BC Hydro creates Aboriginal Relations Department

1992 The First Nations Congress, Canada, and BC establish the First Nations Summit and the BC Treaty Commission to implement the BC Treaty Process. The Treaty Process strives for final agreements in which Indigenous Peoples surrender 95 percent of their territories to Canada in exchange for compensation and specific treaty rights. Within ten years, 120 bands enter negotiations, borrowing $250 million to be paid back out of their compensation packages.

1993 BC Court of Appeal rules Gitxsan and Wet'suwet'en have unextinguished Aboriginal title

1995 **Province of BC introduces its traditional use studies policy**

1995 Federal government acknowledges First Nations inherent right to self-government

1996 **The Royal Commission on Aboriginal Peoples releases its Final Report recommending a redistribution of political authority and economic resources to reform the relationship between Canada and Indigenous Peoples. Condemning Canada's Comprehensive Claim policy, the Commission recommends a policy that recognizes Aboriginal rights and emphasizes shared ownership and jurisdiction over land. Canada shelves the $58 million report for two years.**

1996 *R. vs. Van der Peet* clarifies Aboriginal rights

1996 *R. vs. Gladstone* clarifies fishing rights

1996 *R. vs. Nikal*, *R. vs. Lewis* and *R. vs. NTC Smokehouse* clarifies Aboriginal rights

1996 The Nisga'a Tribal Council, BC, and Canada sign an agreement-in-principle that forms the basis of the first Comprehensive Claim agreement signed in BC.

1996 Joint First Nations/Canada Task Force (JTF) discuss reforming specific claims policy

1997 *Delgamuuk'w vs. British Columbia* upholds aboriginal title (SCC) On appeal from previous BC Court decisions, the

Gitxsan and Wet'suwet'en hereditary Chiefs amend an original assertion of ownership and control over their territories, replacing it with claims of Aboriginal Title and self-government. BC argues that Aboriginal Title does not exist. Alternatively, BC argues, Aboriginal Title is not a right of ownership, but a right to engage in traditional subsistence practices such as hunting and fishing. The Supreme Court of Canada rejects the trial judge's ruling that Aboriginal rights had been extinguished before 1871. The Court does not decide whether the Gitxsan and Wet'suwet'en still hold title to their land and instead clarifies that Aboriginal Title is not a right of absolute ownership, but a proprietary right to "exclusive use and occupation of land" that "is a burden on the Crown's underlying title." Once Aboriginal Title is proven, federal and provincial governments may infringe upon it for valid reasons, including resource extraction, economic and infrastructure development, settlement of foreign populations, and environmental protection. Aboriginal people must be consulted and compensated for any infringement or extinguishment of Aboriginal Title.

1998 Minister of Indian Affairs makes statement of reconciliation re residential school abuse

1998 Nisga'a sign agreement with federal and provincial governments

1999 Supreme Court decides that off-reserve members should have voting rights in on-reserve elections, Corbiere Decision

Here again, let's reflect upon moving into the 20th century, examining the state of Aboriginal affairs and the connection between the development of British Columbia as a province and the establishment of Canada as a country. *Rights-based, legal-based, advancement of assertion. Answering of the Aboriginal Question.*

It is here we see the *Settlers' Rights Act*; we see a direct Aboriginal approach concentrating on England's throne to address the Aboriginal Land Question. The 1910 position on rights and title origins, alienated for mining. No hiring of lawyers, more colonial shenanigans. Oil and gas boom, roads and transportation systems continued to set up for moving resources, structures (Acts) to support the resource extraction and proper elimination of the Indian. Connection between Indian Affairs and natural resource management structure is established. Dams need to power up, create electricity. We see the first land claim by the Nisga'a. We see the White Paper in the first Trudeau government and the Federal government taking over residential schools from the churches.

2000	The Nisga'a Final Agreement becomes Canadian law. The Nisga'a surrender 92 percent of their territory in exchange for expanded reserve lands and $190 million cash. The Nisga'a Lisims government is subject to provincial and federal laws. Nisga'a living in the settlement lands will be subject to BC, Canada, and Lisims taxation.
2004	**Nuu chah nulth win right to commercial fish**
2005	Prime Minister Paul Martin promises a transformation of Indian policy in Canada before reducing the Department of Indian Affairs budget by $260 million.
2005	BC continues to aggressively promote oil and gas drilling, ski resort development, logging, mining, and other forms of resource extraction in Indigenous territories.
2012	Largest Indigenous uprising called Idle No More. Sparked from Harper's Omnibus Bill de-protecting water systems in Canada. Goals include stopping environmental degradation and economic and social inequality
2014	Williams Case – Third definition of Title established
2017	239 legal cases First Nations have won against Canada in the Supreme Courts

This is a sample of the demonstration of the real lived experience of Indigenous economic displacement timeline: a history that was never taught in schools, across each province and territory of this country. This is the history of the establishment of Canada as seen through the lens of only one province, with other provinces and territories following very similar pathways but earlier.

This timeline clearly demonstrates that the establishment of the Province of British Columbia was shaped through the development of securing energy sources, transportation systems, access to resources, and the overall "managing" of the Indians without addressing the Land Question, the formative question of Canada's development.

Progressing through this timeline, it is important to recognize the themes that emerge from transportation, resources, and the establishment of acts to support their extraction are key processes to establish early authority. Essentially, the "Indians" had to be "dealt with"—put on reserves and out of way of extraction, development, and "progress" itself. The truths of this timeline are simple, demonstrating the direct connection to the establishment of Canada as we know and experience it today as well as how we relate to our understanding of Indigenous issues and conflict.

It is important to understand, in choosing to highlight only BC in this timeline for the purpose of being succinct, each province and territory has distinct yet similar developments across Canada, spanning back as early as the 1600s that relay the same pathway to deal with the "Indians," through the establishment of the numbered treaties, gain access to land and resources, develop transportation, energy systems, and governance processes.

The development of this timeline is directly connected to Canada's origin story. As Katherine Mahoney notes, in "The Roadblock to Reconciliation: Canada's Origin Story Is False," "The accepted story of Canada's origin tells us the nation came into being on July 1, 1867. Thirty-six 'Fathers of Confederation,' representing the British and the French colonial powers, signed the British North America Act, setting out the governance structure for the new country."[3]

Mahoney identifies the problem through the simple statement: "Our origin story is false." She notes:

> In 1996, the Royal Commission on Aboriginal Peoples observed, "A country cannot be built on a living lie." After over 150 years in denial, coming to terms with our true origin story is long overdue.... Indigenous Canadians are invisible in this origin story even though they were present on the land for thousands of years prior to Confederation and without their contributions Canada would not be the country it is today.[4]

As Mahoney articulates:

> Origin stories are important. Every country, every community, every family, has an origin story to express who they are and where they have come from. A nation's origin story serves as a script for citizenship; it helps citizens navigate their world,

form relationships, and solidify their identities. But when a nation's origin story ignores the existence and contributions of those integral to its founding, it can create a deep sense of alienation, isolation and hostility.[5]

Today requires the re-storying of Canada through the recognition that Indigenous Peoples were the founders of this great nation. It is this intersection, the power point between our past and our future as a country, that "This must be acknowledged in a formal, legal way. Only then will there be a solid foundation for Canada to reconcile its past and lay the foundation for a new relationship with its first peoples."[6]

Through her leadership, Mahoney is calling Canada into this new reality through the recognition and visibility of the Aboriginal relationship in Canada, right from its origins. That's the thing with recognition, once established, everybody has to move over, make room.

The parallel processes of the establishment of the Indian Act and the establishment of Canada revealed a specific narrative. While the name of the Indian Affairs ministry may have changed over time, the name Indian Act remains within the act and still references the Indians themselves.

REFLECTION

1. What stood out for you on this timeline?

2. What does a "new truth" mean in relation to Canada's origin story?

3. What does "re-storying" mean to you?

The Indigenous Economy

We are tired of being economic hostages in our own homelands.
—MELINDA LABOUCAN-MASSIMO[1]

I once heard an Elder from the Paul Nation in Alberta wisely reflect: "We as Indigenous people are the continuity the world is looking for. We come from the old world, the old ways of the old ceremonies. The world has evolved, but the drum beat has stayed the same. We as Indigenous peoples are the constant the world seeks." This is a brilliant depiction of the role of Indigenous Peoples in modernity—"We are the constant the world seeks."

There are over 370 million Indigenous Peoples worldwide, making up just over 6% of the population. Identifying as Indigenous is confirmed through ancestral connections, genealogical lineages, and connection to lands, culture, traditions, ceremony, and languages reaching across entire continents and regions from Brazil, Bolivia, to Greenland, Canada, across Africa, India, to Australia, to the Māori in New Zealand, the Hawaiian people, the Navajo, or the Inuit in the North. Two key facts: Indigenous Peoples make up approximately 6% of the world's population yet account for over 10% of the global poverty; Canada specifically has over 1 million identified Indigenous Peoples.

For thousands of years, Indigenous Peoples across countless generations have ensured collective culturally focused, lands-centered traditional economies. These traditional economic activities were based in distinct spiritual, social, and cultural values; knowledge systems; and ways of being. They become activated from within an

Indigenous economic framework that has embedded within it an Indigenous worldview as a way of seeing and experiencing the world and reality.

It is these foundational elements of an Indigenous worldview that has ensured the continuity of Indigenous Peoples across thousands of years. It is this very continuity that builds on the United Nations Declaration on the Rights of Indigenous Peoples (UNDRIP)—specifically, the right to self-determination, the right to an economy, and the right to continue our way of life as Indigenous Peoples across time. Indigenomics is centered in this concept. Indigenomics is a modern Indigenous economic paradigm.

In contrast to the Indigenous economy, today's mainstream market economy is commonly described as the production, distribution, trade, and consumption of goods in a geographic area. An Indigenous economy, however, has an entirely different meaning and context. An Indigenous economy falls outside the standard definition of the concept of market economy as it is known today. The concept of an Indigenous economy stretches the imagination to form an alternative reality beyond the measurements and indicators of growth and productivity. Instead it is formed on the ethics of the core principles of an Indigenous worldview.

Kelly's work enhances the concept of an Indigenous relational economy:

> In my work, I didn't seek to define an Indigenous economy but instead tried to understand the nature of the Indigenous economy. This distinction is about understanding the way or why we "exchange" in particular ways. If we only think about economics in terms of "how," the "why" question can be lost, and all of that activity and all of that investment in resources and all of that time spent doing the economy will be all for naught if you don't understand why you are exchanging. What emerged in looking at the Coast Salish Indigenous economy was recognizing that what happens in our economic systems of exchange, actually aligns with our institutions that are embedded in ceremony.[2]

The nature of exchange within an Indigenous economy is derived from a distinct Indigenous worldview that is formed through cultural values, protocols, and ceremonies that reaffirm these relationships.

In further examining the concept of the Indigenous economy, Kelly says:

> In terms of what an Indigenous economy is and in understanding the nature of this economy, we can begin to understand why and how we as Indigenous peoples "exchange," which then helps to answer what the Indigenous economy actually is. It is something that connects us for very important purposes. If we don't have Indigenous economies and if we don't have economies as human beings—we don't have the systems to be able to draw these connections, and we won't have institutions to be able to grow our governance around. The economy is fundamental to being human.[3]

The Indigenous economy exists outside the confines and boundaries of all that we know today about modern economics and its measurements of growth. Instead, the Indigenous economy exists within our relationship to ourselves, to each other, to the Earth, to our past, and to our future. Indigenomics questions assumptions in regards to the Indigenous experience of poverty and colonization itself. Kelly continues in centering the concept of the Indigenous economy:

> Today's Indigenous economies are an articulation of economies that are very old. For historical and political reasons, these economies have kept operating but somewhat silently within our own communities. But now Indigenous economy is about questioning some assumptions around the dominant paradigms and AngloWestern economies that permeate within the Canadian economic landscape.[4]

This is relational economics. While the Western mainstream economy is geared toward monetary transactions as a source of exchange, the Indigenous economy is based on relationship. Indigenous economies are the original sharing economy, the original green economy, regenerative economy, collaborative economy, circular economy, impact economy, and the original gift economy. The Indigenous economy is the original social economy.

At the center of Indigenous economy is ceremony, a form of collaboration, protocol, and agreement within both the physical and the spiritual realms. It is through ceremony the expressed relationship with others and everything around us can be acknowledged.

It confirms that the individual is neither the source nor the owner. This connection of relationships forms relational accountability or relational economics. It is from this concept that Indigenomics is shaped from.

Characteristics of an Indigenous Economy

It is important to gain insight into the foundational elements or characteristics of an Indigenous economy. Outlined here are ten key characteristics of an Indigenous economy, stemming directly from the elements within an Indigenous worldview:

1. An Indigenous economy is an economic system that is place-based. It recognizes and values origin as the relationship to space and people through the deep and lasting connection to place. It is this continuity that forms the sense of responsibility to place and time.

2. An Indigenous economy forms the basis of relational account-ability. It is centered in an inherent sacred sense of responsibility and long-term impact for inter-relational decision-making.

3. An Indigenous economy is future-based. It is framed in multigen-erational thinking. It focuses on long-term thinking and decision-making for the seventh generation and beyond. Decision-making is focused on long-term impact.

4. An Indigenous economy focuses on equality in all universal re-lationships. It focuses on the inter-relationship of species and re-spect for life as a core value. The quality and nature of "exchange" encompasses the protocols of life, the agreements of place and responsibility.

5. An Indigenous economy works to connect and value both the natural and supernatural world – all of the physical, spiritual, and tangible and intangible components.

6. An Indigenous economy is based on the concept of reciprocity. It focuses on giving and receiving as core structures for wealth pro-duction and distribution that forms the basis of exchange and the future value of wealth.

7. An Indigenous economy is restorative or regenerative in nature. It focuses on economic progress as a parallel process to respon-sibility for lands, resource management, conservation, and long-term conservation of resources.

8. An Indigenous economy focuses on the core value and teaching of "only taking what is needed." This is a core premise of governance and decision-making—that future generations require this of us today. Management systems are established from this concept. Indigenous knowledge systems and ways of knowing form relational decision-making.

9. An Indigenous economy both focuses on economic interdependence and builds economic sovereignty (right to an economy) as a mechanism of modernity. Economic sovereignty works to facilitate and uplift the retention of cultural and spiritual identity and the continuity of connection and interdependence.

10. An Indigenous economy measures wealth through relationship and community and across time. Prosperity is confirmed though recognition, protocol, ceremony, the exchange of gifting, and distribution. The future value of wealth is based on giving and wealth distribution.

The wealth distribution of an Indigenous economy unfortunately can no longer be inherently activated in their entirety within today's modern economy. This is due to such intrusions as the Doctrine of Discovery, as mentioned earlier, that continue to ensure the economic displacement of Indigenous reality and sense of responsibility. Further, the disruption of the Indian Act into Indigenous governance systems, as well as current government regulations and policies, continues the practice of Indigenous economic and cultural distortion.

It is now possible to begin to describe the Indigenous economy of today and to reflect on what kind of economy we want in the future. The characteristics of today's modern Indigenous economy is articulated by Indigenous business leader Shannin Metatawabin, CEO of the National Aboriginal Capital Corporation Association, who focuses on building the Aboriginal Financial Institution Network to ensure that Aboriginal businesses have the capacity and access to the capital to grow the Indigenous economy.

Some of the characteristics of an Indigenous economy today include: (1) our monies staying within our community, (2) that it's not going one way out of the community and our people being left in a constant state of poverty, and (3) we are doing

Indigenous-to-Indigenous trade. Our communities are actually not only trading in Canada but trading with other Indigenous groups in this world. In looking at Indigenous peoples globally in areas like Australian, New Zealand, Africa, and South America, it is plain to see that we have the same social and economic issues. Today we can create our own economy amongst ourselves. To begin, we have to create that economy within our communities. This is a difficult thing as most of the communities are in a state of economic unsustainability with no economic base or resources. This is the unfolding process we are seeing today in building an Indigenous economy.[5]

Indigenous business leader Clint Davis speaks to the emergence of Indigenomics as an economic paradigm: "Indigenomics is taking the economics component or taking the national and global view of economics and economy and looking at it and applying Indigenous components to it, in particular, Indigenous value. This provides a very unique perspective to the concept of an Indigenous economy today."[6]

Four essential elements a modern Indigenous economy can achieve today are:

1. Strengthened business relationships based on recognition
2. Operate from constructive, purposeful economy, meaning that builds relevance to the future
3. Lead a shift in how economy is experienced
4. Facilitate a return to inherent Indigenous responsibility and decision-making, in the risk management of land and resource development

Indigenomics is the return to human values in our economic relationships. It draws on ancient principles of life that have supported Indigenous economies for thousands of years and works to include modern practices in business and economic development.

REFLECTION

1. What does relational economy mean to you?

2. What stands out to you in key characteristics of an Indigenous economy?

6

Indian Act Economics

The Indian Act is anti-family, and thus stands in the way of love.
Love forges and welds family ties in the present and through
the generations. The Indian Act does not. Love would promote
legislation and community approaches that recognized and
affirmed family relationships, like husband and wife, parent
and child, grandparent and grandchild, aunts and nephew,
uncles and nieces, cousins, siblings and other kinship bonds.
We are spiritually and sociologically a people of
extended kinship and clan relations.
The Indian Act currently severs these traditions.
—JOHN BORROWS[1]

The Indian Act is anti-love. What a brilliant depiction of collision of worldviews. There is economics, and then there is Indian Act economics. The two are entirely different and have different implications and very different economic outcomes.

It is through the Indian Act that Indigenous Peoples have been effectively and systematically legislated out of the mainstream economy through the imposition of laws, regulations, and "Indian policies" that were developed and imposed upon Indigenous communities without their consultation or consent. This is demonstrated in a powerful depiction by the Algonquin people on the establishment of the Parliament of Canada: "A huge castle, which Canadians called Parliament, stood on top of Algonquin land. In its magnificence, it made the poverty of our people nonsensical even to young minds. What was going on with the Algonquin? Were they invisible? Were our grandmothers even people? Were we?"[2]

In 1876, the Indian Act was established to regulate almost every aspect of the "Indians" life and placed the "Indians" on reserves. It defined and limited who is an Indian and regulates band member-ship and governance system, taxation, lands and resources, estates and money management. The Indian Act disrupted entire cultural ways of being and knowledge systems and displaced the economies of Indigenous Peoples across Canada.

The authority established within the Act ranges from overarching political control, such as imposing governing structures on Indige-nous communities in the form of band councils, to control over the rights of Indians to practice their culture and traditions. The Indian Act micro-managed the life of the Indian, and as an example, in its early days required individual passes for permission to leave the reserve. It enabled the government to determine the land base of Indigenous communities into reservations. In a parallel process, as the Indian Act established reserves, it opened up the rest of Canada for development, productivity, settler fee simple ownership, and resource extraction. The placing of the Indians, the singular act of Indigenous economic regression, was the primary tool to dis-invite Indigenous Peoples to a seat at the economic table.

The Indian Act remains Canada's only race-based legislation. It established the conditions for both economic segregation and the economic regression of the Indigenous Nations, the consequences of which are still being felt today. The Indian Act was created as a tool to serve the invisibility of Indigenous Peoples. The Indian Act by its very nature creates Indigenous economic regression. If the Indian Act is anti-love and anti-family, economic apartheid and economic regres-sion are first cousins. Indigenomics is the response.

Under the Indian Act, there have been over 150 years of economic regression. Economic regression is a statistical measure used in finance and investing that is used to determine the strength of the relationship between one dependent variable (usually denoted by Y) and a series of other changing variables (known as independent vari-ables). Economic regression established within the Indian Act serves the continuous economic metrics of the underdevelopment of the Indian reservation.

The Indian Act was and continues to be a primary tool to serve In-digenous economic exclusion. It has shaped a long history of assimilation policies intended to terminate the cultural, social, economic, and political uniqueness of Indigenous Peoples by purposely absorbing them into mainstream Canadian life and values. This is the uncomfortable space at the heart of Canada's origin story that Canada is built upon—the formation of economic apartheid. The "Indians" were systematically dis-invited to the economic table through the establishment of the reserves and other measures within the Indian Act. The Indian Act remains the primary tool for the continued economic regression of the Indigenous Peoples today. While not every First Nation is currently under the Indian Act, the historical effect of it remains. It is this truth that must be at the heart of re-storying Canada's economic narrative.

The Indian Act is and has always been a tool for economic segregation. The very definition of "apartheid" is racial segregation, specifically, best known as a policy of segregation and political and economic discrimination against the non-European groups in the Republic of South Africa for a land and resource economic grab.

> Economic apartheid exists by the very concept of the Indian Act. The underlying provisions of the Indian Act are there to ensure that Indigenous peoples certainly would become economically dependent upon the federal government and not have any level of independence. Indigenous communities were put into areas of the country which was seen that the land was useless with no value whatsoever and that ensured that Indigenous peoples would be solely dependent upon government.[3]

Indian Act economics establishes a "not allowed to" paternalistic authoritarian approach across generations of Indigenous reality. It is this externalized authoritarian approach that has manifested a community thought process of external approvals and dependency, further perpetuated through the removal of inherent sense of Indigenous responsibility for place. This expresses itself in the margins of this country, from the social and economic gap as an "are we allowed to?" mentality deeply entrenched within a poverty mindset spanning generations across Indigenous reality. Today, whether an Indigenous Nation is self-governing, treaty, or non-treaty, the Indian Act has had impact across time. Indigenomics works to facilitate the space for modern Indigenous economic design as the response to now and the past 150 years and for Indigenous Peoples to take a seat at the economic table of this country.

The Indian Act
and the Aboriginal Question

What the Indian Act did not and cannot address is the Aboriginal Question. At the heart of the Aboriginal Question remains conflicting positions on land and resource rights, conflict of worldviews, and conflict of national economic cohesion. But what is the Aboriginal Question of this century? Indigenous economic design must shift toward addressing standards of well-being, access to economic opportunity, and the continuous evolution and application of legal rights.

One of the earliest demonstrations of the impact of the Indian Act and the early pressure for recognition of Indigenous land rights and in addressing the Aboriginal Question can be seen in *The Memorial to Sir Wilfred Laurier* that was led by the Shushwap and Okanagan peoples in central interior British Columbia:

> In a petition signed by fourteen of our chiefs and sent to your Indian department, July 1908, we pointed out the disabilities under which we labor. Owing to the inadequacy of most of our reservations, some having hardly any good land, others no irrigation water, etc., our limitations regarding pasture lands for stock owing to fencing of so-called government lands by whites; the severe restrictions put on us lately by the government re hunting and fishing; the depletion of salmon by overfishing of the whites, and other matters affecting us. In many places we are debarred from camping, traveling, gathering roots and obtaining wood and water as heretofore. Our people are fined and imprisoned for breaking the game and fish laws and using the same game and fish which we were told would always be ours for food. Gradually we are becoming regarded as trespassers over a large portion of our country. Our old people say, "How are we to live?"[4]

"How are we to live?" This is Indian Act economics. A brilliant yet startling depiction of economic disparity from 1908. This is Indigenous economic regression, a clear picture of the conditions for economic marginalization with the impacts still being felt today. This is the beginnings of what is today called the "socio-economic gap." It is an important historical narrative that speaks to the Indigenous experience of the early days of the establishment of Indian reserves under the Indian Act and systemic economic exclusion and polarization from Canada's GDP. The Indigenous socio-economic gap is the metric of economic displacement.

The Sir Wilfred Memorial text continues: "We will share equally in everything—half and half—in land, water and timber, etc. What is ours will be theirs, and what is theirs will be ours. We will help each other to be great and good."[5] This laid the potential of this early economic relationship that never came to be.

While most Canadian legislation and regulations evolve and are updated over time, the Indian Act has been relatively static and inflexible, serving its original function of economic displacement hundreds of years later. This has left Indigenous Peoples with outdated, paternalistic, discriminatory, and limiting laws that have not kept pace with the modern economy or social, cultural, and economic needs of Indigenous communities. Through the structures of segregation, Indian Act economics have created an environment of Indigenous economic dependencies.

> This new emerging economic reality is creating a level of discomfort within Canada. Everybody around the world knows what apartheid is and certainly would equate that to South Africa in referring to economic apartheid. Today this concept must capture our attention because it's time to realize we need to do something differently and create the conditions for Indigenous economic well-being instead."[6]

While the Indigenous Affairs department has undergone various changes in name and structure with time and different governments, the name of the Indian Act has stayed the same and still refers in its language to the "Indians." The Indian Act remains a significant disservice to the further development of Canada. It is time to move beyond the effects of Indian Act economics; Indian Act economics is the effect of the development and application of Indigenous segregation and economic regression it was created in. If there is any such thing as the opposite of economics, it is Indian Act economics.

The following highlights some key characteristics of Indian Act economics as the foundation for establishing the conditions of continued economic regression of Indigenous Peoples in Canada today:

- The Indian Act limits decision-making from Indigenous Nations referred to as Bands by externalizing, creating geographic removal, and establishing a top-down administrative burdensome economic environment. It creates a paternalistic process of dependency requiring "permission" and layers of bureaucratic red tape.
- The Indian Act establishes that Indian Reserve lands are held by the Crown for the use and benefit of band members. *The Indian Reserves established a "postage stamp" approach to land distribution with very little to no economic base and remains cause of both Indigenous economic displacement and regression.* A key feature of the Indian Act is that reserve lands cannot be leveraged as collateral, or used to guarantee large equity loans. This essentially has prevented Indigenous Peoples from coming to the business table as equals.
- The Crown defines who is and who is not a member of a band or a status Indian. The Indian Act establishes the structure and process for the historical and current declining Indigenous population by defining and limiting who is a certified status Indian and who is not. The Indigenous person is reduced to a number. These numbers, in turn, reduce fiduciary duty by limiting the population by definition.
- Gender inequality within the Act has also furthered economic regression. The Indian Act created lasting fallout from gender inequality through imposed female membership elimination, limitations, and removal of property transfer rights.
- Under the Indian Act, status Indians living on reserves cannot own the land they live on. This facilitates land de-valuation.
- With some exceptions such as Certificate of Possession lands, Indian reserve lands are communally held by the membership of a Band making the lands development process tedious.
- The Indian Act established the processes for the management of the Indian to be "productive" without an adequate land or resource base to sustain an economy for a growing population.
- The Indian Act established the historical and current removal of access to resources, externalized authority, and removed decision-making from the communities.

- Through the Indian Act, assets on reserve are not subject to sei-zure under legal process, making the process of borrowing money for development projects more difficult.
- The Indian Act does not allow for fee simple title on Indian re-serve lands; however, Certificates of Possession (CP), which limit the CP holder to only a partial degree of property rights, are issued by the federal Minister of Indigenous Affairs and Northern Devel-opment.
- Reserve lands cannot be sold; however, they can be leased by third parties after the completion of a lengthy and expensive land des-ignation process managed externally by the federal department.
- Ownership and the transfer of real property (sale or inheritance of land and buildings) located on reserve are transferable only to other members of the same Band and administered externally through the Act. This has resulted in considerably lower market value for reserve lands and complex land transfer processes all externalized to the federal department.
- Under the Indian Act, inheritance rights are not allowed on transfer of real property to heirs who are not members of the same Band of the deceased. This has also resulted in the ongoing perception of lower market value of reserve land by the fiscal in-stitutions.
- Strict restrictions are applied on security pledged as collateral for a loan assumed by an Indian living on reserve. The Indian Act established that only leasehold interests on designated lands can be mortgaged. While property ownership is deemed a threshold value indicator in the rest of Canada, it remains seemingly elimi-nated through the Indian Act.
- The Indian Act structure prevents a tax base that is foundational for a modern economy. The personal and real property held by an Indian on reserve is exempt from any taxes levied by the govern-ment of Canada or a province.
- The Indian Act establishes that the Government has authority to expropriate portions of reserve lands for roads, railways, and other public works for "national interest" as well as move an entire reserve away from a municipality if it is deemed advanta-geous to the "national interest" at any time.
- The Indian Act establishes paternalistic mechanisms to control oversight of any land or resource developments on reserve. For

example, developments requiring infrastructure like roads or services such as water, roads, sewer, or electricity must first obtain a permit or license through the form of a Band Council Resolution that has to be approved externally through the provisions of the Indian Act. In this externalized, top-down administrative environment, if these services were to be incorporated into a lease agreement, these would then be dependent on the lease remaining in good standing. Thus follows a high-risk perception that a potential service development partner may not be willing to invest in the infrastructure necessary. This establishes an environment of seeing lending to Indigenous communities as high-risk, resulting in higher costs and lower capital accessibility or flow for basic infrastructure, further accentuated with no tax base to support it and a government program and service long-term funding approach steeped in high demand.

- The Indian Act establishes "trusts" on behalf of First Nations that serve as externalized long-term controls of money flows. Here the future value of the community's money management is externalized.
- Annual federal transfer payments, established as agreement for the development of the original reserve, are perceived as Indigenous Peoples being a burden on the fiscal system of the country.
- The Indian Act further establishes fiscal dependency through funding models that are service/program or non-profit oriented, annually based and non-profit in structure.

Each of these features highlights the conditions for economic regression that the Indian Act has created over time for Indigenous Nations today who are trying to build economies and come out from years of the conditions that have established Indigenous experiences of poverty. This is not an exhaustive list but highlights some areas that formed and continue to shape Indigenous economic regression under the Indian Act. These are the fundamentals of Indian Act economics.

It is also important to understand the vast differences in Nations' governing status across the country—from self-government, to signed treaties, to modern-day treaty, to Indian Band governance. However, regardless of current governance status, all Nations across time have been impacted in some way, shape, or form by the early establishment of the Indian Act.

As the antithesis to economics, Indian Act economics requires the polarization of Indigenous Peoples. Indigenomics serves to facilitate a positive investment climate and demonstrate economic independence. It is also important Indigenous-led institutions such as the First Nations Lands Management Board create the legal, administrative, and infrastructural legal framework to replace 32 specific sections of the Indian Act that relate to land management and thus impact the process of economic development. Other organizations such as the First Nations Tax Commission and the First Nations Financial Management work to facilitate the market function and fiscal structure of reserve lands and Indigenous communities. These processes are often referred to as "coming out from underneath the Indian Act."

Each of these characteristics of the Indian Act perpetuates the underpinnings of Indian Act economics, and how it serves the ongoing underdevelopment of the Indian reserve and further serves to facilitate or perpetuate the false narrative of the modern Indian Problem—the fiscal burden of Indigenous poverty.

The Indian Act Economics Effect:
The Conditions for an Indigenous Economic Market Failure

The Indian Act is the basis for the existing regulatory regime on First Nations lands and governs almost every aspect of economic activity on those lands. Not surprisingly, given its advanced age, it is almost completely anachronistic and anathema to doing business in today's highly globalized, post-industrial economy.

—HAROLD CALLA,
President of the First Nations Financial Management Board

This speaks to the perfect conditions for market failure. Here "anachronistic" refers to belonging to a period other than that being portrayed and "anathema" means to vehemently dislike a "thing devoted to evil, an accursed thing." Market failure is an economic situation that is defined by the inefficient distribution of goods and services in the free market. This often leads to a net loss of economic value.

This concept of market failure parallels the concept of Indigenous Peoples taking our seat at the economic table of this country. This is the opportunity.

In demonstrating this concept for the condition of an Indigenous market failure, Arthur Manuel, in *Unsettling Canada: A National Wake-Up Call*, refers to reserve lands under the Indian Act:

> When you add up all the Indian reserves in Canada, the land we got is less than 0.2 per cent (reserve) of total lands and we are expected to make a living off of that. The rest of the land is the 99.8 per cent which is under federal, provincial jurisdiction and that's one of the main reasons why Indigenous communities are mostly poor.[7]

This speaks to the foundation for the continued economic regression of Indigenous Peoples. Manual continues: "This land is big enough to sustain both Indigenous people and settlers. There's no reason why the 200,000 Indigenous people in B.C. alone should be totally impoverished, generation, after generation after generation when the land is that large."[8]

This is Indian Act economics. It is time to honestly reflect on addressing the reality of marginalization, dependency, and its social and economic symptoms. The perception and common narrative of viewing Indigenous Peoples as a fiscal burden to this country is a direct reflection of the historical and current underdevelopment of the Indian reserve and is a direct outcome of Indian Act economics.

The Indian Act faces a design issue. While new measures are being developed to understand the size of the emerging Indigenous economy, understanding economic dependency, economic regression, and economic growth under the Indian Act is important to be able to measure economic growth against. This is the heart of Indigenomics, and the growing need for designing a different response: modern Indigenous economic design. This is the intersection of Indigenomics and Indian Act economics.

> For the last 130 years, the rest of Canada has created systems and frameworks that make buying and selling a home, researching an opportunity, zoning a property and building a residential or commercial development relatively simple. You

take public institutions that support a market economy for granted. You do not even realize that we are missing similar institutions.[9]

It is time for the financial architecture of the modern Indigenous economy.

Bill Gallagher, in *Resource Rulers*, aptly notes in referring to the Indian Act:

> It has created such an extensive body of jurisprudence that the underpinnings of the Indian Act (and its department) are no longer relevant in the Canada of the 21st century. The Indian Act serves no go forward purpose. Indeed, it is hindering Canada's economic progress at this critical juncture as native legal wins continue to mount.[10]

Perception of the Indian Act

While the Indian Act remains a mystery to the majority of Canadians, it establishes the perfect conditions for the potential market failure of the Indigenous economy today. It is time to bring Indian Act economics into visibility. When will we start talking about this? It is important to understand the Canadian perception of the Indian Act. According to the Indigenous and Northern Affairs website version of the historical development of the Indian Act:

> The relationship between the Crown and Aboriginal people in Canada is one which has been in near constant evolution since it was first established over 300 years ago. It has been impacted by commercial and economic pressures, by shifting alliances and external threats, as well as by policies of protection and subordination. Initially created to manage the military alliances, the Indian Department has been transformed over time into the Department of Indian and Northern Affairs, managing not only Canada's relationship with First Nations, the Inuit and Métis, but also all of Canada's North. Indian and Northern Affairs Canada continues to change to meet the needs and challenges faced by Canada's Aboriginal People.[11]

We have the Indian Act for the good of Canada, for the protection, security, trade, and relationship with First Nations according to Indigenous and Northern Affairs. The overly simplistic explanation of the purpose of the Indian Act continues: "The Indian Department, under the leadership of Sir William Johnson, quickly rallied the Iroquois Confederacy to the British cause, negotiated treaties of neutrality with France's Aboriginal allies, and struggled to maintain peace and good trade relations once hostilities ended."[12]

And that, according to the Ministry of Indigenous Affairs, is how we came to have the Indian Act—for allyship, to maintain peace and good relations. While as laughable as this statement is in its simplicity, the realities of Canada's only race-based legislation play into the reality of every single Canadian, aware of it or not, since the establishment of the Act itself and the establishment of Canada as a whole and its continuance to this day of Indian Act economics.

Indigenous Nations continue to deal with the difficulty of developing economies under the Indian Act that was never intended or designed to accommodate Indigenous economic progression and instead outlines every condition for economic regression. Indian Act economics is long-term purposeful economic distortion. Indian Act economics is race-based economics. Indian Act economics is the foundation for the market failure of the Indigenous economy. The space for Indigenomics exists outside of the Indian Act. Indigenomics is the creation of space in our modernity and our economic empowerment of today as modern Indigenous economic design.

This form of race-based legislation that was a fundamental tool in building this country has overrun its purpose as Indigenous Peoples are emerging today as economic powerhouses. The questions that remain today include: Does Canada deserve better than Indian Act economics? and How does the the Indian Act impact Canada's GDP? It is time to identify what specifically does the growing Indigenous economy need from the Indian Act today. Can the Indian Act ensure a healthy prosperous people? If the answer is no, this is the foundation for modern, constructive, generative Indigenous economic design.

The crossroads this country is at is to address the processes and structures of economic segregation and shift toward modern Indigenous economic design. Canada is living with the effects of Indian Act economics. It is time to move beyond the language and measurements of the Indigenous socio-economic gap and begin measuring Indigenous economic strength.

While many of the Indigenous Nations today have devised strategies to overcome the structural barriers to development, still many experience significant economic challenges, often related to the Indian Act and/or its regulations and oversight, persist in keeping the majority from achieving their development vision and staying economically dependent. Every single Canadian is impacted by the Indian Act and the Indian Act economics of this country. The immediate question arises: Do we want Indian Act economics or Indigenomics for the next 150 plus years of Canada? It is time to bring into the light the design flaws of Indian Act economics.

REFLECTION

1. What does it mean that the Indian Act is Canada's only race-based legislation?

2. What does that mean to you? "Canada deserves better than Indian Act Economics."

3. What can Indigenous economic empowerment look like beyond the Indian Act?

4. Why is it important to measure Indigenous economic strength?

The Indigenomics Power Center

Indigenomics is a great word or hashtag to focus attention on the intersection between Indigenous rights, environmental stewardship, Indigenous land management and economic strength. This is the new reality in this country that this economic growth is happening through these Indigenous rights. It is really quite incredible as it is a succinct term to capture what is going on right now.

—DON RICHARDSON,
Managing Partner at Shared Value Solutions[1]

Indigenomics is the collective economic response to the lasting legacy of the systemic exclusion of Indigenous Peoples from the economic table of this country. It is the process of claiming a seat at the economic table to center Indigenous modern existence as an Indigenous right to an economy, a right to our modernity, a right to be consulted and to provide consent. It is interwoven with the establishment of legal pressure points for economic inclusion, higher standards of stewardship, collaborative decision-making, and reciprocal prosperity. Indigenomics is the power center of Indigenous economic inclusion.

Canada is at an important intersection. History continues to not bode well for Canada in the courtrooms as Indigenous rights and title are being further defined daily. The evolution of these legal rights and recognition is in continuous development for Indigenous

Peoples, who carry the legal burden of proof. The Indigenous modernity continues to be tested and defined while continuously pushing recognition, jurisdiction, authority, and ownership. This definition plays out within the government, corporations, and the economy.

It is here we can examine the Indigenomics power center, the sweet spot, of increased Indigenous economic activity and the emerging modern economic presence and increasing economic influence. This is an important intersection centered at the heart of the story of Canada, the Canadian economy, and the emerging Indigenous economy.

Canada's collective national history has created this intersection: a power center of Indigenous resilience and struggle for legal visibility, recognition, the struggle for a place in modernity and relevance to now. This intersection focuses on growing our collective understanding and building a collective national economic response to now. This is the power center where the Indigenous relationship and modern economy collide. This is Indigenomics. We are a powerful people.

In "'Reset' on Canada's Roads to Resources," Bill Gallagher describes this power center: "A reset is required in our national thinking in order to take into account these dynamics of massive native legal empowerment and their ramped-up environmental priorities. No project has a chance of succeeding today until we factor this new reality into the power-sharing equation."[2]

What is happening, or what can be observed at this power intersection? The legal and business environment has shifted considerably in recent years, and the disruption can be seen even within the fiscal equation of this country. Providing insight, Gallagher, an expert legal adviser, exclaims:

> All future resource projects, if they are to succeed, have to have Indigenous peoples on-board. Bankers who lend to proponents, who haven't earned the native seal of approval, are being reckless in the current environment. Governments will not always be there to de-risk a poorly executed project. Moreover, the number of projects today that either don't make it out of the gate, or across the finish line, verges on a national crisis. A reset is required to reignite our national imagination.

Great swathes of the country are now mired in resource grid-lock. Once the envy of the world, Canada has foregone great-ness—for gridlock. The remedy lies in extending the hand of reconciliation on our road to resources.[3]

The emerging role of Indigenous Peoples and the Indigenous econ-omy is constantly evolving. It is here that this shift can be observed through the increasing role and visibility of Indigenous Peoples play-ing out in a constant push/pull relationship with Canada. This is the Indigenous economic paradigm. It is here the Indigenomics effect can be viewed.

The Indigenomics Push/Pull Dynamic

At the center of this Indigenous economic progress and development has been a constant "pushing" of Canada toward the development of legal recognition as it is entrenched within the constitution of this country. The "pull" dynamic has taken the form of years of gov-ernment policies and practices. These have formed the systemic invisibility of Indigenous Peoples that has been expressed through the continued denial, resistance, and rejection of Indigenous rights and economic exclusion over time. This push/pull dynamic centers Canada's current and emerging relationship with Indigenous Peoples today.

The "push" for recognition by Indigenous Peoples has taken the form of over 275 court cases, many in the resource sector, which Canada lost through the systemic reluctance for recognition of In-digenous rights. This push/pull dynamic has established a new legal and economic space for Indigenous Peoples. This is the emerging space that has been created for our modernity by Indigenous Peoples' leadership within this country today. We are a powerful people.

Building understanding and visibility of the history of Indige-nous Peoples' removal of rights, and the evolution of these rights, forms the basis of the power center of Indigenomics: the modern Indigenous economic playing field. The rules, while historically one-sided, are now being redefined. The old system and structures are dismantling and the new reality is emerging as Indigenous economic power and influence grow.

7 Rs of the Indigenomics Power Center

These form the 7 Rs of the Indigenomics power center of the evolving Indigenous relationship.

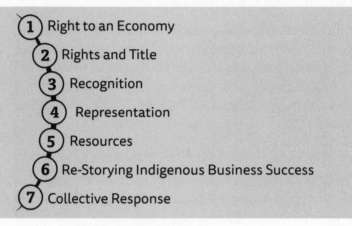

1. Right to an Economy
2. Rights and Title
3. Recognition
4. Representation
5. Resources
6. Re-Storying Indigenous Business Success
7. Collective Response

Right to an Economy

The first R in the Indigenomics power center is the "Right to an Economy." As previously referenced, this is a fundamental right as described in the United Nations Declaration on the Rights of Indigenous People. Indigenous Peoples are the only ones in this country who have had to determine the right to an economy.

Reflecting upon the question "What does it mean to have a right to an economy?" Indigenous business leader Shannin Metatawabin articulates:

> The Indigenous right to an economy—it's putting it out there in the open that we have the same rights as any other cultural group in this world. Through the Declaration, the United Nations affirms that all the countries in the world recognize that 370 plus million Indigenous peoples in this world require economic focus today. This means that governments need to support Indigenous nations so we are economically progressing to be successful in the future. The United Nations Declaration on the Rights of Indigenous Peoples outlines the minimum of what governments need to do for Indigenous groups. It refers to the right to establishing Indigenous-led institutions so that we are responding to the needs of our own communities.

UNDRIP is a framework that countries, specifically Canada here, need to support the development of institutions that support the Indigenous economy. That is the best way to ensure that we are all successful.[4]

A specific example I draw on that demonstrates both the evolving legal environment and the right to an economy is the *Ahousaht v. Canada* case in which the Nuu chah nulth won the right to a modern commercial fishery. With over eight years of negotiations, and an ongoing court case, Canada spent millions of dollars minimizing Indigenous economic rights, holding Indigenous rights in historical limitations rather than a modern right to a commercial economy and modern commerce. Every single Canadian needs to understand that we live in a country that argued Indigenous Peoples do not have a modern right to the economic function of a commercial transaction as a means of exchange. The Nuu chah nulth won the case through the eyes of the Spanish explorers, funded by the Spanish Crown who, at the time, witnessed and documented the original economy of exchange in that first encounter. Nuu chah nulth won the right to a modern economic commercial transaction. This is colonial shenanigans. There is no socio-economic gap, only Indigenous economic displacement and the upholding of the conditions of Indigenous economic regression. This is Indigenomics—to address the systemic economic displacement and economic regression.

The historical denial of Nuu chah nulth people to have a seat at the economic table is what was tested in the courts in this case. The expression of recognition of this right to a modern First Nation-based commercial fishery demonstrates how Indigenous Peoples are winning through legal means our seat at the economic table of this country. Nuu chah nulth people have pushed Canada into a new reality—we have a right to a modern commercial transactional function. We have a right to an economy and a seat at the economic table of this country. We are a powerful people.

As Indigenous business leader Clint Davis reflects: "Today, the right to an economy means the right to participate in the labor force. It is having the right to make decisions on economic activity that impacts my community from anything from resource development to infrastructure activity."[5] It is this right to an economy today that is facilitating a space at the economic table for Indigenous Peoples today. From coast to coast, from the Mikmak peoples to the Nuu chah nulth, the Indigenous right to an economy is increasing in application and strength. Indigenous Peoples are taking our seat at the economic table.

Rights and Title

The second R of the Indigenomics power center is "Rights and Title." Aboriginal rights and title refers to rights that existed prior to the establishment of Canada itself. Title refers to the inherent Indigenous right to lands and territory. As of 2019, Indigenous Peoples in Canada alone have won over 275 Supreme Court cases, each further defining our continued existence, our modernity, and our relevance to the next 150 plus years of Canada. As Bill Gallagher describes in a *Corporate Knights* article: "Indigenous peoples have racked up the greatest winning streak in our legal history—ringing in at over 275 rulings and impacting resource projects coast to coast."[6] These were won only 66 years after gaining the "right" to obtain counsel. Now that's a power play!

These consistent legal wins and development of Indigenous rights and title have considerably shifted the Canadian economic landscape. As Gallagher notes, "This country is at a point where bankers will not advance major funding on projects that have a question mark over the whole business of First Nations involvement and First Nations dialogue and support of projects."[7] This is the effect of the increase of rights and title development in this country.

Recognition

The third R in the Indigenomics power center is "Recognition." As Indigenous Peoples continue to win legal case after legal case, what is being established is the requirement or space for recognition. As Indigenous recognition is shaped by these cases, it is forcing the hand of this country. It is this created space that has established the requirement for this emerging foundation for both legal and economic recognition.

This development forms a basic premise of Indigenomics: Canada is in a legal and an economic relationship with Indigenous Peoples. Emphasis needs to be placed on both the legal and the economic relationship. The economic table has been set. These Indigenous legal wins have forced the hand—bringing increased visibility and participation into the establishment of the infrastructure of this Indigenous economy forming the basis for recognition.

This forced play is facilitated in the legal field and is expressed in the economic field, thus mandating a significant shift in the relationship between Canada, industry, and Indigenous Peoples. It is through this shift that the need to address the changed requirement of the resource economy and corresponding industries and labor markets is established. Further, it is here that can be seen the beginning of addressing the limitations of the regulatory environment at the heart of Canada's resource economy. It is these forces that are shaping the future of work for the Indigenous population in Canada. This is the great power play that even Sir John A. MacDonald could not have seen coming. This is Indigenomics.

From 1867, with the establishment of Canada, it took 115 years for Indigenous Peoples to gain full recognition within the Constitution in 1982. It is only now the potential for application and actualization of "recognition" as a framework for the continued development of Canada's modern relationship with Indigenous Peoples is being defined. It is time to get ready.

In February 2018, in the House of Commons, Prime Minister Justin Trudeau announced the establishment of a "Recognition and Implementation of Rights Framework." It outlined the federal government's leadership in establishing a new pathway for Indigenous recognition. He stated:

> For too long, Indigenous Peoples in Canada have had to prove their rights exist and fight to have them recognized and fully implemented. To truly renew the relationship between Canada and Indigenous Peoples, the Government of Canada must make the recognition and implementation of rights the basis for all relations between Indigenous Peoples and the federal government.[8]

Riddled with controversy, the concept challenged the "nothing about us without us" approach of Indigenous leadership across the country. While this framework did not continue in its development, it speaks to the increasing significance of "recognition" in a national context. The establishment of "recognition" as both a tool and as a process requires a new approach. This approach needs to address the slow yet emerging realization of the need to validate "recognition" as a process that is at the very heart of the constitution of this country. This is the uncomfortable space. A point of honest reflection today asks but is Canada ready?

The emerging Indigenous legal and economic space is causing an uncomfortable space. What is exactly is the source of this discomfort? Why does the idea of "recognition" cause discomfort? Is it because recognition is already defined within the Constitution? Is it because of the long history of broken treaties? Or is it the over 275 court cases that Indigenous Peoples have won through the absence of recognition? Is it the socio-economic gap? Or because the "right to an economy" has yet to be defined today? Economic fragility? Is it because a high number of on-reserve Indigenous children live in poverty in Canada? Or because it might have been cheaper to "recognize" First Nations rights sooner? Is it because maybe Canada has outgrown the Indian Act? These questions all form the foundation of this uncomfortable space that recognition as a tool and a process is beginning to address.

It is here in the Indigenomics power center that Indigenous visibility and economic and legal recognition are being firmly established and Indigenous Peoples are securing the rightful place in our own modernity. This is the power center of Indigenomics. The collective response must set up both the ability to operate from this power center and to identify the perfect storm, the economic conditions for the market failure of the Indigenous economy. We are a powerful people.

Representation
The fourth R in the Indigenomics power center is "Representation." Indigenous Peoples have struggled every step of the way for representation, for the right to represent our rights, our existence, and our place within this country. Through this growing recognition of Indigenous rights is the parallel concept of invisibility. As Indigenous rights grow, so does the entry into Canadian consciousness, into community life, corporate life, and governance systems.

The increased representation that Indigenous Peoples now have acts as an economic platform to dismantle Canada's long-term relationship with Indigenous Peoples that has been based on economic regression. This is a forced hand, one requiring consideration of the creation of economic space and a voice to represent Indigenous right to continuity as a people and a right to an economy.

Resources

The fifth R in the Indigenomics power center is "Resources." Canada was built on the extraction of these resources, starting with the fur trade, forestry, fishing, mining, and oil and gas. In the relationship with Indigenous Peoples, today's legal and business environments are directly connected. What that means today is establishing an economic and business foundation that ensures Indigenous Peoples receive financial value within the resource sector as it relates to lands, traditional territories, ways of life, and treaties.

> With these legal wins First Nations have actually been physically redrawing the map of Canada one ruling at a time. It has now come to impacting the bottom lines of so many companies, provincial governments, and Bay Street finance issues that this message is finally getting home—that First Nations are in fact the gatekeepers on Canada's road to resources.[9]

Taking a look further at the implications of Indigenous relations in a resource-focused economy, the British Columbia government made a commitment in its 2017 mandate:

> Our government fully recognizes that the Declaration is essential to the future of Indigenous peoples here in British Columbia. That is why we are committed to working in partnership with Indigenous peoples to embrace and implement UNDRIP, which has been accepted by 148 nations globally, including the Government of Canada. [10]

Premier Horgan declared:

> We're ready to do the hard work together with Indigenous peoples to build healthy communities, and to create jobs, economic stability and shared prosperity that benefits all British Columbians. As part of that work, all B.C. cabinet ministers have been tasked with reviewing policies, programs and legis-

lation to determine how to bring the principles of the UN declaration to action in British Columbia.[11]

This is becoming the new normal—leadership for Indigenous inclusion and the growing realization for the requirement for new actions and thinking.

Re-storying Indigenous Business Success

Many Canadians do not even realize that a thing called the "Indigenous economy" exists, has a value, and is growing exponentially. From the experience of historical economic regression, today there is a growing story of modern Indigenous business success. Formed on the basis of having modern rights that have never been extinguished, the right to an economy is fundamental to the development of Indigenous Nation building today. This emerging Indigenous economy balances rights with resource, conservation, and protection measures that must ensure the right to continue as people through cultural practices and access to traditional lands and resources.

Indigenomics is working to re-story the common narrative away from "Indigenous peoples are a fiscal burden" toward "We are an economic powerhouse; we are powerful people!" Indigenomics is working toward naming and addressing the conditions of an Indigenous economic market failure—where the cost of doing nothing outweighs the risk of doing nothing. The time is now.

In the power shift no one saw coming, today over 20 percent of Canada's land base is controlled directly by Indigenous Peoples, either through settlements or self-governance agreements. This is a demonstration of the shifting sphere of influence for the foundation of Indigenous economic empowerment.

The Collective Economic Response

The final R in the Indigenomics power center is for collective economic "Response." Indigenomics is modern Indigenous economic design. This country faces the potential of an Indigenous market failure without action for Indigenous economic inclusion and reconciliation. The economic intersection this country is now at is where the risk of doing nothing outweighs the cost of doing nothing. A market failure is described as the economic situation defined by an inefficient distribution of goods and services in the free market. This is the need for a collective response to support the focused growth of the Indigenous economy.

These 7 Rs of the Indigenomics power center collectively form the context and narrative for the emerging growth of the Indigenous economy. Indigenomics focuses on this emerging space of Indigenous economic empowerment. Collectively, they are reshaping Canada's relationship with Indigenous Peoples—essentially forcing the hand for inclusion, recognition, and a seat at the economic table. Indigenomics is a strength-based approach to support Indigenous economic design and inclusion.

This power center also lays out the uncomfortable space—the unknowing, the fear of dismantling colonial thoughts, systems and structures of authority, and worldview as it plays out in the economy and the Indigenous economic and political relationship.

These 7 Rs form the collective expressive impact of the emerging new Indigenous economy as the foundation of the movement toward the establishment of Indigenous rights and the emergence of a modern economic platform.

REFLECTION

1. Describe the Indigenomics power center.

2. Where are you seeing shifting Indigenous economic influence?

3. What is important about re-storying narrative to Indigenous Peoples are an economic powerhouse?

The Dependancy Illusion

The distinction between the past, present and future
is only a stubbornly persistent illusion.
—ALBERT EINSTEIN

Illusion: a false idea or belief. An illusion is something that is or is likely to be wrongly perceived or interpreted by the senses. An illusion is the state or condition of being deceived. An illusion is something that deceives by producing a false or misleading impression of reality. At the heart of Canadian consciousness is the Indigenous dependency illusion.

In the words of human rights activist and lawyer Katherine Mahoney, "This country is built on a myth. One can see that the establishment of the colonial structure parallels the economic regression of Indigenous peoples over the long term."[1] For the illusion to begin to be addressed at a collective level requires the establishment of new truths and new actions. The way forward has to address the historical and current systemic economic displacement and regression of Indigenous Peoples. Indigenomics is the collective response.

An illusion is a distortion of the senses, something that is wrongly perceived or interpreted by the senses. Every illusion about Indigenous reality and the Indigenous burden offers an insight into the illusion. It is time for the great debunk—to face the illusions this country suffers from that exist deep within the collective psyche—that Indigenous Peoples are a burden on the fiscal system of this country.

Indigenomics is about debunking the collective myth. In response to the Indigenous illusion, this chapter brings into visibility the Great Debunk which serves to expose the falseness or hollowness of the illusion and beliefs distorting reality. Debunking the collective illusion allows room for new perspectives and actions.

The Great Debunk: Addressing the Illusion

The following identify some common illusions pervading Canadian consciousness regarding Indigenous Peoples.

Illusion 1: "It's not my problem if my ancestors did it." (Short form of this myth is also often expressed as "Not my problem.")
This mentality is still alive and well today, and it is important to recognize its role in maintaining the status quo instead of focusing on economic reconciliation and the designed growth of the Indigenous economy. The underlying tone of this is to set the stage for taking no responsibility for the current state of Indigenous poverty.

The Great Debunk: Again, the Doctrine of Discovery must be referred to as the self-serving legal principle whereby Europeans claimed rights of sovereignty and ownership of entire regions they claimed to "discover." "Under this Doctrine, Indigenous peoples could not claim ownership of their lands, only the right to occupy and use the land, based on not being baptized and therefore not considered human. "The impact of this misguided, racist doctrine is the origin story that has left Indigenous peoples marginalized, dispossessed, and unrecognized and the rest of us wondering who we really are."[2]

The Doctrine of Discovery is central to the ongoing colonial saga of "how the west was won." The structures, policies, and regulations that exclude Indigenous Peoples from a seat at the economic table are still in place today. It is time to get over that.

In the truth telling of social entrepreneur and author Shaun Loney, in *An Army of Problem Solvers*:

> Most of non-Indigenous Canadians, if we admit it, can trace our privilege back to the demise of First Nations. Many of our ancestors settled on ill-gotten land or benefited from resources to which Indigenous people had legitimate claim. We

are part of a system that has worked better for non-Indigenous people than for Indigenous people. In other words, the economy and society itself is made for people like to me to the exclusion of people who are not like me.[3]

It is when this truth is built upon that economic reconciliation begins. It is time to ask the uncomfortable question: Where is the real myth located in the identity of Canada?

Illusion 2: "Why don't they just get over it already, that was a long time ago?" (Also expressed as "It was my ancestors fault, not mine.") The illusion we face as a country is that we live in a post-colonial world and the policies of the past are no longer relevant or applicable.

The Great Debunk: The colonial structures that exist within governing laws, policies, and regulations are still causing the conditions for Indigenous economic displacement, exclusion, and regression. The role of leadership in economic reconciliation is to address these truths and how they continue to be expressed as Indigenous economic regression.

In a *Policy Options* article, "First Nations Should Have Control of Their Own Revenues," Allan Clarke notes: "The Crown still collects, receives and holds a considerable amount of money on behalf of the 'Indians' because legal title to reserve lands still rests with the Crown, and federal bureaucrats continue to sign leases, permits and licenses on behalf of First Nations (or 'Indians')."[4] While this has shifted for self-government Nations, the paternal nature of the relationship and its structures still exist for many Nations.

The work of bringing this dynamic into visibility is essential to Indigenous economic design. The following demonstrates the lack understanding of what really needs "getting over."

As of 2016, more than $676 million of so-called Indian moneys was being held in the Consolidated Revenue Fund and, based on data from 2006 to 2016, approximately $200 million of these "Indian Moneys" is being deposited into this fund annually. To gain access to this—their own—money, First Nations are required to follow strict, time-consuming procedures. The provisions of the Indian Act that permit Nations' access to these revenues evoke the most odious characteristics of a colonial relationship, including, perhaps most offensively, "any other purpose that in the opinion of the Minister is for the benefit of the band." The money largely sits idle, effectively punishing First Nations. The interest paid by the government of Canada on Indian moneys in the fund is well below what it costs First Nations to access financing from conventional sources. This interest-rate differential costs First Nations more than $45 million annually in higher interest costs by some estimates. Over a generation, these entirely unnecessary higher interest costs could amount to $2.1 billion wasted.

That is just the cost of idle capital.[5]

This is the foundation for both the underdevelopment and under-capitalization of the Indigenous economy. Yes, it is time to get over it. The seat at the economic table is only being established today through the evolution of the legal environment led by Indigenous Peoples.

Illusion 3: "Natives do not pay taxes." (Also served up vaguely as the means for "Justification for economic inequality."

The Great Debunk: The underlying current of this myth is that Indigenous Peoples do not contribute and are unproductive; in other words, bad for the economy and the bottom line.

A better truth: some do, some don't. This is a more accurate truth. It is important to clearly understand that the Indian Act has laid out that the property of an "Indian" or a "Band on a reserve" only is tax exempt. The expression of the Indian Act tax exemption is very narrow and applies only to personal property and income located on a reserve. First Nations pay all other taxes not covered by this constricted exemption. Adding to the complexity is varying degrees of removal or separation from the Indian Act, from self- government agreements to modern treaty nations.

First Nations peoples without status, registered First Nations peoples living off-reserve, Métis people, and those under self-governance agreements definitely pay taxes. With over 60 percent of the approximately 1.6 million Indigenous population living off-reserve, Native peoples definitely do pay taxes. Registered First Nations peoples working off-reserve pay income tax, regardless of where they reside. Inuit and Métis peoples and self-government Nations also pay taxes. It is time to get over this illusion. Natives don't pay taxes—it's time to get over that.

Illusion 4: "Natives get everything for free."
(There is no alternative to this myth; it is served straight up.)

The Great Debunk: The underlying current of this persistent illusion that Indigenous Peoples cost this country money or are a burden on the fiscal system is widespread in Canadian's perception. Native peoples are on the cost side of the equation. In debunking this myth, it is essential to understand the construct of "economic rent" as the basis for the establishment of the strength of Canada's natural resources economy, and as central to economic success measures. "Economic rent" is defined as the net social benefit accruing from the exploitation of natural resources and, therefore, the potential income accruing to the "owner" of the land.

Let's look to a Fraser Institute report headline, "Taxpayers Are Generous to First Nations," that works to establish a trend line of "Indigenous spend," perpetuating the illusion that Indians are a fiscal burden. A headline and story of this nature remain ignorant to the concept of Canada's fiduciary duty. The report notes:

> In the federal department of Aboriginal Affairs and North-
> ern Development Canada, with data gleaned from federal
> archives, department spending per registered First Nations
> person jumped to $9,056 per person by 2012 from $922 in 1950
> (and the figures are already adjusted for inflation so this is an
> apple-to-apple comparison). That is an 882 per cent increase![6]

This is an old and stale unconstructive illusion perpetuating Indigenous Peoples to the cost side of the equation. This narrative no longer serves Canada's economic future. It is time to view Canada's growing Indigenous economy as generative and constructive. It is time to build the business case for the Indigenous spend—we can continue to fund the social cart that is currently pulling the economic horse, or we can invest and design the Indigenous economy. This is the intersection of Canada's future relationship with Indigenous Peoples. It is time to center our leadership as citizens, governments, and industry in Indigenous economic design as the future of Canada. This is Indigenomics. It is time to demonstrate the business case for the growth of the Indigenous economy today.

It is also here that the age-old ongoing Aboriginal Question comes into play in the evolution of Aboriginal rights and legal status in the development of Canada. The concept of economic rent has a central role in the answering of the Aboriginal Question in the legal development and recognition of Aboriginal rights over time. Large-scale development in the resource sectors, such as forestry and mining industries, generates significant economic benefits both nationally and regionally. The distribution of this economic rent between corporations, governments, and Indigenous Nations, however, has been and continues to be grossly unequal. Indigenous Peoples have shared very few of the economic benefits and borne an extraordinary share of the costs economically, ecologically, culturally, and socially. Putting economic rent in the context of "free" is essential to debunking this myth of "natives get everything for free." It is time to get over this myth.

Illusion 5: "Natives are a fiscal drain on Canada. Look at all that money that goes to the Indians."

The Great Debunk: The pervasive myth is that the Canadian economy subsidizes Indigenous communities, when in reality it is the opposite. This myth is perpetuated through media articles such as *The Costs of the Canadian Government's Reconciliation Framework for First Nations* in which Tom Flanagan leaves Indigenous spending in the hands of public opinion, saying, "Canadians would probably find these increased expenditures worthwhile if they raised the standard of living of Indigenous peoples and brought about a better relationship with other Canadians."[7]

One of the louder myths in Canadian reality is that the more than 600 Indigenous communities live off subsidies from the government. Dru Oja Jay addresses this myth in a Media Co-op article, "What if Natives Stop Subsidizing Canada": "Though it is loudly proclaimed and widely believed, is remarkable for its boldness; widely accessible, the verifiable facts show that the opposite is in fact true. Indigenous people have been subsidizing Canada for a very long time." Oja Jay further argues: "The wealth of Canadian society as a whole could not be built without massive subsidies of Indigenous land, resource wealth, and the incalculable cost of generations of suffering over time."[8]

Illusion 6: "Those Natives don't have to pay for post-secondary education. They get it for free!"

The Great Debunk: Western expansion was a vital part of the development of Canada's economic future. Based on this critical expansion, there are eleven historical treaties signed across this country, referred to as the numbered treaties or post-Confederation treaties that addressed this in the relationship to the Crown. These treaties were signed between the Nations and the reigning monarch of Canada (Victoria, Edward VII, or George V) between 1871 and 1921. While primarily focused on land, these treaties also carried within them the intent to ensure access to education. The Indian Act served to displace these original agreements of these treaties.

Here it is also important to increase visibility of the concept "We are all treaty people" in this country, which emphasizes the treaty rights and responsibilities of the government and Canadians in upholding the relationships with Indigenous Nations. What the concept refers to is engaging in understanding these rights and responsibilities, including understanding the role of education and Indigenous historical agreements with the Crown. Access to education is not "free"—it was directly connected to western development in the establishment of Canada itself.

It is also important to put in context the growth of the Indigenous population in relation to education and the on-reserve population. First imposed by the federal government in 1996, a two percent cap was the limit Indigenous and Northern Affairs placed on annual increases to Nations' education budgets. Many Nations cannot meet the current student demand that far exceeds the money that they receive for post-secondary education. Economic development dollars support Indigenous student education.

Illusion 7: "A native veto will take over Canada." (Also serves up as a fear-mongering narrative, suggesting in its undertones that "Those natives have too much power!")

In building a more solid picture of Indigenous Nations as "contributing" instead of being solely on the cost side of the equation, of the more than 630 First Nations across Canada currently, over 120 have on-reserve property tax regimes that generate over $70 million in revenues annually. Understanding the evolution of the fiscal relationship with Indigenous Nations is a more constructive narrative than simply viewing Indians as a cost to the system. It's time to get over this myth.

The Great Debunk: It is time to address the misconception around Indigenous consent that is rippling fear across this country. It is important to understand Indigenous law is still developing, case by case, testing the colonial assumptions of the establishment and continuation of Canada. Indigenous business leader JP Gladu speaks to this:

> There is a misperception that our communities and businesses are opposed to natural resource development when quite the opposite is true. Many of our community leaders and businesses see the opportunity in natural resource development, for example in oil and gas, mining and forestry. It is not that we are opposed to it, but our communities and businesses have to be integrated into all parts of the value chain of a business. Our voices must be heard when it comes to mitigating environmental impact and businesses should make sure that our communities are benefiting. Long gone are the days when truckloads of natural resources would go by without us being decision makers in how they are developed and how we benefit from them.[9]

The fear of the implications of implementing the United Nations Declaration on Indigenous Peoples (UNDRIP) is further stirred by the media. A *Financial Post* article sends fear into Canadian consciousness with the headline "The Trudeau Government signs on to give Aboriginal veto rights nobody else has." Within the article, this sentence—"Making all laws consistent with UNDRIP...would give

Aboriginals rights not enjoyed by other Canadians"[10]—illuminates and uplifts fear and wreaks havoc on the "right-mindedness" of the equality for all narrative that was surprisingly not found in the establishment of Canada.

While irrelevant to the evolving Indigenous legal rights, authors Harry Swain and Jim Baillie use their voice in this article to facilitate an opinion around inequality and further spread fear:

> Making all Canadian laws consistent with UNDRIP, as C-262 demands, would not just give Aboriginal Canadians rights not enjoyed by other Canadians, it would concede to small groups of them an absolute veto on many issues of resource development. This would be carrying the Supreme Court's rebalancing of negotiating strength too far.[11]

Indigenous rights exist outside of popular opinion. It is time to become informed on the foundation of the development of these rights. Further to this understanding are the distinct concepts of veto and consent. The term veto creates unnecessary fear or confusion. In the 2004 Haida decision, the court clarified that the process of consultation "does not give Aboriginal groups a veto over what can be done with land pending final proof of the claim."[12] This is the evolving legal environment that Indigenous Nations are forcing the hand on historical definition and development.

Respected thought leader Roshan Danesh, who writes on the distinction between veto and establishing consent within Indigenous project development, states: "We must reconcile pre-existing Aboriginal sovereignty with assumed Crown sovereignty."[13] He describes the real work of today:

> We need...to build the relationships, structures, processes, understandings and agreements between Indigenous peoples and governments that ensure collaboration, alignment and effectiveness in reaching decisions and moving critical shared work forward together. This simply means refocusing our work on the infrastructure of positive and collaborative Indigenous and Crown relations, rather than the adversarial approaches of litigation and negotiation on which hundreds of millions of dollars are currently spent.[14]

In the *Policy Note* article "Distinguishing consent from veto in an era of reconciliation," Jon Tockman writes:

> If handled appropriately, the process of achieving consent can prevent many of the lawsuits filed to challenge projects on Indigenous territory. That said, we non-Aboriginal Canadians need to accept that our domestic and international commitments to Indigenous rights will sometimes mean that projects and policies will not advance because they have not secured the consent of affected Indigenous communities.[15]

This is the new normal in this country. Fear has no place in the rise of Indigenous economic empowerment and in taking a seat at the economic table of this country. The Natives are not "getting too much power," instead it is a return to the origin of Indigenous rights and expressed within the ascent of the Indigenous economy and reflected in the GDP.

Illusion 8: "Why do natives get special rights? Aren't we all equal?" (This myth is often disguised as: "Aren't human rights Indigenous rights?")

The Great Debunk: Canada is suffering from a chronic misunderstanding or lack of education on the origin or source of Indigenous rights. Through the formation of Canada and specifically from 1982, through the revision to the Constitution, Aboriginal and treaty rights were formally entrenched and recognized within the law of Canada through Section 35 of the Constitution Act. Largely the work of defining these rights has fallen to the courts, much to the expense of Canadians.

The lack of education on Indigenous rights breeds a lack of understanding as well as perpetuates fear and racism about Indigenous communities and Peoples. This myth further serves to falsify the cause of Indigenous socio-economic conditions. Again, there are over 600 Indigenous Nations in this country, not one homogenous group of Indigenous Peoples.

These illusions distort the perception of Indigenous Peoples and the need for a collective response to the growth and design of the Indigenous economy because it is deemed there are already government programs targeted to Indigenous communities or the use of policy to improve indicators such as labor market participation outcomes.

Conclusion: Addressing the Illusion

Whose worldview does the word "marginalized" represent? Who has been left out of the economy? Who is being included in the economy? Asking the question—Who is left out?—can generate a degree of discomfort. That is the work of Indigenomics movement: to bring visiblity to the processes of inclusion and confirming the rightful seat of Indigenous Peoples at the economic table of this country. This is the new truth in front of this country—the untold history of Canada is playing out in the economic field. Addressing the myths—this is what a seat at the 21st century economic table means. Addressing the illusion and taking a seat at the economic table—this is Indigenomics.

REFLECTION

1. How can Canadians learn about the origin and scope of Indigenous rights if they did not learn this in the school system?

2. How can you as an individual address these myths in your workplace, home, and conversations?

3. What is the role of the education system in an age of reconciliation?

9

The Power Play

An idea is like a virus. Resilient. Highly contagious.
And even the smallest seed of an idea can grow.
It can grow to define or destroy you.

—COBB, in *Inception*

Let's face it, Canada loves power plays! The play, the setup, the excitement, the one-man advantage, the hype, the strategy! It all starts with a wrongdoing, the play or strategy is developed, and the advantage is created. In the power play situation, one team has a greater number of players on the ice because the opposing team has a player or players in the penalty box; the team has a scoring advantage, also known as a "man advantage." The idea is to move the puck among the offensive players until a player has an opening and can shoot and score. Scoooooooooooore!!!!

There is a power play happening right before our eyes! It can be seen in the emerging Indigenous legal landscape and the growing strength of economic empowerment. What does a power play require? A wrong, a strategy, and a defensive. Canada has no defensive strategy. Canada has hit the penalty box over 275 times and lost. Let's face it, First Nations have won more times than the number of years of Canada's age. Each of these power play legal wins has opened the door wide to the requirements of a growing Indigenous economy and the evolving legal landscape. What is unfolding in this power play is a beautiful real-time demonstration of the United Nations Declaration on the Rights of Indigenous Peoples—the right to our continuation into the future and the right to an economy played out in the Canadian court systems.

And Then Indigenous People Went to Court!

Prior to the 1956 changes to the Indian Act, Indigenous Peoples were not allowed to seek legal counsel or to assemble in groups of more than three. Over a span of more than 60 years, Indigenous Peoples have won this continuous and impressive series of major court decisions that have reshaped the political and economic map of Canada. This is the great power play of today. This is the foundation for the setting of the stage of Indigenous economic empowerment.

Aboriginal rights were first outlined in 1763 in the Royal Proclamation that set out guidelines for European settlement of Aboriginal territories in what is now North America. Aboriginal rights are distinct collective rights of Indigenous Peoples that focus on the continued use and occupation of certain areas. They are inherent rights that Indigenous Peoples have practiced since before European contact. These "include rights to the land, rights to subsistence, resources and activities, the right to self-determination and self-government, and the right to practice one's own culture and customs including language and religion."[1] The Royal Proclamation was the foundation for the Supreme Court of Canada to rule in favor in a series of Indigenous focused cases.

In *Resource Reckoning*, Bill Gallagher centers the concept of Indigenous Peoples as resource rulers in Canada in referring to the over 150 court wins by the year 2012:

> With over 150 legal wins to their credit, Indigenous peoples have redrawn the map of Canada not only at the expense of the resources sector, but at the expense of the national economy. The rise of native empowerment has gone almost completely unacknowledged in the corridors of power and likewise remains under-reported in mainstream media. Canadians have yet to appreciate the socio-political and economic consequences of this failure on such a grand scale.[2]

Today and over 275 legal wins later, Gallagher boldly presents in *Resource Reckoning* the concepts that Canada is a G8 country and is at war with itself over resources. He establishes that gridlock is the defining feature of many resource projects, which have become mired in regulatory and legal limbo with Indigenous Peoples: "Natives have amassed the longest running, most impressive legal winning streak over resources access in Canadian history. The success in the courts have accorded them de facto control over their traditional lands, making them resource rulers, throughout broad regions of the country."[3]

Gallagher further notes the impact of these wins:

> This means, sizable tracks of territories across Canada cannot be opened up without the direct support of the affected First Nations. This has forced the hand of this country: First Nations have become key players in the resource economy. First Nation support or opposition can determine the future of a proposed mine or construction of a pipeline or any resource extraction or land development.[4]

In an interview, Gallagher states: "The rise of native empowerment is dramatically changing the political map of Canada. New rules for engagement are needed." This is the biggest power play this country has ever seen and it's happening right before our eyes. Gallagher yields caution that while First Nations may have won court cases, they have yet to "commercialize" and fully "monetize" these wins. This is the emerging space of Indigenomics.

The Legal Spectrum

From the spectrum of Indigenous cases being tested and won in the Supreme Court, the growing space of the expression of modern Indigenous reality and application into the economic field can be viewed.

British Columbia in particular is a laser for Aboriginal rights development. It is home to great leaders, innovators, designers, and architects of the modern experience of the Indigenous economy. Some of greatest architects of our time include George Manuel, president of the Indian Brotherhood of BC; Gudjaaw of the Haida Nation's case that laid the foundation for the duty to consult; and Roger Williams, plaintiff of the Tsilqot'in Aboriginal title lands case. It is important to reflect upon what space each of these legal wins created: ownership, jurisdiction, responsibility? The legal and economic landscape of Canada shifts and evolves with each win.

Looking at the emerging legal landscape, there are new economic pressure points being created. The legal environment is the primary business context between government, industry, and Indigenous Nations. The continuous unfoldment of this ongoing legal story has focused on the accommodation of Indigenous interests through consultation and consent. In the legal precedents that Indigenous Peoples have set over the past years, each case is an insertion into the reality of the Canadian economy. This is opening of the door to a modern economic reality, new economic space effectively taking a seat at the economic table of this country.

Today, a shift is happening with new patterns and economic trends emerging. Today's legal conditions set the requirements for the government's duty to consult. The insertion and influence of Indigenous perspective has seen a growing importance of Indigenous values and approaches in resource management and governance decision-making. While this legal context is a duty-oriented relationship, it is from this context that new opportunities can be leveraged within the business environment. This is Indigenomics.

A current example is the Stk'emlupsemc of the Secwepemc Nation (SSN). In filing a title claim in B.C. Supreme Court, the Tk'emlups and Skeetchestn have started what may become a precedent-setting court case. In the assertion of title in court, this case could establish that the Nations have the right to direct use on its land—including resources. This push dynamic has the potential for the Nations to address the status quo of the current unilateral process of decision-making on natural-resource development as identified on SSN lands, pushing Canada into a new legal and economic reality. We are a powerful people.

Another example is the Tsilquotin Williams case: the great watershed moment, the opening of the light box, the insertion of title into the ego of the colonial construct of title. This case served as the entry point for the inception of a third classification of Indigenous title, dismantling the Western-Euro long-held stance on title—of our rules, our game—there are only two, fee simple and Crown lands. We are a powerful people.

As noted historian and academic Ken Coates highlights in "Indigenous Support For Development Is Being Heard":

What a difference a few decades and real political and legal power can make. Companies, reflecting the 21st century approach to corporate social responsibility, are reaching out to Indigenous communities. The duty to consult and accommodate requirements in the *Haida* and *Taku* decisions increased Aboriginal authority and led to new collaboration and impacts and benefit agreements. Indigenous communities previously ignored along the development frontier found themselves courted by companies eager to get them engaged with the projects.[5]

These legal outcomes are all residue from the colonial period, outcomes of the ego of the descending economy. Indigenomics is about the creation of space for Indigenous economic modernity, relevance, and application of Indigenous values and worldview. This is the intersection of the emerging Indigenous rights and the connection to emerging Indigenous economy.

I once heard a story about the owner of the West Edmonton Mall taking the local Nation to court over their intention to build a casino nearby. The problem was that the Nation's new casino would be in competition with the existing casino in the mall. The owner, holding all the cards, power, and money, exhausted all lobbying efforts to prevent this new casino from being built and ended up in court with the local Nation. The judge's ruling favored the side of the Nation, allowing the casino to be built. The story goes upon hearing the judge's ruling; the owner crossed the courtroom floor, shook hands with the Chief, and said "Anyone that can beat me in court, must be powerful, and I want to work with them. I want to work with you." We are a powerful people.

The Push/Pull Dynamic:
An Inception into a New Economic Reality

There is a constant push/pull dynamic within the assertion of Aboriginal rights. This dimension highlights the ever-shifting power dynamics and the need to redefine the evolving legal requirements.

As noted previously, the Nuu chah nulth court case illustrates this push/pull dynamic. Through the Indian Act, the Nuu chah nulth experienced economic displacement from their traditional territories and were forced to live on little tiny reserves in B.C. These were not big enough to sustain a local economy, forcing dependency and economic isolation. B.C. has much smaller reserves, particularly on Vancouver Island, which were intended to be small because Nations were supposed to be able to access the resources from the ocean. Nuu chah nulth built the case from the perspective "the ocean is our garden." The development of the case focused on the historical application of the Fisheries Act and licensing systems that prevented the Nuu chah nulth people from accessing resources based on the traditional economy of harvesting and fishing. They took Canada to Court because the Nation was no longer able to access the traditional economy or undertake economic activities. The case serves to demonstrate the connection between the devastation of the Nuu chah nulth's fishing culture and economy to the development of the modern commercial fishery. It was a loss of economic access case.

The claim was based primarily on Aboriginal rights to fish and sell fish based on traditional activities. The case focused on the Crown's duties arising from the reserve-creation process in which tiny fishing station reserves were set apart for the Nuu chah nulth. The Court defined that Nuu chah nulth people have the Aboriginal rights to fish in their traditional territories and sell that fish into the commercial marketplace; essentially, the right to an economy.

The judge found that the right to sell fish (other than clams) had been infringed both legislatively and operationally by the cumulative effect of Canada's complex regulatory and policy regime applicable to fisheries management. She concluded that Canada must now consult and negotiate with the Nuu chah nulth plaintiffs over their proposed fishery, including allocation of fishing opportunities and the appropriate methods by which that fishing should take place. This formed a new Canadian reality: Aboriginal rights are modern legal rights that are founded upon the pre-contact practices of an Aboriginal group.

Canada vehemently argued against the Nuu chah nulth modern right to sell fish. The judge noted: "In my view, the plaintiff's ancestral practices translate into a broader modern entitlement to fish and to sell fish than captured by 'exchange for money or other goods.' In my view, the most appropriate characterization of the modern right is simply the right to fish and to sell fish."[6]

There is a story Canadians never hear about: Canada is still in court fighting this right to an economy, the right to sell fish. The Nuu chah nulth prepared for 10 years for this case, won it in 2009, and are still in court negotiating these rights another 10 years later. We live in a country with a high percentage of Indigenous Peoples living in poverty, with a proven right, still fighting the modern right to sell a fish, the right to commerce, and the right to an economy. Nuu chah nulth won a seat at the economic table. There is no socio-economic gap; it was constructed through Indigenous economic exclusion. This is the power play.

A case like this demonstrates that the fiscal equation of this country does not make sense. At the heart of the myth of the fiscal burden that Indigenous Peoples in Canada are perceived through, the federal government is arguing against the modern Indigenous commercial function, fundamental to the success of any economy. Canada has no legal strategy operating from within the illusion of its own making: the invisibility of the Indian. It does not make sense because Canada is built on an illusion. To address the illusion requires the entering of the power center, the intersection of the evolution of Aboriginal assertion. This insertion is the point of the 275 plus current legal winning streak that Nations across this country have attained.

"We also need to recognize that Canada needs a new legal strategy in regards to First Nations that has that economic framework to it."[7] We can't have it both ways: a narrative that puts Indigenous Peoples on the cost side of the equation of this country, but on the other hand, Canada is fighting the Indigenous right to an economy, a modern economic function: the commercial transaction of the right to sell fish today. Indigenous Peoples are the only people in this country who have had to fight for the right to an economy. This is the power center. The power struggle. The power play. This is Indigenomics.

Canada is still negotiating Nuu chah nulth space at the economic table. This points to the heart of the "Indian Problem" of today: What does it mean for Indigenous Peoples to have a right to a modern economy? It should not still include Canada in court arguing against the modern right to commercial transactions. Maybe the "Indian problem" is a perception problem, one steeped in the ego of the economics.

Canada has no defensive strategy because the falsity of its origin story prevents it from having one. Through examples like these, Indigenous Peoples are taking our seat at the economic table of this country. Business models based on this legal framework can transition toward an equity benefit model between Indigenous Peoples and industry that respects Indigenous cultures, values, and roles as stewards. This is the opportunity, not the problem.

Indigenomics acts as a vehicle for understanding, creating meaning, and expressing our Indigenous relationship and right to an economy. Indigenous Peoples are defining our modern presence and our need to delineate our future through participation in the Canadian economy. With the recent win of the Tsilhqot'in decision, and numerous other court rulings, the redefinition of wealth within the economic system of this country through the rise of Indigenous economic empowerment is slowly being realized. What is directly in front of us is the question, what new thinking is now required of us? This is the evolution of assertion. Pay attention. The time is now. The economic table of the 21st century has been set. We are a powerful people.

REFLECTION

1. What does Canada need to learn from this unfolding power play of Indigenous legal and economic empowerment?

2. What does it mean for Indigenous Peoples to have a right to a modern economy?

10

The Power Shift:
A Seat at the Economic Table

It's that economies do better when everyone has a chance to succeed. For a long time, it was thought that countries had to choose between economic growth or economic inclusion.
—BARACK OBAMA, 2016 Parliamentary Address[1]

Indigenous Peoples have been in an economic depression—a sustained, long-term downturn in economic activity since the formation of Canada and the establishment of the Indian Act. The emerging success of the Indigenous economy today is in spite of the Indian Act effect. It is the most significant economic power shift this country has ever seen, and it's happening right before our eyes. Are we paying attention?

> Look out there, the native elder said to the young man and tell me what you see. The young man looked out and responded, Well I see a tree, a fence and someone walking out there. Yes, the old man answered, when you figure out the relationship between the three come back and see me again.[2]

This is simple Indigenous wisdom, a reflection of identifying our relationships, of making the connections. The relationship and connections between the establishment of this country, the structures that support it, and the emerging Indigenous economy—these are the connections of today. From out of the margins, from the periphery to the power center of Indigenomics, this is the center of the unfolding Indigenous economic power shift.

With the shift in the Indigenous legal environment, much confusion has arisen around the expression of Indigenous rights. In "There Should Be No Confusion About Aboriginal Consent," lawyer Roshan Danesh speaks to the insertion of this emerging economic power shift into Canadian consciousness: "simply stated, Aboriginal title's relationship to the economy is like a building storm—every time we use lands and resources without consent, the storm strengthens and increases in force."[3]

This is the power center of Indigenous economic strength, the power shift.

It is this storm that Canada is positioned within today—the intersection of old thought that formed the development of Canada and the new thought of today that will shape its continued development. This is the center of the storm, the space for economic transformation. The storm is strengthening and increasing in force and requires a collective economic response. This is Indigenomics.

It is at this intersection that we find ourselves at this new social field. It is at this critical intersection that we encounter the blind spot in Canadian consciousness. It is here where the building of understanding within the emerging Indigenous economic power shift must occur. This new visual landscape highlights a blind spot in Canada's evolution and the evolution of the Indigenous economy. The untold history of Canada's origin is playing out in the economic field today.

This blind spot is where the collective view is obstructed. A blind spot refers to a subject matter of which a person or group is ignorant, prejudiced, or inefficient in its response. In his work, Otto Scharmer, co-founder of the Presencing Institute, focused on bridging the ecological divide (disconnect of self from nature), the social divide (disconnect of self from other), and the spiritual divide (disconnect of self from self) to shape the context in large system change today. In "The Blind Spot: Uncovering the Grammar of the Social Field," he writes:

> When people experience a transformational social shift, they notice a profound change in the atmosphere, in the texture of the social field. But in trying to explain it, they tend to fall back on vague language; and even though people can agree on a surface description of what happened, they don't usually know why it happened or what words to use to describe it.[4]

There is an undeniable transformational social shift happening in Canada's conscious awareness of its Indigenous relationship. An underlying intention of Indigenomics is to address system change needed to transform social meaning. The transformative shift must occur from the perception of Indigenous Peoples as a burden on the fiscal system to Indigenous Peoples as economic powerhouses in their own right.

With the emerging Indigenous legal and economic empowerment, one of the outcomes is increased recognition, one of the R's within the Indigenomics intersection as previously highlighted. Recognition is the acknowledgment of something's existence, validity, or legality. With the establishment of Indigenous legal recognition, this is the inception into Canadian consciousness—a now that requires a new response, new actions, new processes, new beliefs within the unfolding of this social field. Indigenous rights are at the center of the continuation and the evolution in this field of possibilities. The Indian Problem of old is now the opportunity.

Fundamental to this emerging Indigenous economic power shift is recognition that is shaping the development of Indigenous legitimacy in the economic field. *Legitimate* means "conforming to the law or to rules." Legitimacy, as the rules have been defined within a colonial context, can only be established through the courts, through the onus of proof, through the strength of claim, through the assertion of Indigenous rights and title, and then through externalized recognition. The evolution of Indigenous legal and economic recognition is shaping the deconstructing of legitimacy that has been built from only one worldview in the Crown/Indigenous relationship over time. There has only ever been one playbook, one dominant worldview—but the rules have changed through the unfoldment of legitimacy and recognition. This is the power shift. The new social field, the rise of Indigenous economic empowerment. This is the intersection we find ourselves facing as a country. This is Indigenomics.

The Effect of the Emerging Indigenous Power Shift

It is through this growing recognition and legitimacy that further understanding of this evolving power shift can be best seen through the growing influence of Indigenous Peoples. Rapidly growing Indigenous economic success is in front of us as a country. As a Macdonald-Laurier Institute report *Indigenous Support for Development Is Being Heard* affirms: "It has become clear that Aboriginal communities have secured real and sustained authority in the resource sector."[5] This is the core characteristic of the emerging power shift.

From the Indian Act perspective, the following chart demonstrates the land base of 2,267 Indian reserves across Canada, approximately 2.6 million hectares or 0.2% of the total land area of Canada. The table below summarizes the Indian reserve and land statistics.

Region	Bands	Reserves	Land Base (ha)	Average Area (ha)
Atlantic	32	68	29,561.6	434
Quebec	26	31	77,131.5	2488
Ontario	113	189	709985.8	3756
Manitoba	53	104	214,803.7	2065
Sask.	69	143	616,815.9	4313
Alberta	40	100	668,880.1	6688
B.C.	200	1606	353,324.2	217
NWT	1	2	562.1	281
Yukon	7	24	499.6	83
Totals	551	2267	2,671,564.5	1176

The Indian Reserve Land Base in Canada, Indigenous and Northern Affairs Canada; www.aadnc-aandc.gc.ca/eng/1100100034846/1100100034847

Reflecting on shifts in the emerging Indigenous economy in Canada, Indigenous business leader Shannin Metatawabin notes:

> With 600 plus nations across this country, each of these nations has the ability to govern its lands and waters and negotiate arrangements with crown agencies and proponents and to build resilient economies. Those resilient economies must also coincide with this thing called Canada, and having a whole collective of growing, vibrant resilient economies in and around this thing called Canada has to be good for Canada.[6]

The effects of the Indigenous economic shift have the following key characteristics.

Increased Indigenous Influence

Canada's land base covers 998,500,00 hectares. Today over 20% of this is directly controlled by Indigenous Peoples, and this is creating a new shifting sphere of influence. Whether through treaty, self-governance agreements, settlements, fee simple, or other means, this percentage of land base, when compared to the size of European countries, is substantial. Control of 20% of Canada's land base establishes a significant shift in social meaning toward seeing Indigenous Peoples as economic powerhouses. Indigenous Peoples now own or control over 15 million hectares in Canada. Inuit own or control over 45 million hectares.

A recent CBC media headline, "Kapyong Barracks Signed Over to First Nations Group," outlines this emerging pattern. The article states:

> The heads of seven First Nations in Winnipeg and the federal government held a signing ceremony at Assiniboia Downs after reaching a settlement agreement for the 64-hectare site west of Kenaston Boulevard. The group reached an agreement in principle to acquire the property from Ottawa, after a protracted legal stalemate over the future of the former military base.[7]

A project of this magnitude establishes a clear shift in the economic relationship for the Nations.

A second example of this trend is demonstrated in the *Financial Post* story, "Canada's Unfinished Business with First Nations Is an Economic Failure," that describes how the 8,000 members of the Mohawk Nation are claiming 25,000 acres of nearby urban land—or billions of dollars in exchange. Mohawk Grand Chief Mike Delisle stated:

> They [governments] call it a land claim, we call it a land grievance. Here the issue is the seigneurs were granted [by France, three hundred years ago] the right to rent the [Mohawk] land and pay us. This revenue eroded. This is about loss of rents, loss of use, loss of economic opportunity, loss of lands. It's big.[8]

A final example of this growing shift in influence is a media story from Ontario where the Whitefish Lake band filed the largest land claim in Canadian history, $550 billion. This amount represented roughly half the historical proceeds that have been derived from the gigantic nickel-producing area around Sudbury, Ontario. The Nation claims that in 1878, the Canadian justice department gave permission for them to sell timber rights to prospectors, who flipped them months later for fortunes because of nickel discoveries. The case rests on the decision of whether the federal government abrogated its responsibility to protect them from being exploited from over 130 years ago in 1878.

Outlining this shift in influence of First Nations peoples within Canada's economy, business leader Don Richardson of Shared Value Solutions explains:

> Because we are such a resource economy here in Canada, today resource revenue needs to flow not just to the federal government and the provinces and the territories but the resource revenue needs to also flow to the Indigenous rights holders as well. Indigenous peoples need to be a part of the decision-making about what gets extracted, how it gets extracted, if there are secondary processes and how that happens within the management of the territory where they have real rights over. This is the new reality we are facing.[9]

This speaks to this growing Indigenous influence that is permeating and influencing the fiscal equation of this country. This is where economic reconciliation needs to occur—within the fiscal equation. This is economic reconciliation.

Increased and Defined Indigenous Rights

With a landslide of Indigenous legal victories, the unfolding definition of these legal rights is shaking up business as usual. This empowered Indigenous environment needs to serve as a wake-up call to all levels of government and industry. Chief Maureen Chapman of the Sto:lo Nation in British Columbia, in a report by Doug Eyford, *A New Direction: Advancing Aboriginal and Treaty Rights*, describes this shake-up:

After numerous court victories by our peoples and the failure of the current treaty-making process in BC to deliver significant results, Canada must move away from a policy of First Nations making claims to the Crown by fully embracing the need for real recognition followed by true reconciliation. Both the future of First Nations and the national economy depends on it.[10]

Gallagher's recent work has focused on tracking and analyzing Indigenous legal wins. He proclaims, "Nations have racked up against all odds the most impressive winning streak in Canadian legal history. They have taken on some serious opposition and prevailed."[11] This is foundational to the growing Indigenous economic power shift.

First Nations Are Local and Regional Economic Drivers

An example that demonstrates the growing local Indigenous economic strength particularly in a rural setting is the Huu ay aht Nation on the west coast of Vancouver Island in BC. Having signed a modern-day treaty in 2011, the Nation has established a pathway for both self-governance and economic independence. In economic activity, two recent key purchases included the acquisition of a local tree farm license and the purchase of a series of significant developmental commercial lots within the nearby town of Bamfield, which has been seriously hindered from development by the downfall of the forestry and fishing industries decades ago. These purchases place the Nation as a core economic driver of the local forestry industry as well the town itself, a significant economic shift for the Nation and the town. Examples like these are becoming common in the growing power shift and the uprise of Indigenous economic activity.

A well-known example is the Ts'ouke Nation on Vancouver Island, demonstrated in a CBC headline, "B.C. First Nation Leads with Green Technology, Sustainability." The article outlines the Nation's leadership in a diverse range of economic development projects from clean energy to a wasabi production and an oyster farm. "We made the decision, which is really easy, that it's a light footprint approach, and we did that for our children, it's all about future generations," Chief Planes describes.[12] This small Nation has established a national lens for its leadership role in driving clean energy and for diversifying its economy with a focus on sustainability. Examples like this, of small towns being transformed by Nations' economic development growth is becoming a common characteristic of the power shift.

Another example is the B.C. coastal town of Powell River that was established next door to the Tla'amin Nation. Economic growth primarily relied on the forestry and fishing industries, and while the community has experienced significant economic and employment transitional issues, there was high conflict and tension and very little collaboration between the town and the Nation. Powell River demonstrated exceptional leadership in developing processes for partnership and collaboration between the local government and the Nation to open up economic opportunities. Their proactive approach established new economic opportunities and outcomes, and a notable transition away from a relationship historically steeped in conflict. Examples like this point to the pathway of leadership and demonstrate the emerging space for economic empowerment.

Another well-known example, the Osoyoos Indian Band, highlights both the high revenue of the Nation and the need to hire outside of the Nation to meet its workforce requirements. As the *Globe and Mail* article "How a BC Native Band Went from Poverty to Prosperity" emphasizes: "In fact, it's arguably the most prosperous First Nation in Canada, with virtually no unemployment among the Nation's 520 members. Job-seekers from elsewhere flock in to work at the Nation's businesses, which last year saw $26 million in revenue and $2.5 million in net profits."[13]

This series of examples draws on the growing economic influence that Nations are establishing in their respective small towns across this country and demonstrates new economic trends to pay attention to in the rise of Indigenous economic empowerment.

Having Indigenous Peoples at the Table Is a Strategic Advantage

A growing economic narrative of this country is that having Indigenous Peoples at the table is a strategic advantage. As a business leader with extensive experience in working with Indigenous Nations, Don Richardson notes, in regard to the strategic advantage of Indigenous economic opportunities:

Today this is about understanding that this is about making decisions together about how land and resources are used. It is starting to happen where we are seeing joint management, co-management and collaborative management agreements and jurisdictional agreements starting to really take hold and that's the basis of the resource economy.[14]

The Canadian Chamber of Commerce weighs in on this new business environment in its Aboriginal Edge Report, *How Aboriginal Peoples and Natural Resource Businesses Are Forging a New Competitive Advantage*, noting:

Canada's Aboriginal peoples will play an increasingly crucial role in the resource industries. Getting these relationships wrong will take a significant toll on Canada's economic competitiveness. But as the examples listed in this report will show, existing best practices demonstrate a way forward that can lead to better outcomes for industry, Aboriginal communities and all Canadians.[15]

Increased Indigenous Authority and Decision-making

This new business environment lays out a significant shift in approach regarding how decisions are made at the regional, provincial, territorial, and national level. This is the systematic deconstruction of authority that consent and accommodation has created for Indigenous Peoples. Bill Gallagher has maintained a consistent voice in naming this growing shift in increasing Indigenous authority and decision-making:

In contemplating the future of resource development, this country needs to make fundamental adjustments to its approach. Indigenous Peoples have to be involved in project evaluation and approvals from the outset and not later in the process. Complete and unanimous agreement from Indigenous nations is as unlikely as it is among the general Canadian population. Difficult political decisions will therefore be required on pipelines and major project approvals, with Indigenous communities likely to be involved on both sides of the debate.[16]

This is the new business and political environment that is in front of this country. Business leader Don Richardson further notes on this new environment:

> At the core of today's Indigenous economy is the coming to-gether and determining how decisions can get made and it's until we get to a point where people realize that this is about joint or collaborative decision-making and that the parties at the table have true decision-making status. This is the new Indigenous economic reality here.[17]

Indigenous consent is now a fully embedded part of Canadian law, and this consent is now paramount within Canadian consciousness. We need to stop pretending it is new. We should have long ago started talking about how to implement and operationalize Indigenous consent. Lawyer Roshan Danesh reflects on the urgency of this understanding in "There Should Be No Confusion About Aboriginal Consent":

> Our economy cannot afford delay in sorting out what consent means and how to implement it. In the Tsilhqot'in Nation case, the court clarified that every time lands and resources are approved for use by the government without consent, massive risk and uncertainty is created that those projects will have to be cancelled in the future and that compensation will have to paid to First Nations.[18]

Increasing Indigenous Market Potential

In 2011, TD Bank estimated that First Nations will have a market potential of over $32 billion by 2016.[19] Almost all of this Indigenous market potential comes from personal and business income generated in a climate of barriers of access to opportunity, education, and capacity. This is a pivotal point in the growing importance of Indigenous economic growth. Indigenomics, as a platform for modern Indigenous economic design, asks the question: "If Indigenous peoples can achieve this when the deck is stacked against us, what economic outcomes can be achieved when we have a solid foundation to succeed?"[20]

Shannin Metatawabin notes, as CEO of the National Aboriginal Capital Corporation, in observing the shifts in the emerging Indigenous economy in Canada:

The big banks in Canada are starting to realize that there is a market potential in this Indigenous economic base because they are starting to create their Indigenous units and starting to target the establishment of Indigenous financial tools to provide loans for infrastructure, for business, for community, even for governance. The banks are starting to see the trend and to respond to the huge potential. That is a huge market shift because even in the 1990s, even some of the big banks were only beginning to respond to Indigenous market opportunities, but it is happening right now, and it is a good sign because of some of the Indigenous entrepreneurs and communities have taken advantage of mainstream financing and have shown some great success. We are seeing the results of this huge potential.[21]

This shift in influence is beginning to demonstrate the increasing role that Indigenous Peoples are taking within the economy, the financial sector, and political processes today, and that is expressing itself within Indigenous market space as Indigenous economic potential.

Shifting Perception: Indigenous Peoples Are Economic Powerhouses

Nations can no longer be viewed only on the cost side of the equation of this country. Indigenomics is about establishing a shift in social meaning. Lawyer Bill Gallagher highlights:

This is new, I maintain that through these legal wins, First Nations have actually been physically re-drawing the map of Canada one ruling at a time. So, it's now come to impacting the bottom lines of so many companies, provincial governments, and Bay Street finance issues, so that this message is finally getting home that First Nations are in fact the gatekeepers on Canada's road to resources.[22]

Gallagher's work is building a fundamental message about the economic shift that is emerging:

The characteristics of the native legal winning streak in fact scared a lot of people. It has scared them into what I call a defensive posture which has been not conducive to having breakthroughs. The rise of native economic empowerment is seen as something to be weary of, fearful of, and not embraced.[23]

Gallagher speaks to this new reality of financial implications in the rise of Indigenous economic empowerment. This is the time to address the fear about this rise through collective action focusing on economic outcomes.

Academic leader Ken Coates, Canada's Research Chair in Regional Innovation, notes: "The new arrangements included tens of millions of dollars in direct payments, settlements, employment and training programs for Indigenous workers, and preferential contracting arrangements for Aboriginal-owned companies."[24]

In an interview, Shannin Metawain responded to this question: In talking about this emerging economy from your perspective and from your work, how do you see this becoming possible?

The Indigenous population makes up over 5% of the Canada's total population. A per capita economic approach looks at where we should be sitting at as Indigenous peoples with a specific population size as a ratio of the size of the economy. The Indigenous population is growing at four times the national average. It is important to understand that back in the 90s economic development through the Federal Aboriginal Business Development Grant Program was funded at about 70 million annually at the time, and today it is only about 25 million dollars. That is a big reduction, and if you take inflation, it almost hits 60% to 70% reduction in funding toward Indigenous business development. Therefore, the government to this date has been working backwards in responding to the needs of the Indigenous market. Our market is growing four times the national average, but our funding for capital gets reduced and reduced. The Indigenomics growth trajectory is on target as Indigenous peoples—we should be able to generate 5% of Canada's GDP.[25]

Instead this lays out the perfect conditions for an Indigenous economic market failure—the failure to fully respond to and capitalize on the growing needs of the Indigenous economy over the long term. The under-capitalization of the Indigenous economy is a market failure of "incomprehensible failure." The underdevelopment or under-capitalization of the Indigenous economy is the only Indian Problem Canada needs to address.

Deconstructing Authority

The significance of the emerging legal environment is that it has established the pathway for the deconstruction of one-sided authority. The realization of the importance of treating relationships with communities from a nation-to-nation perspective must be an integral part of continued Indigenous economic growth.

In an interview, business leader and advisor Clint Davis affirms this trend:

> There are nations with their own economic interests, their own economic potential, their own economic destinies. In parts of Canada and within the Canadian government they need to understand this. There is a trend toward more people really understanding that this is about nation-to-nation arrangements, it's about nation-to-nation governance and stewardship of lands, waters, and resources.[26]

The growing strength of Indigenous consent and participation in the decision-making process of the regional and national economies is an essential part of this process. The legal and economic context is directly connected. Gallagher reflects on the question: What do you think Canadians need to understand about the legal shift that is happening in Canada?

> There is a legal shift happening. Everybody knows that First Nations have stopping power. Again, there's this fear thing, the first reaction is fear, but Canadians need to know that if we want to have a resources sector, that First Nations have to be up in the front seat with the opportunity to put their hand on the wheel. It's as simple as that. Nothing, no resource company will come on anywhere in the country without any First Nation involvement. This is way beyond just environmental priorities and being stewards of the Earth. No, the nations

have to have equity where they have skin in the game. There is growing pressure now for Nations to commercialize their economic empowerment before they squander their legal successes.[27]

It is when economic reconciliation happens in the fiscal equation of this country that the growth potential of the Indigenous economy can be reached. This is the now that Canada faces; Indigenous nations are beginning to actualize and commercialize the growing strength of economic empowerment.

These are some of the key features of this emerging power shift that point toward a need for collective attention to grow the Indigenous economy.

The Risk of Doing Nothing

At this table of 21st century economics, this new Indigenous business environment establishes the need for a collective economic response. This country is currently at a tipping point where the risk of doing nothing outweighs the cost of doing nothing. Roshan Danesh notes:

> As in real life, you can never simply ignore the storm. If you do, the consequences are massive, perhaps irreversible. The smartest course is to take action to mitigate exposure and damage. Consent is the clear, legally endorsed path to face the building storm of Aboriginal title. Rather than being feared, consent should be embraced and aggressively implemented, as the solution to a basic common challenge.[28]

This is the power shift, the center of this intersection of where we are at as a country. This is the center of the storm that we must face as a country. We must address the perception of fear, the myths, the illusions; see the patterns and facilitate the conditions for Indigenous economic empowerment. Demonstrating this changing narrative, these several media headlines help provide insight into this changing perception. It is these headlines and stories that permeate Canadian consciousness and perception of the Indigenous relationship.

As a *Financial Post* headline clearly states, "Canada's Unfinished Business with First Nations Is an Economic Failure," which is to reconcile the rights and create a role for the country's 603 nations.[29]

The article's central point is that the failure to have done this after centuries not only impedes national economic development but is at the root of much of the misery and squalor on and off reserves. This is the intersection we find ourselves at as a country—where the risk of doing nothing outweighs the cost of doing nothing.

Another headline that outlines this risk of doing nothing is from a *Calgary Herald* article, "Federal Government Blasted Over Native Land Claim Inaction." It describes the federal government's lack of action to resolve land claims that has created serious investment risk and continues to put industry at a disadvantage when it attempts to develop natural resources and projects on these lands. The article highlights the key pressure point:

> The vast majority of impact-benefit agreements are solely between industry and the Aboriginal groups. The government is not at the table. I describe that as trying to solve a trilateral problem, a trilateral relationship, with bilateral negotiations. That's inherently challenging because the courts repeatedly tell us the duty to consult, for example, is a legal obligation on the Crown, but industry carries the lion's share of the effort in getting it done the majority of the time.[30]

The underlying premise of this shifting economic narrative is that the cost of conflict with Indigenous Peoples is high. The article refers to the longevity of conflict "because of the mud of the 20th century, some companies are still unwilling to come and sit at a table across from us and have a serious discussion on what Aboriginal title is and how we utilize our growing stack of chips at this table of 21st century economics."[31]

Building upon this demonstration of the concept of risk and the cost of doing nothing, a *Tyee* article by Chief Ed John, "Mining Is Key to BC's Future, Done Right," outlines a 2010 Fraser Institute global survey of 429 mining executives that positioned B.C. as the second-worst jurisdiction in Canada in which to do business and only 26th of 50 locations worldwide. In the survey, more than 90% cited jurisdiction issues with First Nations as a prime concern.[32] The situation where the cost of doing nothing outweighs the risk of doing nothing is becoming more apparent. This is the perfect storm, the blind spot, and the place to shape the collective response to the rise of Indigenous economic empowerment.

The Collective Response to Now

In this unfolding power shift, the core objective is to converge upon a collective response to the growth of the Indigenous economy. New actions are essential, and the dependency on Indigenous economic health and Canada's economic health are now intertwined.

Lastly, bringing into focus the media narrative, a *Globe and Mail* article, "Canadian First Nations Becoming Less Prosperous," quotes the well-known Chief Clarence Louie of the Osoyoos Nation: "I am telling First Nations we have to make the economy the No. 1 issue, just like non-native people do. Non-native people don't stand for double-digit unemployment. Neither should we. The original treaty relationship in this country was a business relationship. That's what we need to get back to."[33]

Part of the collective response needs to be the ability to accurately frame Indigenous economic growth. "The federal government considers economic development for Aboriginal communities to be discretionary. But I don't know which town, city, or province would call their economy 'discretionary.' White people don't call their economy discretionary.... We want economic development funding to be non-discretionary. That means it's a focus, it must be a priority."[34]

There is now an increasing recognition of the role of Indigenous Peoples in development projects that is being better portrayed. Ken Coates notes in an *Inside Policy* article, "Indigenous Support for Development Is Being Heard":

> Government action is essential now. A coordinated effort by federal and provincial governments and Indigenous peoples is required. The starting point is simple—Indigenous peoples, by right of law and political necessity, must have a central, early stage role. The new systems must find the delicate balance between protecting the right of governments to govern while recognizing the unique status of Indigenous communities. Any attempt to marginalize Indigenous peoples or to put them in a subordinate role in decision-making processes will almost inevitably result in greater conflict and delays. There are solutions available. The new decision-making structures and processes must be co-created with Indigenous peoples, not decided behind closed doors by government.[35]

Coates refers to this as the new normal, the new political and business environment of today. Indigenomics points to the pathway for building economic solutions. What is emerging is a pathway for Indigenous economic inclusion that is igniting growth. This is the choice in front of this country—it is time to select an approach to Indigenous economic growth that reflects the 21st century's legal and political reality of Indigenous inclusion. In only a few short years, Indigenous Peoples have achieved taking a seat at the 21st century economic table. Without a collective economic response, this further establishes the conditions for an Indigenous market failure. A pathway for collective response is the underlying intention of Indigenomics.

The leadership of Danesh points us to the vital conversations: "What these points illustrate is that we are having the wrong conversation. We should not be debating whether consent is relevant or necessary. Rather, we should be focusing on how we implement consent collaboratively and constructively. Implementing consent will require a host of mechanisms—agreements, policies, laws, protocols, and new structures and processes."[36]

This struggle to keep up with the growth of the Indigenous economy says more about our society's need to come to terms with Canada's colonial past, lingering racism, and need to achieve recognition and reconciliation than the idea that consent is something unfamiliar to be feared.

A Strategic Response to Now:
Areas of Innovation in Growing the Indigenous Economy

Growing a strategic response to now is essential to nurture the foundation of Indigenous economic growth. Some of these key components include:

- Developing a body of knowledge about Indigenous economy
- Connecting forecasting, information, data, immediate actions, and future outcomes
- Identifying and measuring economic outcomes and a pathway to a growth trajectory
- Federal Indigenous procurement strategy
- Connecting to the Truth and Reconciliation Commission Calls to Action

- Connecting to the action pathway for the implementation of UNDRIP, the United Nations Declaration on the Rights of Indigenous Peoples
- Call to Action: Implementation of collaboration between corporate Canada and Aboriginal business
- Establishing fiscal policy and budgets with attention to investment and structures for Indigenous economic growth

Indigenomics is a platform for constructive, generative economic design. "Indigenous Peoples make up over 4% of Canada's population. If the next government invests as much into that 4% as it has into the 4% of Canadians who make over $150,000 per year, our economy would be supercharged."[37]

As this platform, Indigenomics has established the concept of the Indigenomics Economic Mix—12 levers or enablers to support the strategic growth of the Indigenous economy toward a $100 billion target. These levers are:

1. Equity ownership
2. Capital
3. Entrepreneurship
4. Trade
5. Philanthropy
6. Procurement
7. Clean energy
8. Technology
9. Social finance
10. Investment
11. Commerce
12. Infrastructure

The Indigenomics Economic Mix serves to focus on the strength of Indigenous economic activities and establish a strength-based approach beyond the socio-economic gap and the "fiscal cost" of Indigenous communities.

Conclusion

Indigenomics is the evidence of our time of the rise of Indigenous economic empowerment. Where are we seeing this evidence? We are seeing this increase in economic visibility in groups such as the Great Bear Rainforest. In 2016, 85% of the rainforest was formally protected through the Great Bear Rainforest Act.[38] Led by First Nations with government, environmental, and industry sectors, this agreement ended 20 years of conflict and put 3.1 million hectares of coastal temperate rainforest off-limits to industrial logging. The agreement formally protects 85% of the coastal temperate rainforest on the British Columbia coast. It provides for government-to-government decision-making with the Province of BC and reflects a vision for healthy First Nations communities, a diverse sustainable economy, and a protected rainforest. The Great Bear Rainforest, home to 74,000 square kilometres of coastal First Nations territory, has the core objectives of conservation, protection, and ecologically balanced economy.

Another example is the establishment of the first Indigenous Business District in Toronto. The city has one of the largest Indigenous populations, over 75,000. The District will serve to create a space where independent business can come to work together, establish visibility, and flourish in a specific area.

This is the time that Canada has an opportunity to get this right. The focus can be on continuously fighting First Nations in courts (the cost of doing nothing) or changing the approach and identify solutions to support the emerging Indigenous economy. In an interview, business leader Don Richardson reflects on the current Indigenous business environment:

> There are incredible opportunities and incredible challenges at the same time. Indigenous leadership is stepping into the challenges and opportunities at the same time and grappling with governance issues, grappling with the land use and environmental management planning issues. There's a lot of human resource challenges and opportunities. Each community is unique and approaches the challenges and opportunities based on their circumstances and histories and treaty rights and so forth. The communities that are doing really well are taking control and working through the issue and building the human resources capacities that they need. Other communities are struggling with that not because of their own issues, because of the external issues of addressing capacity needs, or the project proponents are not providing the capacity required. Often what I see is that the quality of the legal advice and legal challenge that they bring to the table really makes a big difference in the nation's ability to manage the challenges and opportunities.[39]

In the words of a Tsilhqot'in youth, who reflected after their nation's title case victory, "It is certain that we must give the opportunity to have them recognize Aboriginal title. The only way we can do that is to be title, to live and to practice title. I am title—are you?"

Canada must face its own construct of the Aboriginal Question today. According to the *National Post* article "Confronting the Aboriginal Question":

> At some point, the leaders will have to address the myriad of Aboriginals' issues that will shape the future of our country. The Aboriginal Question by far is the most complex and consequential one for Canada today and for the foreseeable future [and] will have to address the myriad of Aboriginal issues that will shape the future of our country.[40]

This is a powerful statement, placing the Aboriginal relationship at the very center of Canada's future. Indigenomics is framed within the context of the application and evolution of the "Aboriginal Question." Today, the Aboriginal Question is cleverly disguised as the "Indian Problem" of yesterday. In *An Army of Problem Solvers*, Shaun Loney notes: "The Indian reality is not an Indigenous problem. It is a Canadian problem. Or, more accurately, it is a Canadian opportunity."[41]

With over a million Indigenous Peoples in Canada, what is the Aboriginal Question of today? With a steadily growing Indigenous economy valued at over $32 billion in 2016, Indigenous economic empowerment can be Canada's story. With constructive, generative economic design and investment into the growth of the Indigenous economy comes the formation of the modern question—How powerful of a people are we? The economic table has been set.

REFLECTION

1. Where are we seeing an increase in Indigenous economic strength and activity? How can this be further supported?

2. If Indigenous Peoples can achieve economic growth with the deck stacked against them, what economic outcomes can be achieved when we have a solid foundation to succeed?

3. What does constructive, generative economic design mean to you?

The Emerging
Modern Indigenous Economy

*How we think determines what we measure. It also determines
how we organize and how we do business. Our thinking,
our belief system, our mindset determines our priorities, our
procedures, our processes, what we expect from people and the
way we deal with them. A distillation of our past thoughts,
observations and experience, our mindset serves as the
foundation for the systems we build and perpetuate.*

—ALBERT EINSTEIN

The recent explosion of the growth of Indigenous business brings a promising future in Canada. Addressing the challenges of the pace of business in today's Indigenous communities must be a central narrative in the re-storying Canada's relationship with Indigenous Peoples. As national Indigenous business leader JP Gladu articulates:

Indigenous people and communities today are challenged with adapting and keeping pace with a world of information exchange, technological advancement, and the interconnectivity of the world's economies and financial systems. They are also faced with the realities of having the youngest and fastest growing population in this country while living in the worst comparable socio-economic conditions, in a time when the gap between the rich and poor is increasing at a rapid rate. Indigenous leaders today are faced with the daunting task of balancing the socio-economic needs and priorities of their people with the finite resources from government and their own source revenues.[1]

Indigenous business leadership today is faced with a rapidly changing, demanding growth environment. This growth is just beginning to be realized and demonstrated through early economic measurements. Gladu continues:

If we look at the last decade, we see there has been an explosion of growth in the number of Indigenous owned and operated businesses, partnerships, joint ventures, and a rapidly growing number of Indigenous entrepreneurs. These are all significant and positive trends in helping close the socio-economic gaps that exist between Indigenous and non-Indigenous peoples. These Indigenous owned businesses are creating employment, economic prosperity, and improving individual and community social well-being.[2]

Connecting the growth of Indigenous business within the context of moving beyond closing the socio-economic gaps offers forward-looking solutions in the design of the growth of the Indigenous economy.

The development of sustainable businesses is vital to the future prosperity of Indigenous people and essential to improving the overall prospects for employment, skill, and capacity development. More and more our leaders are realizing that education is not the only "buffalo" of today, but so is Indigenous business.[3]

Setting a Target for
Indigenous Economic Growth

The Indigenous economy is growing rapidly. A TD Economics Special Report in 2011 estimated that the combined total income of Aboriginal households, business, and government sectors was $12 billion in 2001, doubling to $24 billion in 2011. This report served as a central marker to begin to measure Indigenous economic growth against. The report forecasted that this combined income would be $32 billion in 2016. It noted, "If achieved, total Aboriginal income would be greater than the level of nominal GDP of Newfoundland and Labrador and Prince Edward Island combined."[4] By the 2016 forecast, the $32 billion tally established the assurance of a lucrative market for non-Aboriginal and Aboriginal companies alike. This launches the context of the forward-looking emerging Indigenous economy. It is time to establish a growth trajectory for the continued development and design of the Indigenous economy. It is time to measure Indigenous economic strength, outcomes, and the reduction of Indigenous economic dependency. This is the new story of Canada—Indigenous Peoples are an economic powerhouse.

The emerging Indigenous economy of today requires careful attention, design, and a strategic national growth framework to meet the challenge with the intention of economic reconciliation in an age of the continued assertion of Indigenous rights. Economic equality must be designed. It doesn't just happen by itself. To pursue a pathway of economic reconciliation requires addressing the conditions of economic inequality. The time is now for laying the foundation for economic equality, as Gladu articulates:

> With economic equality, Indigenous peoples have the potential to unlock hundreds of billions of dollars for the Canadian economy. Without economic reconciliation, this unequal relationship will continue on with the status quo. We are facing this unique opportunity to re-make the relationship between Indigenous peoples and businesses in Canada. This is the opportunity.[5]

Understanding the Growth of the Indigenous Economy

The resulting power play of Indigenous economic empowerment has resulted in a significant increase in Indigenous economic activity. This increase takes on the shape of a hockey stick with a sharp uptake in recent years.

In demonstrating this hockey stick growth curve, Indigenomics is driving the narrative of the space between the current value of $32 billion and the potential of the emerging $100 billion target.

Gladu articulates what has contributed to this hockey stick growth curve:

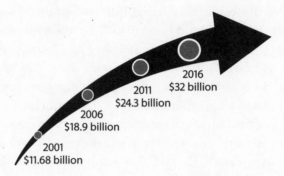

2001
$11.68 billion

2006
$18.9 billion

2011
$24.3 billion

2016
$32 billion

Sources: S. Gulati and D. Burleton, *Estimating the Size of the Aboriginal Market in Canada*, Toronto: TD Economics, 2011; and S. Gulati and D. Burleton, *The Long and Winding Road Towards Aboriginal Economic Prosperity*, Toronto: TD Economics, 2015.

The Aboriginal economy is growing faster than Canada's. There are a few factors that have made our businesses grow faster, on average, than the wider Canadian economy. One is recognition—as Indigenous people, we are the only people to be recognized in Canada's constitution. When companies are looking to advance projects, especially in natural resources, which constitute 16% to 17% of Canada's GDP, they are looking to develop certainty, which Indigenous businesses can provide. Ninety percent of court cases fall in favor of Indigenous communities, so Canadian companies are starting to understand that it is better to partner than to litigate.[6]

Business leader Don Richardson weighs in on this hockey stick growth curve:

I continue to be surprised by the strength of this Indigenous economy. It is growing so quickly it will be difficult for people to even understand what is going on. It is going through a metamorphosis in what's happening with the impact benefit agreements, approaches to co-management, revenue sharing, joint management of resources and land and waters. This shift is happening quickly, and a lot of people may not even understand it is happening, but it is happening and it is happening fast.[7]

The State of Indigenous Economic Research: Money, Meaning, and Metrics in the Emerging Indigenous Economy

There is a growing body of research that focuses on the character-istics of the emerging Indigenous economy and serves to frame the urgent need to pay attention to both its development and design. This Indigenous economy is now starting to be measured and better understood. The following examples highlight Indigenous economic research core metrics that offer insight around the growth and de-sign for the future Indigenous economy.

Aboriginal Economic Benchmarking Report Series: 2012, 2015, 2019
Published in 2012, the Aboriginal Economic Benchmarking Report was the first of a series that outlined the focus of identifying socio-economic indicators to assess the state and progress of the growing Indigenous economy in Canada. The report posited, "Aboriginal prosperity is increasingly linked to Canada's overall prosperity, re-flecting the vital role the Aboriginal population has in ensuring the long-term collective success of the Canadian economy."[8] This is a central theme in the narrative of Indigenous economic success being tied to the success of Canada. This report served as the first national effort to set bold ten-year targets for tracking the economic progress of Indigenous Peoples in Canada. Building understanding of regional Indigenous economic performance is a growing story.

The 2015 report established that while some initial progress had been made between 2006 and 2011, Aboriginal peoples are not on track to achieving parity with non-Aboriginal Canadians and that more efforts by all are required to attain these results.[9] The report set out to assess how the overall core and underlying outcomes for the Aboriginal population have compared with the non-Aboriginal population. It identified the need to focus on better data collection and assessment of policy measures that stimulate economic devel-opment in order to provide more detailed insight into the state of the Indigenous economy and what needs to be done.

The 2019 report also established that while some progress had been made, it was not enough to achieve parity with other Canadi-ans.[10] It is unclear what the pathway was for this progress, how to replicate it for further impact, or who is doing the "progression." The report set out additional indicators. There is currently no clear indi-cation of action or outcomes of this report at this time.

Reconciliation: Growing Canada's Economy by $27.7 Billion,
by the National Indigenous Economic Development Board

This report outlines a clear message that Canada is missing out on a whopping $27.7 billion annually because of its "under-utilized" Indigenous workforce. It highlights the economic gap between Canada's Indigenous and non-Indigenous population in terms of income, education, and training:

> If all Indigenous people had employment, income, education and poverty rates comparable to that of all Canadians, Canada's GDP would grow by 1.5 % or $27.7 billion. For this report to be actualized is bigger than any other economic growth plan in Canada today. And realistically, this target is attainable within existing means and systems.[12]

The report articulates:

> Over 1.4 million people in Canada identify themselves as Aboriginal. It is estimated that $32 billion a year is generated by this group in combined income across households, business and governments. This is as much as two small provinces. The employment targets are not unreachable if scaled across various provinces, territories, industries and entities across Canada. To achieve employment parity, there are 135,210 new Indigenous jobs required.[13]

This report narrative is centering the Indigenous workforce somewhere between being a problem and being an opportunity. It further voices the growing need to align the Indigenous labor market with the growing Indigenous economy. These are some key points:

- Indigenous business success in Canada's labor market is, or should be, of great interest to *all* Canadians.
- The Indigenous population is demographically young, underemployed, and growing rapidly at a time when the rest of the population is aging and growing slowly. This dynamic points to a greater role for Indigenous people in the labor force of tomorrow.
- The economic implications of demographic change depend, among other things, on the size of the labor force, the participation rate, the employment rate, and the unemployment rate.[14]

The report concludes with a clear recommendation:

> The level of spending on Indigenous economic development
> programs should increase to 10% of the total federal spend-
> ing on Indigenous peoples; federal Indigenous economic
> development program funding should be categorized as non-
> discretionary; and that Indigenous economic development
> is a valuable path to a renewed nation-to-nation relationship
> between Canada and Indigenous peoples.[15]

This report points to the fiscal relationship with Indigenous Peoples.
Indigenous economic research must move beyond headline numbers
like $27.7 billion and actually establish a pathway forward for Indig-
enous economic design and outcomes. There is no clear indication
of action or outcomes of this report at this time. To not activate the
potential of $27.7 billion is an indication of the conditions of market
failure in the designed growth of the Indigenous economy. This is the
opportunity.

"Indigenous Economy in Atlantic Canada Exceeds $1 Billion in Annual Spending," Atlantic Policy Congress Report

This report identified that, when accumulated, Indigenous band,
community, organizational, and business spending, as well as net
household spending, have a total regional impact of $1.144 billion
annually.[16] This served to bring visibility to the growing strength
of the regional Indigenous economy that creates 16,733 full-time-
equivalent employment positions, contributes $184.5 million total
tax revenues ($73.2 million federal taxes, $92.7 million in provincial
taxes), and generates $710.9 million in household income in Atlantic
Canada. This report demonstrated early leadership in understanding
the growing strength of regional Indigenous economies.

"$1.14 Billion Strong: Indigenous Economic Performance in Atlantic Canada"

The 2016 Atlantic regional specific measurements report identified
the Indigenous economic annual participation at $1.44 billion. This
demonstrated the real economic contributions of Indigenous communities, businesses, and development activities to the broader

Atlantic Region economy. The study's co-chair, John Paul, commented on the report findings: "The project has confirmed for us what we've known for years, the Indigenous communities in Atlantic Canada are significant contributors to the region's economy."[17]

Highlighting Successful Atlantic Indigenous Businesses

Following the previous report, *Highlighting Successful Atlantic Indigenous Businesses* by the Atlantic Provinces Economic Council brought Indigenous business success into focus:

> Indigenous businesses in Atlantic Canada are making a sizable contribution to the regional economy and are expanding rapidly, but financial obstacles remain a significant barrier to future growth. This report highlights successful Atlantic Indigenous businesses and the impact they have on Atlantic Canada's economy. The study notes that Atlantic Indigenous business revenues were valued at $1.6 billion in 2016, almost 137% more than in 2012. These firms are benefitting the region, creating jobs and income for both Indigenous and non-Indigenous workers: 40% of employees are non-Indigenous workers receiving $118 million in wages.[18]

Indigenous Contributions to the Manitoba Economy

This report highlighted the strength of contributions to the provincial economy. It noted that Indigenous spending in Manitoba totaled $9.3 billion in 2016, the equivalent of contributing 3.9% to the provincial GDP—greater than the regional oil and gas (including mining), food and accommodations, or the manufacturing sectors.[19]

This report serves to bring into visibility the growing strength of regional Indigenous economies. These numbers can serve as markers to establish targets for Indigenous economic success.

The National Aboriginal Capital Corporations Association and Business Development Bank of Canada (BDC) Report

This report showed Aboriginal entrepreneurs face significant barriers in a financial ecosystem that provides support for Aboriginal entrepreneurship in Canada. Data detailed in the report highlighted the important contributions made by investing in Indigenous entrepreneurs. A key metric established in this report was that with each dollar lent under the Aboriginal Business Financing Program (ABFP), $3.60 is added to the Canadian gross domestic product (GDP).[20] This is a significant number to be paid attention to as Indigenous businesses continuously struggle with access to capital and there is a growing army of Indigenous businesses. Reading a significant metric like Manitoba or the Atlantic Indigenous economic contributions leads to the question: Where is Alberta's report on Indigenous economic strength? BC? Saskatchewan? Quebec? How much would the collective three territories demonstrate in Indigenous economic activity?

These report examples above serve to demonstrate the growing significance of Indigenous economic performance metrics as baseline information and the need to connect to a clear trajectory of Indigenous economic strength going forward.

Building a Collective Economic Response: The Emerging $100 Billion Indigenous Economy

Indigenomics is a platform for modern Indigenous economic design that is facilitating a research narrative that supports the knowledge base of the emerging $100 billion annual Indigenous economy. It is essential in re-storying Indigenous economic growth and design to establish a clear trajectory or target. Indigenomics focuses on pushing the narrative of this country to establish a clear economic agenda as the collective response to now.

Indigenomics asks how we establish a focused Indigenous economy without a forecast or clear trajectory pathway. What do we need to learn from the current growth trajectory? If the Indigenous economy met and exceeded the 2016 projection, what are forecasts for 2021? What can be expected in five more years? How can we collectively respond to the potential of a $100 billion Indigenous economy? Indigenomics asks the core question, how can we collectively make possible a $100 billion Indigenous economy? Indigenomics is about future pacing the economic reality of this country to get ready for the emerging $100 billion Indigenous economy.

Understanding the shifting context of the emerging Indigenous economy is important to be able to create the focused attention and design framework that are essential for supporting the continued success of this growth. As Aboriginal business leader JP Gladu notes:

First Nations are coming to the table hungry. There is a need to invest and build solid business and economic structures that are inclusive to Canadian First Nations and lets them participate, and to be recognized. These structures need to be built on the foundation of our role in the history of the development and the continuation of Canada.[21]

The time is now for a collective economic response. Indigenous business is reaching new markets at a rapid rate. "Today Indigenous business is more than just a local gas station or campground. It is regional, national and international in scope. Indigenous peoples from around the world are organizing themselves to take advantage of growing global markets."[22]

The current challenge is to identify the collective strategic response to now. Indigenomics as a platform for modern Indigenous economic design serves to:

- Connect current data and measurements to establish Indigenous economic growth forecast
- Establish a forward-looking growth target
- Establish a national economic baseline to determine Indigenous economic strength
- Future pace the trajectory to forecast the foundation of the $100 billion Indigenous economy
- Understand how to operationalize the shift from the legal relationship to the economic relationship with Indigenous Peoples
- Establish the Indigenomics Economic Mix as 12 levers to support the growth and design of the Indigenous economy. Facilitate these hot spots to increase Indigenous economic activity.

Conclusion

Through the growth of the Indigenous economy, this is the time of re-storying this narrative of the Indigenous relationship in Canada. "There's this growing concept that if you don't have First Nations at the table, you're at a strategic disadvantage."[23] This is the new story of Canada. It is time for modern, constructive economic design.

In an interview, Indigenous business leader Clint Davis explains the significance of the growing concept of Indigenomics:

I love the concept of Indigenomics which talks about the actual metrics, design, and the research for understanding Indigenous economic strength and development. We need to tell this new success story and outline the needs in responding to this emerging growing economy. Indigenomics is an economic platform to connect to the GDP, identify targets, create collective actions that support wealth generation within our communities. $100 billion Indigenous economy—that is the number we need to be paying attention to.[24]

REFLECTION

1. What else can be measured besides Indigenous socio-economic gap?

2. What is significant about the $100 billion Indigenous economic target for Canada's economic future?

3. How can money, meaning, and metrics support the designed growth of the Indigenous economy today?

12

Indigenomics and the Unfolding Media Narrative

The great themes of Canada are as follows:
Keeping the Americans out, keeping the French in,
and trying to get the Natives to somehow disappear.
—WILL FERGUSON, humorist and 2012 Giller Prize winner

Indigenomics serves as a platform to examine how media stories are currently being told about Indigenous business and the economy. Indigenomics emerged from social media, specifically on Twitter, as a thread that focused on the content areas of Indigenous business success, economic development, industry project conflict, and the constant push for economic growth and further access to lands and resources.

Indigenomics emerged from the hashtag #indigenomics. The hashtag evolved through the constant scanning and distribution of the everyday news articles around the content and relevance of the Indigenous relationship to national identity in the social, business, and economic context.

The Indigenomics hashtag highlights stories of high conflict projects, legal challenges, and economic development success. It evolved as a thread of content that examines the thinking and connection to an Indigenous worldview. The media stories reveal some insight into initial patterns and themes of the emerging Indigenous economy, both nationally and globally, that demonstrate the increasing economic presence and visibility of Indigenous Peoples.

The scanning of media stories across the country and globally in the Indigenous legal and business environment is an important means to understanding the basis of the emerging yet ongoing narrative of Indigenous business success. These stories indicate at a sample level how the Canadian media portrays the Indigenous experience and sets it against the background of Indigenous economic growth. Understanding how these types of stories influence our understanding as Canadians is a core question and function of Indigenomics.

The Indigenomics hashtag thread highlights media stories that are often fear-based, sensationalized, or focused on the perceived uncertainty in the business environment or the markets. Indigenomics focuses on how the core question of how the media narrative creates an environment that furthers racism or facilitates inclusion. It explores the question, what is the space created within media to highlight Indigenous business and economic success?

It is also important to examine the language of media regarding the growth of Indigenous business success and challenges. This language strongly reflects the shifting power structures at play. Controlling the narrative power structure of the media collective story has facilitated the underlying image of Indigenous Peoples from a perspective of social and economic struggle.

The invisible thread that ties the development of Canada to the current economy plays out daily in the story of the Indigenous relationship in the Canadian media. This chapter highlights some pivotal moments about the unfolding story shaping the conscious awareness of the Indigenous economy and shaping our collective pathway forward.

Indigenous Business Media Themes

The common thread among these sample stories highlights the success, struggle, development of rights, barriers, tone, complexity, history, justice, and the new legal requirements as story lines within the constant media narrative.

The following section looks at recent media reports that exemplify a cross section of the emerging themes of Indigenous business success growth and its deeply interwoven connection to the Canadian economy and national consciousness. These themes demonstrate dominating narratives that reflect only a minute sliver of the constant emerging stories around the evolving Indigenous business context.

Media Theme 1: Growing Indigenous Business Success

This theme is framed within a simple narrative: Indigenous business is growing. With an increased focus on partnership and the legal environment, the growth of Indigenous business forms a constant story theme in Canadian media, as demonstrated in the following four examples.

"Huge Lineups for Toronto's New Anishinawbe Restaurant," from *Blog Toronto*

This story, which speaks to the demand for indigeneity within the culinary industry, describes lineups around the block on opening night of an Indigenous restaurant. With an increased focus on local Indigenous foods and styles of cooking, Indigenous business success must be paid attention to today.[1]

"Fort McKay First Nation to Put $350M into Suncor Oilsands Tank Farm," *CBC News*

This is an example of a seismic shift in the playing field of Indigenous nations being central powerhouse players in the Canadian energy market. The context of this story is the development of a $1 billion storage facility that is part of a larger $13.5 billion project. This is a significant business entry into the value chain of the energy industry, a value chain that is at the heart of the Canadian economy and also of growing Indigenous participation in the capital markets.[2]

"Canada's First Indigenous Business District Is Coming to Toronto," *Huffington Post*

This story demonstrates the powerful opportunity to increase the visibility of the Indigenous Peoples in one of Canada's major cities. While there have historically been cultural areas for Chinese or Italians, this initial Indigenous business district will demonstrate the growing collective strength and prominence of Indigenous business entrepreneurs and build their presence in the heart of Canada's largest city.[3]

**"B.C. Coastal First Nations Conservation
Economy Booming,"** *DeSmog Magazine*

This article highlights the ecological and business structure of British Columbia's Coastal First Nations, an alliance of nine nations in the heart of the Indigenous-led structure of the Great Bear Rainforest area. Coastal First Nations President Chief Marilyn Slett notes, "For the coastal economy to continue to grow, the key is recognizing the link between economic and ecological sustainability. It is not possible to achieve one without the other."[4] This story highlights the combined business and environmental leaders driven by Indigenous inclusion in the governance and stewardship decision-making and economic structures of the region.

Media Theme 2:
Conflict and Risk in Industry Project Development

Indigenous communities are constantly engaged in a struggle for recognition of rights, implementation of rights, and having a voice or role in the stewardship and development of projects within their traditional territories. The heart of this struggle deals with the "right to continue way of life" and the possibility of disruption to a traditional way of life through current and future ecological and cultural impacts. The following stories demonstrate this central theme of conflict and challenging existing government and processes in industry project development.

"Indigenous Law Banishes a Giant B.C. Mine," *National Observer*

This story highlights a conflict in the mining industry and the rise of Indigenous law and exercising of authority. As Chief Ignace of the Skeetchesn Nation outlines, "The days of colonial authoritarianism are over. It's time for Canada to recognize that we are nations, and as nations we have rights to our land, and if we are approached honourably, we can sit down and come to a fair and just conclusion."[5]

**"Island First Nation Bans Mining
and Clearcutting,"** *Times Colonist*

This story speaks to the growing role of nations in establishing a firm no in proposed project development. It highlights the growing trend of nations taking responsibility for short-term and long-term ecological impacts, decision-making, and stewardship within the traditional territories.[6]

"Tseshaht Demands Termination of
Raven Coal Project," *Ha-Shilth-Sa* newspaper

This story speaks to the Nation's experience of the regulations and policies negatively impacting the Nation's lands. Here the Tseshaht Nation publicly voices their demands that the provincial Environmental Assessment Office officially terminate the proposed Raven Underground Coal Project and, in doing so, establishes an environment in which it is potentially difficult for the proponent to go forward with the proposed project without the Nation's support.[7]

"Canada, Aboriginal Tension Erupting Over
Resource Development, Study Suggests," *Huffington Post*

Framing the experience of risk to Indigenous Peoples and lands is essential to building understanding of the significance of the Indigenous economic relationship in this country. This article headlines the Indigenous Rights Risk Report regarding the treatment of Indigenous rights and resource development around the world, which singled Canada out as the country with the most risk of conflict with Indigenous communities.

> "Canada is a developed country and it is having an implosion of the sort that we've only seen in the developing countries," said Rebecca Adamson, president and co-founder of First Peoples' Worldwide, the group that conducted the study.
>
> "We've always seen this conflict erupt when a government refuses to be clear in upholding Indigenous land tenure."
>
> The Indigenous Rights Risk Report studied 52 U.S. resource companies and 370 projects around the world, including 16 companies and 76 projects active in Canada. The aim of the survey was to assess how likely it is that conflict with Indigenous communities could result in costly shutdowns.[8]

It identified that Canada is home to six of the 21 projects deemed to be at highest risk of collapse—more than any other country.

The Canadian government is "operating like a third-world country," Adamson said, adding that its approach to Indigenous rights more closely mimics the Philippines and Brazil than the U.S. and Australia.

Signs are pointing to an increasing number of protests and possible violence in the country, the article highlights.

Canada's risk level was graded three out of five—medium risk—higher than other industrialized countries like the U.S., New Zealand and Australia, which had a risk level of two.

"The Canadian government may be pro-business but its policies towards First Nations will have very anti-business results," Adamson said.[9]

Media Theme 3: Tone of Media Headings

Examining the "tone" of a sample of Indigenous-based headlines can bring some attention to the role of fear in the Canadian media narrative in regard to Indigenous Peoples. These headlines can perpetuate negative perceptions of Indigenous Peoples and serve to imprint doubt, fear, and myths into the consciousness of the reader.

"Wynne Pushes Ring of Fire Chiefs for Decision on Regional Road," *Globe and Mail*

This story highlights the economic push/pull dynamic of government and Indigenous project development. Here Premier Wynne warns the remote fly-in Nations in Northern Ontario that they must "quickly agree" on the construction of a road into their region. This road would also serve mining interests in the Ring of Fire mega project to access resources. The article proclaims the Premier will "negotiate unilaterally with those communities that want the project."[10] A heading of this nature has the undertone of "making those pesky natives agree."

Cash for Pipelines: "How Energy Companies Woo First Nations on Controversial Energy Projects"

This article highlights the experience of industry "wooing" First Nations, in its economic imperative of getting to yes and obtaining their consent for project development. It outlines the role of contracts extended by a corporation offering big money to the traditional Chiefs in exchange for supporting the pipelines and the division between traditional and Indian Act systems of governance and decision-making.[11] This headline leaves just enough room for speculation but a lasting negative impression instilled by the common and less than positive narrative, "There those natives go again getting money!"

"First Nations Staking Their Claims in the B.C. Economy," *Vancouver Sun*
What is your response upon reading a headline like this? "Staking a claim" is leftover colonial language that instills fear in the reader of the growing economic strength of First Nations. While less than constructive, this story speaks to the increasing economic space of Indigenous business.[12]

"No Wealth, No Justice in $1 Billion LNG Offer to First Nation Band," *The Tyee*
This headline's tone speaks to a sensationalized payout offer, highlighting the increasing value of Indigenous project consent. "The proponent of a liquefied natural gas plant on British Columbia's north coast offered more than $1 billion to obtain the consent of a First Nations community, a ground-breaking proposal that could establish the new price tag for natural resource development in traditional Aboriginal territories."[13]

Resource projects of this size and impact largely disrupt a nation's ability to go into the future with their identity and practices and beliefs intact. They focus on economic generation whereas Indigenous opposition identifies that the number one priority is fish habitat protection. Nation members reflected the company could give $2 billion instead of $1 billion and the answer would still be no because fish are more important than money.

"Our Warrior Problem: Militant Natives Are Causing Trouble, and They Aren't Going Away," *London Free Press*
This headline is referring to the highly visible fracking conflict in the Atlantic, and the tone of the story does not hold back and puts it right out there: "Those pesky natives!" The language and tone of "aren't going away" leaves very little unsaid and is particularly problematic with its racist undertone.[14]

Media Theme 4:
Aboriginal Legal Challenges and New Requirements

With a constant stream of stories that outlines Indigenous legal challenges, this common theme resounds loudly in the Canadian media narrative. The following four examples describe an environment of legal challenges and the facilitation of new requirements emerging in the legal realm that is empowering Nations.

"This Is a Watershed Moment": Chief Vows to Be
Arrested As Fight Against Site C Dam Ramps Up," *The Narwhal*

This headline addresses the role of Indigenous conflict in project development. The article refers to a growing sentiment noted by esteemed Indigenous leader Stewart Philipp of the Union of BC Indian Chiefs: "If push comes to shove, I for one, being a grandfather of 14 grandchildren who I absolutely adore—I am more than willing to be arrested as long as that will contribute to stopping this project.... I know when that moment comes I will not be alone." These sentiments demonstrate the degree of conflict and commitment to the opposition within this mega project.[15]

"Northern Gateway Decision a Huge
Victory for First Nations Rights," *The Tyee*

This headline serves to demonstrate the growing influence of First Nations in major project development. This particular project was under a national microscope focusing on the quality of Indigenous consultation that eventually resulted in a no-go for the proponent and a significant problem for Canada in its quest to get resources to market.[16]

"Court Decision Affirms First Nations
Landowner Rights," *Journal of Commerce*

This headline outlines a new environment where Aboriginal title must be given the same rights as any other private landowner, as the B.C. Court of Appeal ruled in a historic decision this month. The case was brought forward by Saik'uz First Nation and Stellat'en First Nation in B.C. "They claim that Rio Tinto Alcan's Kenney hydroelectric dam on land they assert Aboriginal title over has severely damaged the Nechako River and its fisheries." They describe "the river no longer flows like a river!"[17]

Media Theme 5:
Indigenous Business Innovation and Leadership

Establishing today's environment of Indigenous business success has required tremendous leadership, innovation, and vision, as demonstrated by the following media stories.

"Tsuut'ina First Nation Plans Major Commercial Development at Calgary's Southwest Edge: Chief Says Project Will Be 'One of the Largest, if Not the Largest' First Nations Developments in Canada," CBC

Chief Roy Whitney offers a strategic insight: "This is why Tsuut'ina people, after much debate and voting, decided to approve the construction of the southwest Calgary ring road—not because of immediate cash benefits, because those are fleeting, but precisely because of a vision of what could be built in the traffic flow throughout our land."[18]

"B.C. First Nation Leads with Green Technology, Sustainability," CBC

This story puts First Nations at the center in support of green sustainable technology, while offering an alternative to energy poverty that many First Nations in Canada experience. This story exemplifies the work of a small 250-member coastal Nation who sells its excess energy from the micro-grid back to the municipality. The Nation is working toward being a net zero community and has become an eco-tourism destination. Stories like these place local Nations as key economic players in developing regions, cities, and towns across the country.[19]

Media Theme 6: Indigenous Worldview

The subtleties of bringing into visibility the components of an Indigenous worldview are often lost within the media narrative. Small glimpses of this worldview can be seen within these specific stories.

"Conrad Black: This Isn't Religion, It's Madness!" *National Post*

This article outlines media mogul Conrad Black's take on the highly visible 2009 court challenge to a proposed ski resort that was contested by the Ktunaxa Nation. It highlights Ktunaxa leadership in declaring their absolute opposition to the project because of the "sacred significance" of the entire area. Little can be said for the emotional response to indigeneity, religion, and freedom clashing in a difference and experience of worldviews and project development. Black's contention that "this isn't religion this is madness" does little to diminish conflict and the experience of the Ktunaxa people against development and impact on their ways of being.[20]

Media Theme 7: Aboriginal Relations/Reconciliation

An emerging theme in Canadian awareness is one of reconciliation and the need to move away from conflict toward positive Indigenous relationships and actions. At the heart of this reconciliation process is the increasing role of corporations and governments with Aboriginal relations. The following examples demonstrate the growing visibility of economic reconciliation with Indigenous Peoples.

As the Canadian media struggles to understand and articulate the rapidly changing Indigenous legal and business environment, the 86th Call to Action of the Truth and Reconciliation Commission states:

> We call upon Canadian journalism programs and media schools to require education for all students on the history of Aboriginal peoples, including the history and legacy of residential schools, the United Nations Declaration on the Rights of Indigenous Peoples, Treaties and Aboriginal rights, Indigenous law, and Aboriginal–Crown relations.[21]

This call to action is essential for furthering the Canadian Indigenous media narrative around the Indigenous economy and the strength of the Indigenous relationship in Canada. The following are three examples of media headlines regarding Indigenous reconciliation.

"Calgary Raises Treaty 7 Flag in a Permanent Move of Reconciliation," Windspeaker

This Windspeaker article highlights actions that support reconciliation. "It's fair to say, and I don't think any Canadian would disagree, that one of our greatest failures as a nation is the inability to include our Indigenous brothers and sisters in the prosperity and growth of us as a people. And that for me is what reconciliation is about. It's about acknowledging the mistakes of the past and moving forward together in a way that involves everybody, includes everybody," said Mayor of Calgary Nenshi.[22]

"City of Vancouver Formally Declares City Is on Unceded Aboriginal Territory," *Global News*

This headline demonstrates leadership in reconciliation. Connecting to the language of "unceded" allows the reader insight into the history of the development of B.C. and of the city itself.[23]

"Energy Projects Fuel Tension Between Trudeau and First Nations," *Discourse Media*

This headline outlines explicit conflict between government and First Nations in resource development. The articles further states, "Experts say approving mega-projects without First Nations consent creates economic uncertainty and hinders reconciliation." It is important to note the growing narrative of connecting economic uncertainty directly to Indigenous consent in an era of reconciliation.[24]

Media Theme 8: Growing Indigenous Economic Influence

A subtle yet powerful emerging media narrative is of the growing Indigenous economic influence. Each of these examples place Indigenous business success as central to regional development. They serve to demonstrate a newfound Indigenous modern economic influence through land ownership, transfer, or ownership within projects.

"It's a Breach of Treaty: Manitoba First Nations Want Promised Land," *CBC*

This article serves to demonstrate the ongoing process of lands being returned to Indigenous control. In this example, the size of lands owed under historical and current treaty breaches is more than half a million acres.[25]

"Elsipogtog Files Aboriginal Title Claim for Sikniktuk to Protect Territory," *Media Co-op*

The Elsipogtog First Nation filed an Aboriginal Title Claim for title to the Mi'kma'ki district of Sikniktuk, which is traditional Mi'kmaq territory covering about 30% of New Brunswick. "We cannot stand by while the government ignores us and makes decisions that threaten the traditional lands of the Mi'kmaq people," Chief Sock said. "It's time for us to exercise our rights and responsibilities to protect our territory."[26]

"Huu-ay-aht First Nation Buys 11 Properties in Bamfield," CBC

This is a story of successful Indigenous business positioning that is increasingly common in rural locations. Indigenous Peoples are becoming key drivers in otherwise stagnant local economies that have been dependent on forestry or fisheries or other natural resources industries for years. The increased capacity of a modern treaty Nation to create clear real estate domination locally speaks to the increased role of communities.[27]

Media Theme 9:
Shifting Aboriginal Business Environment

Understanding the growth of the Indigenous business environment gives key insight into the labor market, unemployment rates, and the growing Indigenous population and workforce. These articles demonstrate these shifting patterns and serve as a wake-up call to pay attention to the growth of the Indigenous economy.

"Reducing Aboriginal Unemployment Could Bring
90 million in Economic Benefits to Saskatchewan," Star Phoenix

This article describes how closing Saskatchewan's education gap is fundamental to reducing Aboriginal unemployment and could potentially provide a $90-billion economic boost. In an interesting comparison, study lead Eric Howe notes, "That's 20 per cent more, for example, than the total value of all potash that's ever been produced in Saskatchewan, (just by ensuring) Aboriginal people are employed at the same rate as non-Aboriginal people."[28]

"Uncertainty Surrounds Rights and
Title Decision," Williams Lake Tribunal

This article offers insight into the experience of rising Indigenous economic empowerment through this watershed decision that speaks to the change in how business is done with Indigenous communities. It outlines a local and government perspective on the application of the case unfolding for non-First Nations living and working in the 1,900-square-kilometer title area. In this new environment, instead of paying the province an annual fee for permits or licenses, for example, those fees will be paid to the Tsilhqot'in Nation.

In an ironic depiction, a public meeting participant noted that, prior to the court decision, 300 square kilometres of his trapline area was removed and returned to the Nation, and after the court decision, he lost another 200 square kilometres, explaining, "I never received any written notice or spoken notice that I lost the right on this area. I think this is absolutely wrong."[29]

Media Theme 10: Indigenous Ownership

There is an increased push to move toward equity ownership in partnership development with Indigenous communities. This facilitated ownership represents recognition of Indigenous rights, values, and need for participation, as well as strategic advantage of Indigenous inclusion.

"B.C. Proposal Aims to Have First Nations Own Chunks of Major Projects," *Vancouver Sun*

The First Nations Major Projects Coalition is leading this charge for increased equity ownership of First Nations in major projects across the country. The loan guarantees process will allow Aboriginal communities to buy equity stakes in major projects. According to the article, "The development of the First Nations Major Projects Coalition is one of the most exciting—and important—developments in indigenous business in recent decades," said institute spokesman Brian Lee Crowley.[30]

"First Nations Are Eyeing Equity Partnerships," *The Province*

This article highlights the growing movement of Nations positioning themselves economically beyond benefit agreement frameworks through equity ownership in resource projects. Ownership can offer consistent and predictable revenues for Indigenous communities. It outlines the growing interest in taking a more ambitious step: going for equity ownership, a share of the corporate action. Equity ownership for Nations can offer the prospect of increasing returns, not just fixed payments, as a resource project hits its full economic cycle and moves away from "impact payments" alone. It can also mean longer-term revenue flows linked to the economic life of the project.[31]

Collectively, these ten media themes serve to demonstrate the storying of Indigenous economy, the language of media, and the visual insertion into Canadian consciousness.

Media Visual Portrayals of Conflict and the Assertion of Aboriginal Rights

The role of conflict in economic development cannot be lessened as Nations continuously experience the minimum standards of consultation and an environment weighted to the proponent for financial gain and the good of the economy or the nation. The following are some of the most impactful media visual portrayals of Aboriginal conflict and the assertion of Aboriginal rights.

The story the media tells about this economic relationship leaves far too much room for uninformed opinion—the smallest unit of measurement. The real measurement is the shift toward impact. What is emerging today is that people are simply expecting more of economy. It is time to move beyond fear. Let's have the courage to do this together—all my relations.

Source: http://globalnews.ca/news/56194/gallery-a-history-of-first-nations-protests-in-canada/

Source: Elsipogtog fracking protest. Photo credit and permission: Ossie Michelin and APTN.

"Understanding First Nations values, worldview, stories, and relevance to the Canadian economy—that's really where Indigenomics role is within Canada. So I think the time is right."[32] Indigenomics is a pathway to pull Canada into a better future.

REFLECTION

1. What is important to pay attention to as you read media stories about Indigenous business?

2. What role can media play in shifting the perception of Indigenous Peoples being a burden on the fiscal system toward re-storying Indigenous economic growth?

13

Building a Toolbox
for Economic Reconciliation

We have described for you a mountain,
We have shown you the path to the top.
We call upon you to do the climbing.
—SENATOR MURRAY SINCLAIR,
Truth and Reconciliation Commission of Canada

Canada is struggling with the complexities of understanding its evolving relationship with Indigenous Peoples. As Indigenous Peoples are establishing an ever-growing shifting and dynamic political and economic presence, it is becoming increasingly important for Canadian citizens to develop a larger knowledge base to better understand this through a toolbox for economic reconciliation.

This is a time when grasping the significance of the growing Indigenous presence and influence is being made visible like never before. Canada's future is implicitly connected to the quality of the Indigenous relationship and must include the process of economic reconciliation as a foundation. Our modernity as a country requires new means for collaboration, new thinking, and new language and innovative actions in this economic relationship.

The Truth and Reconciliation Commission Report was a call for action for individual and collective leadership into the Indigenous relationship requiring honesty, reflection, and new action. This concept of reconciliation emerged into Canadian consciousness which was formed through the Commission documenting the voices and experience of thousands of residential school survivors. Through this process, reconciliation has been established at the forefront of

Canadian consciousness and is a driving force for social, political, and economic change within communities, organizations, corporations, and governments.

Reconciliation is a word that comes loaded with historical baggage—the burden of broken promises, mistrust, and lived court challenges, the desecration of lands and resources over time, and the ongoing lived socio-economic realities of poverty levels experienced by Indigenous Peoples. While there are distinct arguments for and against from within Indigenous communities and within Canada overall, this is undoubtedly the time for economic reconciliation. There are a lot of misconceptions and narratives of what reconciliation is and is not. There is reconciliation done well, and there is reconciliation done poorly, and reconciliation that desperately needs to be done.

Reconciliation is an ongoing process of establishing and maintaining respectful relationships. It is also about embedding the importance of the Indigenous relationship into the Canadian consciousness. At its foundation, reconciliation has to be an exercise in truth telling. Truths are rooted within the social and economic lived realities of Indigenous Peoples who have been rendered to the sidelines of the negative statistics of this country. Truth is the parallel process of reconciliation. This is the uncomfortable space. For Canada, this means the need to build the collective response to now, which can no longer be based on governments spending millions of dollars in court fighting Indigenous rights and title.

From an Indigenomics perspective, economic reconciliation is defined as the space between the lived realities of Indigenous Peoples, the need to build understanding of the importance of the Indigenous relationship, and the requirement for progressive actions for economic inclusion.

The lived realities of Indigenous Peoples can only shift towards well-being through renewed economic and fiscal strength. The need for understanding of the legal and economic relationship Canada is in with Indigenous Peoples is paramount for the designed emergence of the Indigenous economy. The leadership to support the constructive, generative economic designed growth requires entering the uncomfortable space of addressing a past built upon Indigenous economic exclusion and making space at the economic table of this country.

Indigenomics is the invitation for a modern economic response to the Indigenous relationship. It serves as a platform for the dismantling of Indigenous economic exclusion and regression and addressing the systemic devaluing of Indigenous knowledge systems from the initial formation of Canada.

Kathleen Mahoney is a leader who was instrumental in her work as an international human rights lawyer and acted as the legal advisor and negotiator for the Assembly of First Nations at the time of the development of the Indian Residential School Settlement Agreement. She voices a key perspective in "Economic Equality Must Be a Part of Indigenous Reconciliation":

> Canada's origin story is the story of the British North America Act, the Fathers of Confederation, and the British/French duality that together formed the bedrock of the free, equal and of the diverse democracy we believe ourselves to be. But here's the problem: our origin story is false. In 1996, the Royal Commission on Aboriginal Peoples observed, "A country cannot be built on a living lie."[1]

This is the leadership and truth telling that the process of reconciliation requires today. After 150 plus years of denial, coming to terms with our true origin story is long overdue. Mahoney asks "Who will be brave enough to write this story?" She takes on the task of truth: "Indigenous Canadians are invisible in this origin story even though they were present on the land for thousands of years prior to Confederation and without their contributions Canada would not be the country it is today."[2]

Bringing a significant voice in the reconciliation process, Mahoney makes the connection:

> When a nation's origin story ignores the existence and contributions of those integral to its founding, it can create a deep sense of alienation, isolation and hostility. Canada is in an awkward position of needing to acknowledge its shaky foundation as the Aboriginal legal environment continuously pokes holes in this accepted origin story and the business as usual approach.[3]

Mahoney's voice leads a growing national narrative of the importance of "the recognition that Indigenous Peoples were the founders of this nation and must be acknowledged in a formal, legal way as an act of reconciliation. Only then can there be a solid foundation for Canada to reconcile its past and lay the foundation for a new relationship with its first peoples."[4]

Building from the truths of the establishment of this country is the beginning of reconciliation. Indigenous Peoples did not receive recognition for their contributions to building Canada, nor a fair share of the ensuing wealth. Instead, they were classified as non-citizens, removed from their lands, and subjected to unequal treatment founded on the racist philosophical and legal justifications of the Discovery Doctrine and the formal equality principle. This is the myth this country was built upon. This is the uncomfortable space.

It is this uncomfortable truth that needs to be addressed within both the history books and the narrative of this country. This voice is central to evolving the legal and economic shift that is bringing Indigenous Peoples into visibility within this country. This is the role of reconciliation—to build from the truths and role of Indigenous recognition in this country. Reconciliation is about creating a new normal—whether through government processes, business, education, justice, or the child welfare systems; in essence, it is about addressing the lived realities of the Indigenous population and the over-told story of negative social and economic statistics and continuous marginalization.

Reconciliation cannot be a feel-good exercise or resolved within a talking circle. The outcomes of reconciliation must produce Indigenous socio-economic well-being. If it cannot do that, then it is not reconciliation. Economic reconciliation must occur within the fiscal equation of this country. Economic reconciliation should serve a dual function: to establish a critical mass of positive action for inclusion and to establish processes "to make right" that builds on the truth that Indigenous Peoples have been systematically denied the right to an economy, access to lands, and resources for the interest of the establishment of Canada. If it cannot do that, then it is not economic reconciliation.

In an interview on Indigenomics, Indigenous business leader JP Gladu observes:

Economic reconciliation is looking at the end game, which is when our communities are no longer managing poverty but creating and managing wealth. The only way to manage wealth is by creating it, and the way to create it is by leveraging our assets—which are our people, our innovation and our lands and resources.[5]

Economic reconciliation must establish the foundation for building an inclusive economy—this is the journey from invisibility to inclusivity of Indigenous Peoples in the formative economic design framework of this country. It is time to move beyond the far too common narrative of "Get over it!" as a response to Indigenous Peoples. Author Shaun Loney offers an important insight into this sentiment: "Some Canadians say 'What is done is done. It's time Aboriginal people let go of what happened and move on.' Instead, we need to understand exactly what has been done to enable us to think creatively about how to move forward."[6] Indigenomics is about leadership of recognition and inclusion.

Canadians are not equipped with the language that says "I understand what free, prior, and informed consent is, I understand what consultation is, I understand what a referral system is, or UNDRIP." It is time to build our toolbox of understanding.

That's where a new language needs to be built from. Canadians need to understand how and why First Nations are important within the regional and national economies.

Economic reconciliation is the process of creating and facilitating meaningful partnerships and mutually beneficial opportunities to support Indigenous economic prosperity and inclusion. Establishing a shared prosperity approach must draw on the values of the community to inform the structures, processes, and environments to stimulate economic action toward community resilience.

Reconciliation and the Pathway to an Inclusive Economy

With economic inclusion and equality, Indigenous Peoples have the potential to unlock hundreds of billions of dollars for the Canadian economy. Without economic reconciliation, our unequal fiscal relationship will continue. We face a unique opportunity to remake the once-vibrant relationship between Indigenous Peoples and businesses in the rest of Canada.

The experience and reality of exclusion are lived daily by Indigenous Peoples. As Chief Terry Paul reflects:

But the reality is First Nations have been excluded from Canada's economy. First Nations have great demographics—a fast
growing young population. The statistics show that 400,000
Aboriginal youth will enter the Canadian workforce by 2025.
There's all kinds of money out there. But First Nations only
have access to 0.1 per cent of one per cent of the available capital in Canada. This is both the challenge and the opportunity
in front of this country.[7]

The Characteristics of an Inclusive Economy

The absence of an inclusive constructive, generative economic design of the Indigenous economy leads to these questions: What is an
inclusive economy, and what does progress toward it look like? An
inclusive economy is one in which there is expanded opportunity for
more broadly shared prosperity, especially for those facing the greatest barriers to advancing social and economic well-being.

Author Emily Garr Pacetti outlines five characteristics of an inclusive economy in "Getting Beyond the Equity-Growth Dichotomy."

1. Participation: In an inclusive economy, citizens are able to participate fully in economic life and have greater say over their
   future. Common knowledge and transparent rules and norms
   allow people to access and participate as workers, consumers, and
   business owners. Technology is more widely distributed and pro-
   motes greater individual and community well-being.
2. Equity: In an inclusive economy, more opportunities are available
   to enable upward mobility for more people. All segments of society, especially poor or socially disadvantaged groups, are able
   to take advantage of these opportunities. Inequality is declining
   rather than increasing. Citizens have equal access to a more solid
   economic foundation, including adequate public goods, services,
   and infrastructure, such as public transit, education, clean air and
   water.
3. Growth: An inclusive economy is increasingly producing enough
   goods and services to enable broad gains in well-being. Good work
   opportunities are growing and incomes are increasing, especially
   for the poor. Economic systems are transforming for the better-
   ment of all, including especially poor and excluded communities.
   Economic growth and transformation not only is captured by

aggregate measures of economic output (such as GDP) but must include and be measured by other outcomes that capture overall well-being.

4. Stability: In an inclusive economy, individuals, communities, businesses, and governments have a sufficient degree of confidence in their future and an increased ability to predict the outcome of their economic decisions. Individuals, households, communities, and enterprises are secure enough to invest in their future. Economic systems are increasingly resilient to shocks and stresses, especially to disruptions with a disproportionate impact on poor or vulnerable communities.

5. Sustainability: In an inclusive economy, economic and social wealth is sustained over time, thus maintaining intergenerational well-being. Economic and social wealth is the social worth of the entire set of assets that contribute to human well-being, including human produced (manufactured, financial, human, social) and natural capital. In the case of natural capital, human use must preserve or restore nature's ability to produce the ecosystem of goods and services that contribute to human well-being. Decision-making must thus incorporate the long-term costs and benefits, and not merely the short-term gains, of human use of our full asset base.

In order to sustain inclusive Indigenous economic growth, understanding Indigenous focused decision-making, the investment environment, and fiscal or economic policies is essential. These characteristics point to the foundation for economic empowerment in an environment of economic reconciliation with Indigenous Peoples.[8]

Indigenous business leader JP Gladu notes:

Economic equality must be part of Indigenous reconciliation. We cannot reverse hundreds of years of unequal relationships overnight. A history of broken treaties, territorial dispossession, reserves and residential schools will take time to overcome. This sad legacy is reflected in contemporary Indigenous culture, education, health and wellness—and in the economic marginalization of First Nations, Inuit and Métis peoples in Canada.[9]

Indigenomics, as a new word, helps to form a new language structure and push an agenda for Indigenous economic inclusion and growth and supports a new narrative that Indigenous Peoples are an economic powerhouse in our own rights.

Indigenous economic exclusion is directly connected to the broader social challenges faced by Indigenous Peoples today and compounded by the trauma of history. Addressing economic disparity can be a vital part of a sustainable solution. The absence of discussion on economic equality establishes a status quo environment and the conditions for economic regression.

The core of economic reconciliation is supporting Indigenous communities so that they have access to the capital, resources, and opportunities needed to succeed today. Addressing the overarching obstacles to economic growth that would unlock the potential of the fastest-growing segment of Canada's population—this is Indigenous economic inclusion. This is Indigenomics. This new economic environment must be based on the United Nations Declaration of Indigenous Peoples and ensure that Indigenous entrepreneurs and companies have business environments conducive to success.

Those words of the Truth and Reconciliation Commissioner, respected leader Murray Sinclair—"We have described for you a mountain. We have shown you the path to the top. We call upon you to do the climbing."—bring clarity to this time of economic reconciliation. We call upon you to do the climbing!

Gladu provides further insight into economic reconciliation:

> The need to foster economic reconciliation cannot exist in a vacuum. As the Indigenous population grows, it's critical that we prepare today for the entrepreneurs and business leaders of tomorrow. This next generation must have access to the right technology for tomorrow. We need to connect Indigenous young people, especially in the North, where access is often limited. Like any other young people, they need to be ready to work in the digital world. Indigenous communities are going through a demographic boom, often in areas that face labor shortages and lack suppliers for local development projects. Canada cannot afford to lose the next generation of Indigenous business talent. The cost of inaction will be heavy, and not just for Aboriginal peoples.[10]

Indigenous Peoples want a pathway to prosperity that most Canadians take for granted. All Canadians need to know that Indigenous business is a growing force. Today's modern Indigenous reality must establish the space to enact our ways of life, culture, and responsibility to our children and future generations.

A *Say Magazine* article, "The Case for Economic Reconciliation in Canada," outlines the growing significance and role of economic reconciliation.

> Growing Aboriginal economic prosperity is essential to Canada's overall prosperity. There is great potential that remains to be realized in the people, in their land, and in their spirit. With a concerted effort, Corporate Canada, small businesses, education institutions, health institutions, and all levels of government, Canada's economic strategy must include economic reconciliation as well.[11]

The Indigenomics Toolbox

The questions immediately in front of this country are how can we better understand our legal and economic relationship with Indigenous Peoples? How can Canadians become engaged in understanding reconciliation and responsibility? It is important to understand that reconciliation cannot be somebody's responsibility, it has to be everybody's responsibility. Reconciliation happens at an individual level, at a family level, at a community level. It happens in the home, the office; as well as local, regional, and federal administration; and governance systems and through businesses and corporations.

The Indigenomics toolbox lays out 13 core concepts in building understanding of the foundation of economic reconciliation for Canadians:

- UN Declaration on the Rights of Indigenous People—What did it say and why it is important?
- The 2008 Canadian Statement of Apology to First Nations peoples—What did it say and why was it important?
- Free, prior, and informed consent—What is it and why does it matter?
- What is the outcome and significance of the Tsilhqot'in court decision?

- Doctrine of Discovery—What is it and why is important to understand it in the context of today?
- Royal Proclamation—What is it and why is it important in the relationship with Indigenous Peoples?
- Truth and Reconciliation Calls to Action—Read the Calls to Action, understand what these are and why they are important.
- "Unceded"—What does this term mean in relation to Indigenous Peoples, Crown land, and fee simple lands?
- "Principles Respecting the Government of Canada's relationship with Indigenous Peoples"—What are they and why are they significant?
- What is the Indian Act? What is an Indian reserve?
- What does it mean that Indigenous Peoples have constitutional rights? What are they?
- What is a treaty nation and a non-treaty nation? What is the difference?

What is the $100 billion Indigenous economic target and how can it support the evolution of economic reconciliation in Canada?

For Canadians, the pathway towards reconciliation means becoming educated about Indigenous issues, demonstrating positive leadership in the face of racism, and promoting system equality. It is about leadership in action.

Now is the time to establish the leadership in building pathways for implementing the Truth and Reconciliation Commission Calls to Action. Reconciliation is about leadership. Reconciliation is about shifting the lived realities and experience of Aboriginal peoples in Canada. Economic reconciliation must occur within the fiscal equation of this country. We all have a responsibility and a role to play. Find your leadership. It is time.

Conclusion

The development of the Canadian economy has been based on the establishment of the structure of authority to ensure access to resources that first required the removal of Indigenous Peoples from the land they used as their economic base. This economic lag is still being felt today as Canada has the legal duty and requirement to now consult with nations and gain consent. Regarding the new economic environment, Gladu notes: "But now the access to resources has shifted considerably, and Canada really needs to be able to identify what is our relationship with First Nations now? The time is right. Those who do not embrace Indigenous partnerships will lose their competitive edge."[12]

A number of years ago, the Stz'uminus First Nation, located in the Ladysmith municipality on Vancouver Island, B.C., was holding an open house for their economic development corporation. The mayor of Ladysmith acknowledged for the very first time in the history of the small town, over 90 years after incorporation, that a mayor went across the bay and onto the reserve to do the opening comments and a welcoming for the community's business open house event. He began the session with these words: "I have crossed the line, the line that prevents us from working together. I am here. It's time to cross the fabricated lines and start a new relationship of working together. Now let's do business together." And he walked off the stage. (Applause)

This is reconciliation. It's time to cross the line, the fabricated line of the reservations that prevent us from recognition, responsibility, and economic reconciliation. It's time to address the fabricated lines of economic exclusion. It is time. This is Indigenomics in action.

REFLECTION

1. What leadership is required today in the relationship with Indigenous Peoples? What does your leadership look like for economic reconciliation with Indigenous Peoples?

2. What does that mean "to be on the right side of history" in regard to the Indigenous relationship? Or the wrong side of history?

3. What if economic development was an act of reconciliation what would change?

4. How can we better understand our legal and economic relationship with Indigenous Peoples?

5. How can Canadians become engaged in understanding reconciliation and individual and collective responsibility?

14

The Global Indigenous
Power Shift

Our economy is at war with many forms of life on earth,
including human life. What the climate needs to avoid collapse
is a contraction in humanity's use of resources;
what our economic model demands to avoid collapse
is unfettered expansion. Only one of these sets of rules
can be changed, and it's not the laws of nature.

—NAOMI KLEIN, *This Changes Everything: Capitalism vs. the Climate*

There is an astonishingly vast spectrum of the degree of recognition of Indigenous Peoples and rights across the world. A power shift is happening in the increasing recognition of the role of Indigenous Peoples in the economic realm.

A power moment is an inception into possibility that stems from the connection between Indigenous worldview and economy that supports increasing inclusion of Indigenous thought and worldview into modernity. The concept of Indigenous power moments allows insight into the role of the Indigenous worldview and its contrast with modern economics, both national and globally. The following examples demonstrate Indigenous global power moments.

Ecuador: The Power Moment

Ecuador was the first country to recognize the rights of nature in its constitution, which was a significant power moment—a first step for humanity toward a change of the modern economic paradigm. With a high percentage of the population identifying as Indigenous, the constitution was ratified in 2008. This established a paradigm that shifted away from treating nature solely as property under the law and toward establishing a formal recognition of the rights of nature. The constitution acknowledges within it that nature in all its life forms has the right to exist, flourish, maintain, and regenerate its vital cycles and that "We—the people—have the legal authority to enforce these rights on behalf of ecosystems."[1] In the constitution, the ecosystem itself can be named as the defendant. This paradigm shift has shaped a new narrative directed at capitalism itself to level the playing field against the experience of big international corporations in the country.

The granting of constitutional rights to nature was driven largely from an Indigenous worldview and is a significant power moment to pay attention to in the contrast between the tension of mainstream economics and the need for ecological balance in humanity's economic equation.

Bolivia: The Law of the Rights of Mother Earth Power Moment

In another demonstration of a significant power moment, Bolivia, also with a majority of Indigenous Peoples, passed the Law of the Rights of Mother Earth that went into effect in 2012. This law was based on the founding principle that Mother Earth is a living being. It outlines "principles for shifting from classic development models to an integral model that is 'in harmony and balance with nature, as a means for recovering and strengthening local and ancestral knowledge and wisdom.'"[2]

In the Indigenous language, the Bolivian people call this *Pacha mama* or "Mother Earth," which inherently describes within it the human relationship to Earth that expresses "We know we cannot live without her." This understanding of ecological dependency is supported by ancient Indigenous spiritual and cultural traditions and also by contemporary science that further reveals the complex interdependence of all life on Earth. This perspective converges into the concept of "Earth jurisprudence"—the philosophy of law and human governance based on the premise that humans are only one small part of a wider community of beings and that the welfare of each member of this community is dependent on the welfare of the Earth and the ecological system as a whole. This is the economic paradigm shift of modern economics.

As a largely Indigenous-based population, Bolivia set out the process for defining this evolutionary pathway of legal rights to express itself directly into the economic field. The insertion of Earth rights into this new legal and cultural reality has implications for the field of economics. This insertion into the dominant worldview is the systematic dismantling of what is impossible from a mainstream economic worldview and acts as the inception of what is possible through a distinct legal structure and the embodiment of Indigenous worldview. This is Indigenomics.

A very important implication of the evolution of the rights of Mother Earth is that it enables the legal system to establish and maintain ecological balance by aligning human rights against the rights of all life-forms. It is this ecological balance that modern economics is in full collision with. As climate leader and activist Naomi Klein articulates, "Our economy is at war with many forms of life on earth, including human life. Only one of these sets of rules can be changed, and it's not the laws of nature."[3]

Centering these rights of nature into a legal framework is also a significant development in economics. Andrew Martin continues:

> If legal systems recognized the rights of other-than-human beings (e.g., mountains, rivers, forests and animals), courts and tribunals could deal with the fundamental issues of environmental contamination rather than being bogged down in the technical details of permitted pollutants and emissions. A rights-based approach could evaluate whether the rights of humans to clear tropical forests for beef ranching should trump the right of species in those forests to continue to exist. Instead of devising ever more complex schemes to authorize environmental damage and to trade in the right to pollute, the focus would shift to how best to maintain the quality of the relationship between ourselves and the Earth.[4]

Martin describes connecting "living well" as a way of life that seeks not to live "better" or at the cost of others and nature but in harmony with all life-forms as the foundation. 'The struggles of Indigenous people and social movements in Latin America have enabled this perspective to be enshrined within the Bolivian constitution."[5] This is a power moment. This is Indigenomics within a global context. Of particular note, Martin points out that it is the struggles of Indigenous Peoples and social movements that enabled this development.

Through this concept, the Bolivians defined Mother Earth "as a dynamic and indivisible community of all living systems and living organisms, interrelated, interdependent and complementary, which share a common destiny."[6]

Clayoquot Sound:
The War in the Woods Power Moment

Going back further in time to another power moment, the War in the Woods in Clayoquot Sound on Vancouver Island was a series of high-profile protests addressing the practice of the forestry company Macmillan Bloedel's clear-cutting forest blocks in the region in 1993. Over a thousand people were arrested protesting industrial clear-cut logging practices of the temperate old-growth rainforest, and is to date the largest act of civil disobedience in Canadian history.

What is significant about this power moment was the Indigenous leadership in these protests which sparked new global best practices for forestry based in both Indigenous knowledge and scientific practice. The Nuu chah nulth people reclaimed a stewardship role, and what emerged was a new collaborative model for co-decision-making, shaping the early days of consultation in Canada. Author and legal expert on the Indigenous relationship Bill Gallagher refers to this as a poetic wake-up and acknowledges the significance of the increasing visibility of Indigenous rights and practices:

> Meares Island, in Clayoquot Sound, is important not only because of the trees but because it is where the line has been drawn. It has become a symbol. This was a wake-up call, permeating Canadian consciousness for years to come. Hypothetically and based on mathematical extrapolation, this win fundamentally redrew the map in terms of native land rights.[7]

Nuu chah nulth inclusion in forestry and land use decision-making and planning marked the early days of the shaping of the requirement for consultation, the beginnings. That was Indigenomics and was a power moment in Canadian consciousness.

New Zealand:
The Rights of a River Power Moment

It is a highly controversial principle in human rights law that allows corporations the same rights and protections as real persons but corporations cannot be held accountable for human rights violations. What is developing globally from an Indigenous perspective is the new legal recognition of legal personhood and the rights of nature.

In a power moment, after 140 years of negotiation, the Māori tribe Whanganui Iwi won recognition for the Whanganui River, establishing that it must be treated as a living entity and granted the same legal rights as a human being. In the words of Gerrard Albert, the lead negotiator for the Whanganui Iwi:

> We have fought to find an approximation in law so that all others can understand that from our perspective treating the river as a living entity is the correct way to approach it, as an indivisible whole, instead of the traditional model for the last 100 years of treating it from a perspective of ownership and management.[8]

This distinct Māori worldview affirms the respect for life itself in the concept of *Ko au te Awa, ko te Awa ko au,* "I am the River, and the River is me," as Indigenous leader Albert articulates:

> We can trace our genealogy to the origins of the universe... and therefore rather than us being masters of the natural world, we are part of it. We want to live like that as our starting point. And that is not an anti-development, or anti-economic use of the river but to begin with the view that it is a living being, and then consider its future from that central belief.[9]

The clear distinction within this development is a starting point of connecting Earth to law and governance and business that is steeped in Indigenous worldview of recognition of life force and building economy from this pivotal principle. Other nations that have included this growing movement of rights of nature are Colombia and India, Uganda, and most recently Bangladesh.

Māori Economy Measured at
$50 billion Annually: Power Moment

Also from New Zealand, another pivotal power moment was the establishment of a clear economic marker to measure the growing strength of the Māori Indigenous economy, currently estimated as worth $50 billion annually.

The growth and development of the Māori economy has emerged from the progressive inclusion of the Indigenous worldview. According to the Chapman Tripp 2017 report, "Māori-owned businesses are unique in that they are driven not only by financial outcomes but by principles of kaitiakitanga (responsibility), manaakitanga (supporting people) and taonga tuku iho mō ngā uri whakatipu (guardianship of resources for future generations)."[10]

The Chapman Tripp report highlights key features:

The Māori economy includes a range of authorities, businesses, and employers who self-identify as Māori. Māori own a significant proportion of assets in the primary sectors: 50% of the fishing quota, 40% of forestry, 30% in lamb production, 30% in sheep and beef production, 10% in dairy production and 10% in kiwifruit production. Products from these sectors typically face the highest tariffs in our export markets.[11]

Building the features and size of the Indigenous economy draws on its characteristics of both distinction and growing strength and emerging role in the larger national economy.

United Nations Calls for
Revolutionary Thinking: Power Moment

In 2011 at Davos, then Secretary-General of the UN Ban Ki-moon called for revolutionary action and thinking to ensure an economic model for global survival to achieve sustainable development. This served as a stern warning that the past centuries of reckless consumption of resources has led to "a global suicide pact," with time running out to ensure an economic model for survival. He articulated:

All this now needs rethinking to secure the balanced development that will lift people out of poverty while protecting the planet and ecosystems that support economic growth.... It may sound strange to speak of revolution, but that is what we

need at this time. We need a revolution. Revolutionary thinking. Revolutionary action. A free market revolution for global
sustainability.[12]

Ban Ki-moon is making the call for action for the new thinking that
is required of today aligns nature with economy. This revolution will
be Indigenous led. This stern warning of the conditions of global economic suicide sees time running out. This is a call for an economic
model for survival that Ban Ki-moon refers to, an economic model to
establish a global interconnected perspective of the issue of sustainability and the threats facing our planet and to start action. This is
Indigenomics.

> "To make it happen we have to be prepared to make major
> changes—in our lifestyles, our economic models, our social
> organization, and our political life. We have to connect the
> dots between climate change and water, energy and food...
> Together, let us tear down the walls," he declared. "The walls
> between the development agenda and the climate agenda. Be-
> tween business, government and civil society. Between global
> security and global sustainability. It is good business—good
> politics—and good for society."[13]

These power moments, as outlined, have forever shifted economics
as it has been experienced to date. We cannot go backwards. We
know too much. Influenced deeply by Indigenous worldview, this
ecological rights approach is a complete break away from law, environmental regulatory systems, governance, and economy in regard
to nature viewed solely as property.

At the center of these power moments is the expression of Indigenous rights, recognition, and economy. The time is now. This is a
power moment. The evolution of Indigenous economic inclusion has
served to reshape economy from its current form. We are a powerful
people.

Examples like Chile, being the only South American country that
does not have recognition of Indigenous Peoples embedded in its
constitution, where the country sees tension in its Indigenous relationship leaving room for the continuous unfolding of Indigenous
recognition and economic inclusion—the time is now. This is a power
moment. We are a powerful people.

15

Indigenomics
and the Great Convergence

The world is being buffeted by multiple global crisis that manifests itself into a climate, financial, food, energy, institutional, cultural, ethical and spiritual crisis. These are the manifestations of unbridled consumerism and a model of society where the human being claims to be superior to Mother Earth. It is a system characterized by the domination of the economy by gigantic trans-national corporations whose targets are the accumulation of power and benefits, and for which the market values are more important than the lives of human beings and Mother Earth.

—Evo Morales, President of Bolivia,
in Deidre Fulton, "Capitalism Is Mother Earth's Cancer"[1]

The myth of this century permeating both Canadian and global consciousness is the myth of economic growth. It is central to Canadian consciousness, breeding the same response, the same mindset, and a pervasive concept of truth as produced within a singular worldview. This myth reaches the core of the evolution of Canada itself. Economics as a field has us blindly believing that corporations really do have the same status as human beings and places extraordinary belief in the invisible hand of the markets and the playing out of competition as the reason for social inequality and poverty.

This global economic myth requires us to blindly believe that there is no credible alternative to the current global economic system. This myth frames for humanity a singular narrative that growth is good, necessary, positive, and natural, and that it is the definitive

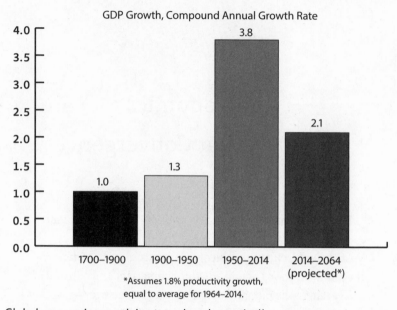

GDP Growth, Compound Annual Growth Rate

*Assumes 1.8% productivity growth, equal to average for 1964–2014.

Global economic growth is set to slow dramatically.

answer and solution to progress and development. This is the illusion. The heart of this myth must be viewed through the illusory current state of national and global economics.

It is well documented in recent years that the rate of global economic growth has slowed substantially. A 2015 McKinsey Global Analytics report sets a serious warning: "Without action, global economic growth will almost halve in the next 50 years."[2] It notes that economic growth has been exceptionally rapid over the last 50 years, but that there is no consensus on prospects for the next 50 years.

This global economic downturn is an outcome of its own worldview. The 2008 economic crash set in motion the framing of a new narrative and approach to the global economy that aimed at the very center of economics itself. At the heart of this warning is the shaping of the emerging "new economy" as an alternative future that is based on measurements beyond GDP and focused on human well-being and ecological balance.

This is a time of calling out both the state of and experience of the global economy system. A report on regenerative economy by the Capital Institute makes a fundamental point: "The current global reality is pressing up against social, environmental and economic collapse. The world needs to move beyond the standard choices of capitalism or socialism."[3] It further emphasized that the world economic system is closely related to and dependent upon the environment: "The failure of modern economic theory to acknowledge this reality has had profound consequences, not the least of which is global climate change."[4]

The article "Beyond Capitalism and Socialism" highlights a key point that the post-2008 global economic crash saw an emergence of viewing economics through a new lens as a way to address this economic growth myth—*mainly*, economic growth and dependency on the environment cannot exist in siloes. Economics is converging upon itself—a product of its own worldview.[5]

> The failure of modern economic theory to acknowledge this reality has had profound consequences, not the least of which is global climate change. The consequences of this economic worldview are vast and far reaching, encompassing a host of challenges that range from climate change to political instability.[6]

Economic Distortion:
Addressing Dysfunctionality in the New Economy

In the words of Indigenous leader President Evo Morales, past president of Bolivia:

> The world is being buffeted by multiple global crisis that manifests itself in a climate, financial, food, energy, institutional, cultural, ethical and spiritual crisis. These are the manifestations of unbridled consumerism and a model of society where the human being claims to be superior to Mother Earth... It is a system characterized by the domination of the economy by gigantic trans-national corporations whose targets are the accumulation of power and benefits, and for which the market values are more important than the lives of human beings and Mother Earth.[7]

This is an honest reflection that points to the global economic crisis humanity is facing and calls out the foundation of economic dysfunction. It is from this questioning of economic power structures and pending collapse that a new economic movement has emerged— a paradigm shift so powerful as to redefine economy, to shift from destruction to construction, and to facilitate a return to human values. What a powerful rendition of experience Fulton describes as caused from "the manifestions of unbridled consumerism." From within the dominant economic worldview stems the fragmentation of reality, separateness, and isolation that originates with the divergence from the unity of life—the very cause of economic dysfunction. It is this response to the economic dysfunction that has caused the uprising of the new regenerative economy movement.

The term *new economy* is broad reaching and can first be examined through the lens of what it does not do. The new economy does not accept the orthodox neoclassical theory that dominates economics: "Humans are perfectly rational, markets are perfectly efficient, institutions are optimally designed and economies are self-correcting equilibrium systems that invariably find a state that maximizes social welfare."[8]

The concept of "new economy" functions as a platform for bringing into visibility the source of economic dysfunction. It is here that the contrast of these economic dysfunctionalities can be named and humanity comes into its own truth, its own reflection of its own finiteness, and the oncoming collision course with its own growth measurements and worldview. What is emerging is its own truth telling, a transformative shift, a great convergence—a time where everything is up for questioning: capitalism, economics, commerce, trade, finance, and global debt. Like encountering a double-headed sea serpent, we can run away in fear or we can stand in our own truth.

The new economy movement is a collective response that enhances the function of humanity itself. This means the collective recovery from the Industrial Age to address the effects of global colonization, the equity/growth dichotomy, the experience of competition in the capital markets, and the nature of capitalism itself. As articulated by Otto Scharmer, author of "Transforming Capitalism": "Perhaps the term 'new economy' could be used more precisely to speak about transforming capitalism toward an economic system that generates well-being and prosperity for all."[9]

Regeneration: The Great Convergence

Addressing the economic myth is directly linked to our collective understanding of the inheritance of worldview. The emerging realization that the current global economic system is fundamentally dysfunctional has framed and solidified the movement of the emerging nature of a regenerative economy. This new economy is calling toward its center a return to our humanity that is based on our human values.

The activation of these human values is establishing leading economic innovations, new relationships and connectivity, and ways of seeing economy through another worldview.

The new economy movement is based on the concept of the economic regeneration process as a return to wholeness, the lack of which has been inflicted through a worldview immersed in division and separateness. This new economy narrative is centered around a driving concept: "The universal patterns and principles the cosmos uses to build stable, healthy, and sustainable systems throughout the real world can and must be used as a model for economic-system design."[10] It questions the authenticity and authority of the "corporation," challenging it to see itself as part of a bigger connected ecosystem and directly connected to nature. The irony cannot be lost that the word "corporation" originates from the word "incorporated" which means "embodied," "collected," or "united as a whole."

The Capital Institute argues what is needed now is a collective economic response:

> A new systems-based mindset built around the idea of a regenerative economy, which recognizes that the proper functioning of complex wholes, like an economy, cannot be understood without the ongoing, dynamic relationships among parts that give rise to greater wholes. In practice, this might lead to close analysis of supply chains, investigations of the effects of water use, circular economy initiatives, community economic development work or a host of other sustainability efforts.[11]

Indigenomics serves to bring into visibility economic inequality, exclusion, the conditions of economic regression, and the underdevelopment of the Indigenous economy. Understanding the development of economic inclusion must play a central role in the emerging economy.

Economic Design for an Inclusive Economy

John Fullerton, in *Regenerative Capitalism: How Universal Principles and Patterns Will Shape Our New Economy*, writes: "The universal patterns and principles the cosmos uses to build stable, healthy, and sustainable systems throughout the real world can and must be used as a model for economic-system design."[12]

The Indigenomics economic movement is an invitation to align economic practice with understanding how the universe and humanity interact. The function of the modern economy must address the myths, structures of economic exclusion, and invisibility of colonialism expressed as capitalism. In practice, this leads to closer analysis of resource use, circular economy initiatives, energy systems, inclusive collaborative community economic development work, and global sustainability efforts. This convergence toward holism brings economics into focus, its shortcomings and its shortsightedness.

In "Rethinking Prosperity: Exploring Alternatives to the Economic System," Jo Confino pointedly notes: "The collective failure to reimagine another pathway results in focusing our intellectual power on trying to prop up the existing system, even though this is akin to putting a plaster on a gaping wound."[13] It is these new pathways that form the economic convergence of today's economic design.

The Great Economic Convergence and the Transformation of Meaning

This is a time for the emerging landscape of economic transformation, a time of the great convergence! How many types of economies can we see emerging? The green economy! The circular economy! The sharing economy! The collaborative economy! The gift economy! The clean economy! The social economy! The impact economy! What are we converging upon? The characteristics of local economy and the new language of economy is shifting toward co-operation, sharing, reciprocity, collaboration, balance, harmony, co-existence, interconnection, sharing, and respect—the foundational values of humanity.

This great economic convergence of our time is a defining moment through the ages of humanity. Never in our history has there been this opportunity to redefine economy. The time is now. What a beautiful opportunity to redefine wealth! This is relational economics: an economy of connection, of relationship, of impact, and of the potential of humanity itself. This is the act of staring the double-headed sea serpent in the eye. As author and environmentalist Paul Hawken writes in *Blessed Unrest*:

Here in this emerging new economy is the collective call for accountability. It is here in the new economy where the very language of economy is being called to move beyond the constructs of supply and demand and the unyielding phenomenon of measurements and performance-based outcomes. This economic movement is a call to return to relationship based on impact. The new economy works to bring impact-driven solutions and serves to *imagine the balance of values-led, purpose-driven marketplace*. It is this recalibration of the marketplace that can demonstrate new human gains and outcomes that achieve market-rate financial returns without entirely trading off on social good. It is here impact can be measured and relationality and accountability can be formed.[14]

In Indigenous reality, there is no externalization of the market, we are the market. This is Indigenomics.

The central points of economic convergence are the redirecting of economics toward impact and meaning and the inclusion of wisdom of Indigenous economies which must shape the thinking that is required in the evolution of humanity's economic modernity. The function of the modern economy must facilitate the transition toward seeing the world in a different way—the shift to an ecologically based economic worldview in which nature is the model.

"The regenerative process that defines thriving, living systems must define the economic system itself."[15] And while the concept is not exactly new to Indigenous Peoples, this is the transition, the transformation—this is the new economic model. This is Indigenomics.

An Economy of Meaning

In "An Economy of Meaning—or Bust!" John Boik establishes the concept of an "economy of meaning" as the space for new insight into the human experience of economy: "In short, 'good' economic systems must produce *economies of meaning* that help us to help one another live meaningful lives—to meet real needs and solve problems that matter."[16] While the world is falsely divided into characterizations of countries as "developed" or "undeveloped" or "first world" or "third world" economies, the concept of economy of meaning better provides the space for our human experience.

This experience of meaning is central to understanding the convergence of the Indigenous experience of "development" and meaning.

From within the Indigenous worldview, economy must connect to our experience of our humanity, of human development, of progess to meaning and to our livelihood. In shifting the narrative of the function of economy, Manfred Max-Neef boldly positions five key operating points of economy:

- The economy is to serve the people, not the people to serve the economy.
- Development is about people and not objects.
- Growth is not the same as development, and development doesn't necessarily require growth.
- No economy is possible in the absence of ecosystem services.
- The economy is a sub-system of a larger finite system—the biosphere—hence permanent growth is impossible.[17]

Max-Neef's work positions the formation of these economic operating points that serve to evolve the modern economy to be able to address global economic dysfunction and both establish new meaning in the experience of economy and serve to address real human needs. His work shines a bright light on the concept that "good" economic systems must produce economies of meaning that help us to help one another live meaningful lives—to meet real needs and solve problems that matter. He identifies nine categories of human need in the establishment of meaning within the experience economy: subsistence, protection, affection, understanding, participation, leisure, creation, identity, and freedom.[18]

This work is a light on the pathway toward aligning the human experience of economic meaning—an economy of relationships and connectivity formed on the deeper structures of the nature of reality and human values as a function of the new economy embedded within the natural world. This is relational economics.

Today, the function of modern economy must widen the boundaries of its existing limitations and reset the rules that connect the human experience of economy. Indigenomics focuses upon the pursuit of answering these questions: How can meaning be established beyond infinite growth that Indigenomics focuses upon? How can the separation of growth and resources be aligned? It is from this economy of meaning that the new economy is converging. An economy of meaning is a return to our human experience—this is Indigenomics.

Drawing from the work of Nuu chah nulth scholar Richard Atleo:

> Today, the experience of "things fall apart" has become a global phenomenon, particularly with respect to two crises: (1) humanities relationship with humanity; (2) humanity's relationship with the environment. We are in a relationship crisis, a crisis of protocol, of relativity, connectivity stemming from a dominant global economic system—symptoms of its own worldview.[19]

There is much to be learned from within an Indigenous worldview as global economies struggle with accountability to themselves. Addressing the disconnect will require nothing less than a transformation of the dominating worldview of economy.

> It's not working! These economies that we know intuitively as Indigenous peoples we have inherited from our ancestors and through our ceremonies. These economies are increasingly becoming important as alternatives to today. Our ways of thinking and being is what allows us to be resilient as Indigenous peoples; these old ways honor our identities and our relationships to land, to each other, and to our territories. They honor our deep obligations we have to one another, and they also honor this kind of greater sense of belonging not only on planet Earth as a part of the cosmos. Indigenomics includes that level of thinking that we are not the only beings on the planet and that we belong within long lineages and lineages to come. What we do in this economic space is closely tied to the bigger picture of who we are today.[20]

This is the great convergence upon the collective human economic response—a return to relationships, to our humanity and connectivity, and to address the myth of separateness and isolation of nature from our current experience of economy. This is a time of a seismic shift, a quantum leap that points to the convergence that we as humanity are embarked upon through the emergence of modern economic meaning. Here is the intersecting space of Indigenomics, Indigenous worldview, colonialism, and economic knowledge systems based in thousands of years of relationship, connectivity, and human values.

> This new economic space is opening up out of necessity from the failings of the current economic philosophies and paradigms. The systems we have in place are showing to be deeply flawed, and in many ways, they are not working for our societies; they are not working certainly for Indigenous communities. Because of these failings, there is an opening to look at other ways of being and knowing. What is required within this new economic space is an incredible opportunity to fill it in a way that is grounded with principles that are very old. At the same time, we can bring our relative energy and context of our world today in line with that of our ancestors.[21]

The underlying principles of these emerging economic constructs parallel Indigenous values and ways of being—at the core of which are human values and a remembering of how to be in relation to each other and to the Earth. What is being named here is a value set, an outline of purpose of how we can experience economy. This is the shift to connectivity, to local relationships, to the economy of meaning. This is the Great Convergence. This is Indigenomics.

Addressing the Economic Disconnect

Economic thinking is changing. "Economic ideas matter" is advanced by Eric Beinhocker in *Evonomics*: "The writings of Adam Smith over two centuries ago still influence how people in positions of power—in government, business, and the media—think about markets, regulation, the role of the state, and other economic issues today."[22]

As humanity, we are facing a formidable economic challenge, he continues:

> The economic challenge of today is to close the disconnect between infinite growth and finite resources. Today, in the course of a year, our planet uses the natural resources of 1.5 planets. Thus, the challenge is to reframe nature as an eco-system rather than a resource. Instead of treating nature's gifts as commodities that we buy, use, and throw away, we must treat the natural world as a circular ecology that we need to cultivate and co-evolve with.[23]

What the great economic thinker Adam Smith did not account for was the growing climate pressures, resource pressures, crisis of capitalism itself, and the population demands of today that cannot be accounted for in the concept of the Invisible Hand. This is the disconnect. The human experience of economic disconnect has been and continues to be felt all over the world whether through poverty, displacement, climate change, or other ways. Perhaps, while peering into another worldview, the Nuu chah nulth peoples have accounted for the invisible hand in the concept of *hiish uk ish tsa walk*—everything is one and interconnected, which forms the basis for meaning, relationship, connectivity, and the protocol of life itself. This is the economy of meaning. This is relational economics. This is the invisible hand. This is Indigenomics.

Conclusion

Indigenomics is a contribution to a new world of thinking where economics, productivity, and prosperity are aligned with human values. It is the economy behind the economy—the values that spin the relationship between nature and human kind—the life force of intention. The concept of *hish uk ish tsa walk*—everything is one and interconnected—is the real invisible hand of the market place called Earth. Indigenomics is a return to the concept of marketplace that aligns humanity to economy—we are the marketplace.

Indigenomics is an economic platform to facilitate Indigenous economic inclusion: inclusion of worldview, inclusion with local economic development practices, and inclusion within the larger economy of this country.

Indigenomics is an infiltration into the system of neoclassical economics that, as a singular approach to economics, relates supply and demand to a human rationality and the ability to maximize utility or profit. Indigenous economics is transforming our relationship to place—as central to innovation, and driving economic solutions through design, relationships, and connectedness. Productivity is centered in community design, ecosystem-based management systems of resources, and output is *generational* management of wealth.

Indigenomics as a concept that is centered within this slowed global economic growth. It serves to highlight the contrast between worldview, economic pace, and the polarization between economic performance of humans and the environment.

Indigenomics is the convergence of the concept of the interdependence and co-evolution of human economies and natural ecosystems over time and space. Is it possible economics is growing up?

Indigenomics is a platform to facilitate the Indigenous economic relationship to collectively reimagine the future we want and redesign the systems to get us there. The pervading question in Canada today that is setting the stage for the next 150 plus years is how do we collectively get ready for the emerging potential of a $100 billion annual Indigenous economy in Canada today? This is the convergence of today, of the applied new meaning of the Indigenous economy—we are a powerful people.

Indigenomics is the landscape for economic transformation where economics and capitalism and Indigenous worldview collide. At the heart of the current global predicament of slowed growth and high conflict is a disconnect and breakdown between the real-world challenges of the widening ecological, social, material, and spiritual divide. The time is now to build a collective response to the current inquiry—to find out what is possible in the search for deeper economic meaning and the increasing relevance of the Indigenous worldview to the new economy.

Hiish uk ish tsa walk—everything is one and interconnected—this is the real invisible hand of Adam Smith. *Hiiish uk ish tsa walk* is the great ecological marketplace. This is nature's household (ecology) and humankind's household (economics).

REFLECTIVE QUESTIONS

1. How can the Indigenous concept of relational decision-making contribute to economics today?

2. How can we collectively get ready for the emerging potential of a $100 billion annual Indigenous economy in Canada today?"

3. How can humanity be better aligned to the concept of the "marketplace"?

16

A Seat at
the Economic Table

Canada is built on the wobbly structure of economic apartheid.
"This country is built on an illusion—there is no legal ground here."
—Louise Mandell, Mandell Pinder lawyer

Indigenomics acts as a vehicle for building understanding, creating meaning, and expressing the significance of the growth of the Indigenous economy today. It is a response to the slow realization of the significance of Indigenous values and the inception into economic theory that allows for another worldview. Indigenous wisdom and knowledge systems are a valuable source of economic innovation and inspiration for Indigenous economic empowerment today.

Indigenomics questions what is beyond Adam Smith's Theory of Moral Sentiments and the human values and principles associated within the current neoclassical economic system. As the arguments that uphold the dominant economic worldview are beginning to form cracks, an Indigenous worldview that embraces intergenerational responsibility begins to make more sense to shape the future of humanity that is on a crash course with its own construct of money, meaning, and metrics. So, like the story of the sea serpent, we have two choices: we can run away in fear or we can stand in our own truth. This time calls on us to be asking the difficult questions while exploring the discomfort zone of a colonial legacy. Directly in front of us is the question, What new thinking is required of us today to shape an economy of meaning?

According to Canadian history, we are not supposed to be here as Indigenous Peoples. We were supposed to have been exterminated through policy and through the tools of genocide and assimilation. But the fact that there is a blossoming, evolving Indigenous population and the uprise of the Indigenous economy today speaks to the need to build a nation-to-nation relationship, based on economic empowerment and recognition. Indigenomics is about shifting our modern reality as Indigenous Peoples—emerging from hundreds of years of colonization toward a positive, healthy, and whole reality.

Through the rise of Indigenous economic empowerment, this power shift in the economic landscape is shaping the future of this country. The way forward must build understanding and awareness, supporting the development of new economic and financial tools and structures for stronger economic outcomes. This is modern Indigenous economic design.

The foundation of Indigenomics is shaping a new narrative that we can cause a different economic course of action and establish the modern relational economy based on our collective future that highlights Indigenous knowledge systems and ways of knowing. These new actions can form and create new measurements and meaning of economy. This is Indigenomics.

Indigenous business leader Shannin Metatawabin speaks of the growing success of the Indigenous economy:

> In order for us to be fully successful and for us to be at a place that meets our population growth, we need to support Indigenous economic development today. We need to invest in its processes and structures today so that we can grow the Indigenous economy to its maximum capacity. That means providing the capital that is required to ensure that every Indigenous entrepreneur that wants to start a business has access to capital and the supports in place to ensure that they are the most successful.[1]

A national narrative built upon the foundation of Indigenous economic success is pivotal to economic reconciliation today. Indigenous economic success must be foundational to the narrative of this country and an underlying intention in both policy and investment into the Indigenous economy. "We are successful in our resilience as Indigenous Peoples. We are successful in our historical business networks, our connectivity. We can bring this into the light after hundreds of years—this speaks to these relationships, to the quality of connectivity, and to the success of our worldview over time."[2]

An invisible thread ties the development of Canada's economy to the emerging Indigenous economy. This thread focuses on supporting economic opportunities to right our past relationship and to continue defining our current legal, financial, and economic relationship in the national economic modernity. Economic reconciliation must occur within the balance sheet of this country. Now is the time to build a collective toolbox to seek answers to our deepest questions: why, how, and what is possible in the search for deeper meaning and relevance to the economy?

Indigenomics is a platform for future pacing the reality of the emerging Indigenous economy. Establishing a collective response means addressing the foundation of Indigenous economic growth. A $100 billion Indigenous economy is only an outcome of Indigenous economic inclusion.

The Collective Indigenomics Economic Pathway

Describing the collective economic pathway must shape key economic outcomes for the emerging Indigenous economy. Indigenomics as a construct of modern Indigenous economic design posits that the uprising of the emerging Indigenous design must focus on constructive generative economic design. To shape Indigenous economic design requires the following:

- Addressing the potential of a market failure. Through taking a minimal response to the growing Indigenous economy, the upswing of Indigenous economic growth will be continuously threatened
- Addressing the structure of the long-term economic regression of Indigenous nations through the financial and economic relationship to the state and regions
- Addressing the structure of the long-term underdevelopment of the Indian reservation currently under the Indian Act
- Addressing the conditions for a holistic market response to facilitate the emergence of a $100 billion Indigenous economy

- Facilitating Call to Action #92 with industry as established with the Truth and Reconciliation Commission
- Establishing a baseline measurement of national and regional annual Indigenous economic strength, outcomes, and performance
- Facilitating the Indigenous right to an economy and the implementation of UNDRIP
- Building the financial architecture for the ongoing capitalization of the Indigenous economy
- Facilitating new actions and principles that support the underlying premise: "We are in a legal and an economic relationship with Indigenous peoples."
- Facilitating an Indigenomics Economic Freedom Index as a structure to measure Indigenous economic self-determination and reduction of fiscal dependency

In the absence of a process for constructive modern Indigenous economic designs lies the instructions on how to fail to grow the Indigenous economy. The consequence of failing to act on the upswing of this growth is a critical consideration facing this country. Failure to support the design, continued Indigenous economic regression, or not addressing the conditions for market failure are all on the wrong side of the economic equation. A lack of Indigenous economic design looks like the following:

1. Do nothing.
2. Act like business as usual.
3. Ignore the rise of Indigenous economic empowerment and new economic space of the Indigenous economy.
4. Continue to measure only the "socio-economic gap."
5. Fund from a problem perspective. Ensure the "social cart" pulls the "economic horse."

To ensure a successful Indigenous economic foundation for design requires new understanding of the idea that Canada is in both a legal and an economic relationship with Indigenous Peoples. Let's create the conditions for Indigenous economic success.

Indigenomics is a callout, an invitation to the four corners of the Earth, for an awakening, for Indigenous economic empowerment and inclusion. An invisible hand is shaping this country—Indigenomics. The economic imperative of our country and within the world begs the question: Is this going to be the time we almost got it and did nothing? Or will this be the time we created mechanisms for Indigenous economic growth, when we built from the foundational truth that the Indigenous economy is directly connected to the national GDP?

Indigenomics is both a callout and an invitation into the new economic reality of the potential of a $100 billion Indigenous economy.

This is the challenge of our time—inclusivity at the economic table. The time is right. Let us work collectively to get out of the margins, to address the illusion, and to collectively create the conditions for Indigenous economic success.

The invitation is here—to build the collective modern response to now, the response to the growing Indigenous economy. Let's have the courage to do this together. Indigenous Peoples are taking a seat at the economic table of today. It's time! Who wants to play Indigenomics? Let's have the courage to do this together.

The Universal Declaration of the Rights of Mother Earth

The Universal Declaration of the Rights of Mother Earth, presented by Bolivia for UN recognition, outlines some of the fundamental rights of Earth.

1. Mother Earth is a **living being**.
2. Mother Earth is a **unique, indivisible, self-regulating community of interrelated beings** that sustains, contains, and reproduces all beings.
3. Each being is defined by its relationships as an **integral part** of Mother Earth.
4. The inherent rights of Mother Earth are inalienable in that they arise from the **same source as existence**.
5. **Mother Earth and all beings are entitled to all the inherent rights** recognized in this Declaration without distinction of any kind, such as may be made between organic and inorganic beings, species, origin, use to human beings, or any other status.
6. Just as human beings have human rights, **all other beings also have rights** which are specific to their species or kind and appropriate for their role and function within the communities within which they exist.
7. The rights of each being are limited by the rights of other beings, and **any conflict between their rights must be resolved in a way that maintains the integrity, balance, and health of Mother Earth.**

Truth and Reconcilation
Commision Call to Action #92

#92. We call upon the corporate sector in Canada to adopt the *United Nations Declaration on the Rights of Indigenous Peoples* as a reconciliation framework and to apply its principles, norms, and standards to corporate policy and core operational activities involving Indigenous peoples and their lands and resources. This would include, but not be limited to, the following:

   i. Commit to meaningful consultation, building respectful relationships, and obtaining the free, prior, and informed consent of Indigenous peoples before proceeding with economic development projects.

   ii. Ensure that Aboriginal peoples have equitable access to jobs, training, and education opportunities in the corporate sector, and that Aboriginal communities gain long-term sustainable benefits from economic development projects.

   iii. Provide education for management and staff on the history of Aboriginal peoples, including the history and legacy of residential schools, the *United Nations Declaration on the Rights of Indigenous Peoples*, Treaties and Aboriginal rights, Indigenous law, and Aboriginal–Crown relations. This will require skills-based training in intercultural competency, conflict resolution, human rights, and anti-racism.

Notes

Chapter 1: Through the Lens of Worldview

1. Leroy Little Bear, "Aboriginal Relationships to the Land and Resources," in *Sacred Lands: Aboriginal World Views, Claims, and Conflicts*, Jill E. Oakes, Ricke Riewe, Kathi Kinew, and Elaine Maloney, eds., Canadian Circumpolar Institute Press, 1998, p. 31.
2. Ibid., p. 26.
3. Frantz Fanon, *The Wretched of the Earth*, François Maspero, 1961, p. 158.
4. Little Bear, p. 32.
5. Dara Kelly interview, 2018.
6. Rucha Chitnis, "Changing the Narrative: Film Series on Public TV Reveals Profound Insights on the Significance of Sacred Lands and Indigenous Worldviews," *Intercontinental Cry*, modified May 15, 2015; intercontinentalcry.org/changing-the-narrative-27940/. Accessed August 15, 2019.
7. Duane Townsend, *The Independent*, April 17, 2019.
8. National Archives of Canada, Record Group 10, volume 6810, file 470-2-3, volume 7, pp. 55 (L-3) and 63 (N-3) 1920.
9. Indigenous Services Canada, Auditor General, *Report 5: Socioeconomic Gaps on First Nations Reserves*, 2018.
10. Lucy Sholey, "Incomprehensible Failure": Auditor General Says Federal Government Not Improving Life for Indigenous People," *APTN*, May 29, 2018. aptnnews.ca/2018/05/29/incomprehensible-failure-auditor-general-says-federal-government-not-improving-life-for-indigenous-people
11. Amy Judd, "Neskonlith Indian Band Issues Eviction Notice to Imperial Metals," *Global News* August 12, 2014; globalnews.ca/news/1505507/neskonlith-indian-band-issues-eviction-notice-to-imperial-metals/

12. Jenna Winton, "Eriel Deranger: Fighting the World's Largest Industrial Project, the Alberta Tar Sands," *Culture Survivor*, February 14, 2014; culturalsurvival.org/news/eriel-deranger-fighting-worlds-largest-industrial-project-alberta-tar-sands. Accessed August 15, 2019.

13. Frances Gardiner Davenport, *European Treaties Bearing on the History of the United States and Its Dependencies to 1648*, Vol. 1, Carnegie Institution of Washington, 1917, pp. 20–26.

14. Ibid.

15. Tonya Gonnella Frichner, "The 'Preliminary Study' on the Doctrine of Discovery," 2010; researchgate.net/publication/49111954_The_Preliminary_Study_on_the_Doctrine_of_Discovery

16. E. Richard Atleo, *Tsawalk: A Nuu-chah-nulth Worldview*, UBC Press, 2007, p. 20.

Chapter 2: The Nature of Wealth

1. Barry Gough, *Father Brabant and the Hesquiat of Vancouver Island: Study Sessions*, CCHA, 1983; cchahistory.ca/journal/CCHA1983-84/Gough.pdf, p. 557. Accessed March 20, 2019.

2. Ibid., p. 558.

3. Ibid.

4. Ibid., p. 562.

5. Ibid.

6. Dara Kelly interview, 2018.

7. Ibid.

8. Ibid.

9. Naomi Klein, "Dancing the World into Being: A Conversation with Idle No More's Leane Simpson," *Yes Magazine*, March 5, 2013. Accessed August 15, 2019.

10. Robert B. Moore, "Racism in the English Language" (February 9, 2006); writework.com/essay/racism-english-language-robert-b-moore, October 28, 2019.

11. Charelle Evelyn, "Better Relationships Between Government and First Nations Possible," *Business in Vancouver*, September 10, 2015.

12. Kristy Kirkup, "60% of First Nation Children on Reserve Live in Poverty, Institute Says." *CBC News*, May 17, 2016; cbc.ca/news/indigenous/institute-says-60-percent-fn-children-on-reserve-live-in-poverty-1.3585105

13. Jordon Press, "Over 80% of Reserves Have Median Income Below Poverty Line, Census Data Shows," *Global News: Canadian Press*, October 10, 2017; globalnews.ca/news/3795083/reserves-poverty-line-census/. Accessed August 15, 2019.

14. Kelly interview, 2018.

15. Clint Davis interview.

16. Facing History and Ourselves, *Stolen Lives: The Indigenous Peoples of Canada and the Indian Residential Schools, The Indian Act and the Indian Residential Schools*, December 2016.

17. Mark Anielski, "Why Forests Matter: The Indigenomics of Forests," Anielski Management, November 5, 2015; anielski.com/why-forests -matter-the-indigenomics-of-forests/

Chapter 3: The Landscape of Indigenous Worldview

1. Dara Kelly interview, 2018.

2. Ibid.

3. Ibid.

4. Māori Marsden and T. A. Henare, *Kaitiakitanga: A Definitive Introduction to the Holistic World View of the Māori*, New Zealand, Ministry for the Environment, Wellington, 1992.

5. E. Richard Atleo, *Tsawalk: A Nuu-chah-nulth Worldview*, UBC Press, 2007, p. xi.

6. Ibid.

7. Ibid., p. 117.

8. Leroy Little Bear, "Aboriginal Relationships to the Land and Resources," in *Sacred Lands*, Kathi Kinew, Elaine L. Maloney, Jill Oakes, Rick Riewe, eds., University of Alberta Press, 1998, p.18.

9. Ibid., p. 35.

10. Wilma Mankiller, *Good Reads*; goodreads.com/quotes/7894694-in -iroquois-society-leaders-are-encouraged-to-remember-seven -generations

11. *David Suzuki: The Autobiography*, chapter 6, Haida Gwaii and the Stein Valley, erenow.net/biographies/david-suzuki-the-autobiography/6 .php

12. Crane Bear, unpublished.

13. Wagamese, goodreads.com.

14. Atleo, *Tsawalk*, p. xix.

15. Ibid., p. 92.

16. Ibid., p. 5.

17. Kimberly M. Blaeser, "Like 'Reeds through the Ribs of a Basket': Native Women Weaving Stories," in *Other Sisterhoods: Literary Theory and U.S. Women of Colour*, Sandra Kumamoto Stanley, ed., University of Illinois, 1998, p. 268.

18. Atleo, *Tsawalk*, p. 117.

19. George Clutesi, *Potlatch*, Gray's Publishing, 1969, p. 80.

20. Steven Point, "Nationhood Keynote Multi-Community Governance Forum," YouTube video, posted by BC Treaty Commission, June 14, 2016.
21. Mel Bazil, Gitxsan and Wetsuweten, source unknown.
22. Leroy Little Bear, "Aboriginal Paradigms: Implications for Relationships to Land and Treaty Making," in Kerry Wilkins, ed., *Advancing Aboriginal Claims: Visions, Strategies, Directions*, 2004, p. 27.
23. David Bohm, *Wholeness and the Implicate Order*, Routledge, 1980, p. 126.
24. Ibid., p. 128.
25. Little Bear, "Aboriginal Paradigms."
26. Little Bear, "Aboriginal Relationships," p. 18.
27. Ibid., p. 6.
28. Oren Lyons, "Second Special Edition on Freedom of Religion: A Time for Justice," *Native American Rights Fund Legal Review*, 18, no. 2, 1993. Accessed August 15, 2019.
29. Harold Cardinal, *The Rebirth of Canada's Indians*, Hurtig Publishers, 1977, p. 84.
30. Kepä Maly, "MÄLAMA PONO I KA "ÄINA: An Overview of the Hawaiian Cultural Landscape"; studylib.net/doc/8252028/mälama-pono-i-ka--äina--an-overview-of-the-hawaiian-cultural 2001. Accessed August 29, 2019.
31. Marsha C. Bol, ed., *Stars Above, Earth Below: American Indians and Nature*, Roberts Rinehart, 1998.
32. Kanaka Bar Indian Band, "The Memorial to Sir Wilfrid Laurier: Commemorating the 100th Year Anniversary"; kanakabarband.ca /downloads/memorial-to-sir-wilfred-laurier.pdf, p. 17. Accessed August 29, 2019.
33. Gary Witherspoon, *Language and Art in the Navajo Universe*, University of Michigan Press, 1977, p. 27.
34. Atleo, *Tsawalk*, p. 130.
35. E. Richard Atleo, *Principles of Tsawalk: An Indigenous Approach to Global Crisis*, UBC Press, 2012, p. 54.
36. Jane Haladay, "The Grandmother Language: Writing Community Process," in Jeannette Armstrong, *Whispering in Shadows*, Theytus Books, 2000.
37. Ibid., p. 14.
38. Ibid., p. 13.
39. Ibid., p. 15.
40. Ibid.
41. Haladay, pp. 175–76.
42. Kelly interview, 2018.
43. Atleo, *Tsawalk*, p. 72.
44. Excerpt from Ktunaxa Creation Story, unpublished.

45. Atleo, *Tsawalk*, p. 96.

46. Atleo, *Principles of Tsawalk*, p. 20.

47. Blaeser, p. 39.

48. Haladay, p. 191.

49. Blaeser, p. 268.

50. Little Bear, *Aboriginal Paradigms*, p. 30.

51. Ibid., p. 12.

52. *Brainy Quote*, "Pope Benedict XVI," www.brainyquote.com/quotes /pope_benedict_xvi_586416?src=t_ethics. Accessed August 29, 2019.

Chapter 4: "But I Was Never Taught This in School"

1. Loney, Shaun. *An Army of Problem Solvers*, self-published, n.d., p. 21.

2. UBCIC timeline; ubcic.bc.ca/timeline.

3. Kathleen Mahoney, "The Roadblock to Reconciliation: Canada's Origin Story Is False," *Globe and Mail*, May 10, 2016.

4. Ibid.

5. Ibid.

6. Ibid.

Chapter 5: The Indigenous Economy

1. Richard Thompson, "New Economy Trailblazer: Melinda Loubacan-Massimo," modified November 7, 2017; rabble.ca/blogs/bloggers /kairos-witness/2017/11/new-economy-trailblazer-melina-laboucan -massimo. Accessed August 15, 2019.

2. Dara Kelly interview, 2018.

3. Ibid.

4. Ibid.

5. Shannin Metatawabin interview.

6. Clint Davis interview.

Chapter 6: Indian Act Economics

1. John Borrows, *Seven Generations, Seven Teachings: Ending the Indian Act*, Research Paper for the National Centre for First Nations Governance, May, 2008.

2. Lynn Gehl and Heather Majuary, "First Nations Finance Their Own Demise Through Land Claims Process," *Ricochet Media*, February 2, 2015.

3. Clint Davis interview.

4. Kanaka Bar Indian Band, "The Memorial to Sir Wilfrid Laurier: Commemorating the 100th Year Anniversary"; kanakabarband.ca /downloads/memorial-to-sir-wilfred-laurier.pdf. Accessed August 29, 2019.

5. Ibid.

6. Davis interview.

7. Arthur Manuel, *Unsettling Canada: A National Wake-Up Call*, Between the Lines, April 30 2015.

8. Ibid.

9. Harold Calla, source unknown.

10. Bill Gallagher, *Resource Rulers: Fortune and Folly on Canada's Road to Resources*, Bill Gallagher, publisher, 2012, p. 29.

11. canada.ca/en/indigenous-northern-affairs.html

12. Ibid.

Chapter 7: The Indigenomics Power Center

1. Don Richardson interview.

2. Bill Gallagher, "'Reset' on Canada's Roads to Resources," *Corporate Knights*, March 26, 2019; corporateknights.com/channels/leadership /reset-canadas-road-resources-15535997/. Accessed August 29, 2019.

3. Ibid.

4. Shannin Metatawabin interview.

5. Clint Davis interview.

6. Gallagher, *Corporate Knights*.

7. Bill Gallagher interview.

8. Justin Trudeau, Prime Minister of Canada, "Government of Canada to create Recognition and Implementation of Rights Framework," February 14, 2018; pm.gc.ca/en/news/news-releases/2018/02/14 /government-canada-create-recognition-and-implementation -rights. Accessed August 29, 2019.

9. Gallagher interview.

10. Office of the Premier, news.gov.bc.ca/releases/2017PREM0083-001562.

11. Ibid.

Chapter 8: The Dependancy Illusion

1. Kathleen Mahoney, "The Roadblock to Reconciliation: Canada's Origin Story Is False," *Globe and Mail*, May 10, 2016.

2. Kathleen Mahoney, "The Rule of Law in Canada 150 Years After Confederation: Re-Imagining the Rule of Law and Recognizing Indigenous Peoples as Founders of Canada," ABlawg.ca, March 29, 2017.

3. Shaun Loney, *An Army of Problem Solvers*, self-published, n.d., p. 40.

4. Allan Clarke, "First Nations Should Have Control of Their Own Revenues," *Policy Options*, December 12, 2018.

5. Ibid.

6. fraserinstitute.org/article/taxpayers-are-generous-first-nations

7. Tom Flanagan, *The Costs of the Canadian Government's Reconciliation Framework for First Nations*, Fraser Institute, November 6, 2018; fraserinstitute.org/studies/costs-of-the-canadian-governments -reconciliation-framework-for-first-nations

8. Dru Oja Jay, "What If Natives Stop Subsidizing Canada," *Media Co-op*, January 2013.

9. JP Gladu, "Indigenous Diversity at All Levels of the Energy Industry Opens Doors," *The Future Economy*, November 13, 2018; thefuture economy.ca/spotlights/energy/jp-gladu/

10. Harry Swain and Jim Baillie, "The Trudeau Government Signs on to Give Aboriginal Veto Rights Nobody Else Has," *Financial Post*, January 26, 2018.

11. Ibid.

12. C.J.C. McLachlin, *Haida Nation v British Columbia* (Minister of Forests), [2004].

13. Roshan Danesh, "Editorial: Confronting Myths About Indigenous Consent," Indian Residential School History and Dialogue Centre, October 22, 2019; irshdc.ubc.ca/2019/10/22/editorial-confronting -myths-about-indigenous-consent

14. Ibid.

15. Jon Tockman, "Distinguishing Consent from Veto in an Era of Reconciliation," *Policy Note*, April 10, 2017.

Chapter 9: The Power Play

1. Indigenous Foundations, Royal Proclamation; indigenous foundations.arts.ubc.ca/royal_proclamation_1763

2. Bill Gallagher, *Resource Reckoning: A Strategist's Guide from A to Z*, Bill Gallagher, 2018.

3. Ibid.

4. Ibid.

5. Ken Coates, "Indigenous Support for Development Is Being Heard," MacDonald-Laurier Institute, June 27, 2016.

6. ratcliff.com/sites/default/files/publications/The%20Aboriginal%20 Right%20to%20Sell%20Fish.PDF.

7. Bill Gallagher interview.

Chapter 10: The Power Shift: A Seat at the Economic Table

1. Remarks by President Obama in Address to the Parliament of Canada, June 29, 2016; obamawhitehouse.archives.gov/the-press -office/2016/06/30/remarks-president-obama-address-parliament -canada

2. P. Colorado and D. Collins, "Western Scientific Colonialism: The Re-emergence of Native Science," *Practice: The Journal of Politics, Psychology, Sociology and Culture*, Winter 1987, pp. 51–65.

3. Roshan Danesh, "There Should Be No Confusion about Aboriginal Consent," *Times Colonist*, October 23, 2016.

4. Otto Scharmer, "The Blind Spot: Uncovering the Grammar of the Social Field," *Huffington Post*, June 6, 2015.

5. Ken Coates, "Indigenous Support for Development Is Being Heard," MacDonald-Laurier Institute, June 27, 2016.

6. Shannin Metatawabin interview.

7. Sean Kavanagh, "Kapyong Barracks Signed Over to First Nations Group, *CBC News*, August 30, 2019; cbc.ca/news/canada/manitoba/kapyong-barracks-signing-ceremony

8. Dianne Francis, "Canada's Unfinished Business with First Nations Is an Economic Failure." *Financial Post*, November 29, 2014.

9. Don Richardson interview.

10. Doug Eyford, *A New Direction: Advancing Aboriginal and Treaty Rights*, Government of Canada, February 20, 2015; rcaanc-cirnac.gc.ca/eng/1426169199009/1529420750631?wbdisable=true

11. Bill Gallagher interview.

12. Martha Trolan, "B.C. First Nation Leads with Green Technology, Sustainability," *CBC*, April 14, 2017; cbc.ca/news/indigenous/tsou-ke-nation-green-energy-leaders-1.4067833

13. Jake MacDonald, "How a BC Native Band Went from Poverty to Prosperity," *Globe and Mail*, May 29, 2014.

14. Richardson interview.

15. Canadian Chamber of Commerce Report, "Aboriginal Edge: How Aboriginal Peoples and Natural Resource Businesses Are Forging a New Competitive Advantage," August 2015.

16. Gallagher interview.

17. Richardson interview.

18. Danesh, "There Should Be No Confusion."

19. Darrell Beaulieu, Denendeh Investments Incorporated; pnwer.org/uploads/2/3/2/9/23295822/beaulieu_-_aboriginal_economic_development.pdf.

20. Ibid.

21. Metatawabin interview.

22. Gallagher interview.

23. Ibid.

24. Ken Coates, "Indigenous Support for Development Is Being Heard," MacDonald-Laurier Institute, June 27, 2016.

25. Metatawabin interview.

26. Clint Davis interview.

27. Gallagher interview.

28. Danesh, "There Should Be No Confusion." About Aboriginal Consent,"

29. Dianne Francis, "Canada's Unfinished Business with First Nations Is an Economic Failure." *Financial Post*, November 29, 2014.

30. Dan Healing, "Federal Government Blasted Over Native Land Claim Inaction," *Calgary Herald*, April 21, 2015.

31. Ibid.

32. Ed John, "Mining Is Key to BC's Future, Done Right," *The Tyee*, March 30 2011.

33. Gloria Galloway, "Canadian First Nations Becoming Less Prosperous," *Globe and Mail*, May 15, 2018.

34. Metatawabin interview.

35. Coates, "Indigenous Support."

36. Danesh, "There Should Be No Confusion."

37. Metatawabin interview.

38. Great Bear Rainforest (Forest Management) Act; canlii.ca/t/8z8m

39. Richardson interview.

40. Irvin Studin, "Confronting the Aboriginal Question," *National Post*, August 19, 2015.

41. Shaun Loney, *An Army of Problem Solvers*, self-published, n.d., p. 21.

Chapter 11: The Emerging Modern Indigenous Economy

1. JP Gladu, "The Promising Future of Indigenous Canadian Business," *Huffington Post*, January 7, 2017.

2. Ibid.

3. Ibid.

4. S. Gulati and D. Burleton, *Estimating the Size of the Aboriginal Market in Canada*, Toronto: TD Economics, 2011.

5. JP Gladu interview.

6. JP Gladu, "Indigenous Diversity at All Levels of the Energy Industry Opens Doors," *The Future Economy*, November 13, 2018; thefuture economy.ca/spotlights/energy/jp-gladu/

7. Don Richardson interview.

8. *The Aboriginal Economic Benchmarking Report*, National Aboriginal Economic Development Board, June 2012; naedb-cndea.com/reports /the-aboriginal-economic-benchmarking-report.pdf, p. 7.

9. *The Aboriginal Economic Benchmarking Report*, National Aboriginal Economic Development Board, June 2015; naedb-cndea.com/reports /NAEDB-progress-report-june-2015.pdf.

10. *The Aboriginal Economic Benchmarking Report*, National Aboriginal Economic Development Board, June 2019; naedb-cndea.com/wp

-content/uploads/2019/06/NIEDB-2019-Indigenous-Economic
-Progress-Report.pdf.

11. Fiscal Realities Economists, *Reconciliation: Growing Canada's Economy by $27.7 Billion*, National Indigenous Economic Development Board, November 2016.

12. Dawn Leech and Terrance Paul, *National Reconciliation: The $27.7 Billion Argument for Ending Economic Marginalization*, National Indigenous Economic Development Board, modified November 21, 2016; naedb -cndea.com/en/national-reconciliation-the-27-7-billion-argument -for-ending-economic-marginalization. Accessed August 15, 2019.

13. Ibid.

14. Ibid.

15. Ibid.

16. Atlantic Policy Congress, *Indigenous Economy in Atlantic Canada Exceeds $1 Billion in Annual Spending*, Nation Talk, April 27, 2016; nationtalk.ca/story/1-14-billion-strong-indigenous-economic -performance-in-atlantic-canada.

17. *$1.14 Billion Strong: Indigenous Economic Performance in Atlantic Canada*, APCFNC, March 31, 2016; apcfnc.ca/wp-content/uploads /2020/06/FINAL_WEBSITE_VERSION_1_14_Billion_Strong _June_1_2016.pdf.

18. Atlantic Provinces Economic Council, *Highlighting Successful Atlantic Indigenous Businesses*, June 19, 2019; apec-econ.ca/publications/view /?do-load=1&publication.id=381.

19. Brandon University, "Brandon University Report Details Indigenous Economic Impact in Manitoba for the First Time," January 10, 2019; brandonu.ca/news/2019/01/10/brandon-university-report-details -indigenous-economic-impact-in-manitoba-for-the-first-time.

20. NACCA, The National Aboriginal Capital Corporations Association (NACCA) and Business Development Bank of Canada (BDC) Report, March 7, 2017; nacca.ca/report-shows-aboriginal-entrepreneurs-face -significant-barriers-in-financial-ecosystem.

21. Gladu, "The Promising Future."

22. Gladu, "Indigenous Diversity."

23. Gladu interview.

24. Clint Davis interview.

Chapter 12: Indigenomics and the Unfolding Media Narrative

1. "Huge Lineups for Toronto's New Anishinaabe Restaurant," *Blog Toronto*, May 1, 2017.

2. Hilary Bird, "Fort McKay First Nation to Put $350M into Suncor

Oilsands Tank Farm," *CBC News*, September 6, 2016; cbc.ca/news /canada/calgary/first-nation-puts-350m-oilsands-project-1.3749640. Accessed August 15, 2019.

3. Joshua Ostroff, "Canada's First Indigenous Business District Is Coming to Toronto," *Huffington Post*, January 12, 2017.

4. Judith Lavoie, "B.C. Coastal First Nations Conservation Economy Booming: New Report," *The Narwhal*, September 16, 2016; desmog .ca/2016/09/16/bc-coastal-first-nations-conservation-economy -booming-new-report.

5. Elizabeth McSheffrey, "Indigenous Law Banishes a Giant B.C. Mine," *National Observer*, April 21, 2017.

6. Sarah Petrescu, "Island First Nation Bans Mining and Clearcutting," *Times Colonist*, January 27, 2017.

7. Shayne Morrow, "Tseshaht Demands Termination of Raven Coal Project," *Ha-Shilth-Sa*, June 1, 2015.

8. Sunny Freeman, "Canada, Aboriginal Tension Erupting Over Resource Development, Study Suggests," *Huffington Post*, October 30, 2013.

9. Ibid.

10. Gloria Galloway, "Wynne Pushes Ring of Fire Chiefs for Decision on Regional Road," *Globe and Mail*, May 11, 2017.

11. Hilary Beaumont, "How Energy Companies Woo First Nations on Controversial Project," *Vice Magazine*, November 30, 2016.

12. Gordon Hoekstra and Larry Pynn, "First Nations Staking Their Claims in the B.C. Economy," *Vancouver Sun*, June 4, 2015.

13. Ian Gill, "No Wealth, No Justice in $1 Billion LNG Offer to First Nation Band," *The Tyee*, May 5, 2019.

14. Kris Sims, "Our Warrior Problem: Militant Natives Are Causing Trouble and They Aren't Going Away," *London Free Press*, November 3, 2013.

15. Emma Gilchrist, "'This Is a Watershed Moment': Chief Vows to Be Arrested as Fight Against Site C Dam Ramps Up," *The Narwhal*, July 12, 2015; desmog.ca/2015/07/12/watershed-moment-chief-vows-be -arrested-fight-against-site-c-dam-scales

16. Judith Sayers, "Northern Gateway Decision a Huge Victory for First Nations Rights," *The Tyee*. July 1, 2016.

17. Russell Hixson, "Court Decision Affirms First Nations Landowner Rights," *Journal of Commerce*, April 21, 2015.

18. Robson Fletcher, "Tsuut'ina First Nation Plans Major Commercial Development at Calgary's Southwest Edge," *CBC News*, July 11, 2016; cbc.ca/news/canada/calgary/tsuutina-development-calgary -southwest-ring-road-1.3673753.

19. Martha Trolan, "B.C. First Nation Leads with Green Technology, Sustainability," *CBC News*, April 14, 2017; cbc.ca/news/indigenous /tsou-ke-nation-green-energy-leaders-1.4067833.

20. Conrad Black, "This Isn't Religion, It's Madness," *National Post*, May 27, 2016.

21. Truth and Reconciliation Commission of Canada, "Calls to Action"; trc .ca/assets/pdf/Calls_to_Action_English2.pdf. Accessed June 3, 2018.

22. Sherry Narine, "Calgary Raises Treaty 7 Flag in a Permanent Move of Reconciliation," *Windspeaker*, March 23, 2017.

23. Peter Meiszner, "City of Vancouver Formally Declares City Is on Unceded Aboriginal Territory," *Global News*, June 25, 2014.

24. Trevor Jang, "Energy Projects Fuel Tension Between Trudeau and First Nations," *Discourse Media*, October 20, 2016; towardreconciliation .discoursemedia.org/investigation/energy-projects-fuel-tension.

25. Austin Grabish, "It's a Breach of Treaty": Manitoba First Nations Want Promised Land," *CBC News*, May 29, 2017; cbc.ca/news/ canada/manitoba/treaty-land-entitlement-committee-manitoba-1 .4136260.

26. Dallas McQuarrie, "Elsipogtog Files Aboriginal Title Claim for Siknik-tuk to Protect Territory," *Media Co-op*, November 10, 2016.

27. CBC, "Huu-ay-aht First Nation Buys 11 Properties in Bamfield," *All Points West*, January 23, 2016; cbc.ca/news/canada/british-columbia /bamfield-first-nation-1.3416342.

28. Alec MacPherson, "Reducing Aboriginal Unemployment Could Bring $90 Billion in Economic Benefits to Saskatchewan," *Star Phoenix*, June 15, 2016.

29. Monica Lamb-Yorski, "Uncertainty Surrounds Rights and Title Decision," *Williams Lake Tribunal*, February 24, 2015.

30. Peter O'Neil, "B.C. Proposal Aims to Have First Nations Own Chunks of Major Projects," *Vancouver Sun*, January 20, 2016.

31. Dan George, "First Nations Are Eyeing Equity Ownership," *The Province*, February 22, 2019.

32. Don Richardson interview.

Chapter 13: Building a Toolbox for Economic Reconciliation

1. JP Gladu, "Economic Equality Must Be a Part of Indigenous Reconcili-ation," *Globe and Mail*, August 1, 2016.

2. Kathleen Mahoney, "The Roadblock to Reconciliation: Canada's Origin Story Is False," *Globe and Mail*, May 10, 2016.

3. Ibid.

4. Ibid.

5. JP Gladue, "The Promising Future of Indigenous Canadian Business," *Huffington Post*, January 7, 2017; huffingtonpost.ca/lougheed-leader ship/Indigenous-canadian-business_b_8930776.html.

6. Shaun Loney, *An Army of Problem Solvers*, self-published, n.d., p. 22.

7. Trina Roache, "Boosting First Nation Economies a Part of Reconciliation," *APTN National News*, June 26, 2015.

8. Emily Garr Pacetti, "The Five Characteristics of an Inclusive Economy: Getting Beyond the Equity-Growth Dichotomy," Rockefeller Foundation, December 13, 2016.

9. JP Gladu interview.

10. Ibid.

11. Dawn Madahbee Leach, "The Case for Economic Reconciliation in Canada," *Say Magazine*, December 23, 2016.

12. Gladu interview.

Chapter 14: The Global Indigenous Power Shift

1. Constitution of Equador; constituteproject.org/constitution/Ecuador _2008.pdf, August 12, 2019.

2. Andrew Martin, *The Universal Declaration of the Rights of Mother Earth*, *Collective Evolution*, August 24, 2014, p. 1; collective-evolution .com/2014/08/24/the-universal-declaration-of-the-rights-of-mother -earth.

3. Ibid.

4. Ibid.

5. Ibid.

6. Seán Dagan Wood, *Positive.News*, June 12, 2011; positive.news/society /justice/bolivia-to-give-legal-rights-to-the-earth.

7. Bill Gallagher, *Resource Rulers: Fortune and Folly on Canada's Road to Resources*, self-published, 2012, p. 258.

8. Eleanor Ainge Roy, "New Zealand River Granted Same Legal Rights as Human Being," *The Guardian*, March 16, 2017.

9. Ibid.

10. Chapman Tripp, "Trends and Insights," "Te Ao Māori" Pipiri, 2017, p. 5; chapmantripp.com/Publication%20PDFs/2017%20Chapman%20 Tripp%20Te%20Ao%20Maori%20-%20trends%20and%20insights %20E-VERSION.pdf.

11. Ibid., p. 3.

12. *UN News*, "Warning of 'Global Suicide': Ban Calls for Revolution to Ensure Sustainable Development," January 2011; news.un.org/en /story/2011/01/365432.

13. Ibid.

Chapter 15: Indigenomics and the Great Convergence

1. Deidre Fulton, "Capitalism Is Mother Earth's Cancer," *Common Dreams*, October 12, 2015. Accessed August 15, 2019.

2. Richard Dobbs, Andrew Jordan, Eric Labaye, James Maniyika, Jaana Remes, Johnathon Woetzel, "Can Long-term Global Growth Be Saved?" McKinsey Global Institute, 2015; mckinsey.com/global-themes/employment-and-growth/can-long-term-global-growth-be-saved. Accessed August 15, 2019.

3. John Fullerton, in *Regenerative Capitalism: How Universal Principles and Patterns Will Shape Our New Economy*, April 2015; capitalinstitute.org/wp-content/uploads/2015/04/2015-Regenerative-Capitalism-4-20-15-final.pdf.

4. Ibid.

5. Jo Confino, "Beyond Capitalism and Socialism: Could a New Economic Approach Save the Planet?" *The Guardian*, April 21, 2015.

6. Fullerton, *Regenerative Capitalism*.

7. Fulton, "Capitalism Is Mother Earth's Cancer."

8. Eric Beinhocker, "How the Profound Changes in Economics Make Left Versus Right Debates Irrelevant," *Evonomics*, n.d.; evonomics.com/the-deep-and-profound-changes-in-economics-thinking. Accessed August 16, 2019.

9. Otto Scharmer, "Transforming Capitalism: 7 Acupuncture Points," *Huffington Post*, April 1, 2017.

10. Fullerton, *Regenerative Capitalism*.

11. Confino, "Beyond Capitalism and Socialism."

12. Fullerton, *Regenerative Capitalism*, p. 9.

13. Jo Confino, "Rethinking Prosperity: Exploring Alternatives to the Economic System," *The Guardian*, September 15, 2015.

14. Paul Hawken, *Blessed Unrest: How the Largest Social Movement in History Is Restoring Grace, Justice, and Beauty to the World*, Penguin, 2008.

15. John Fullerton and Hunter Lovins, "Creating a Regenerative Economy to Transform Global Finance into a Force for Good," *Fast Company*, October 29, 2013.

16. John Boik, "An Economy of Meaning—or Bust," *Common Dreams*. Accessed August 16, 2019.

17. Manfred Max-Neef, "The World on a Collision Course and the Need for a New Economy," Contribution to the 2009 Royal Colloquium, *Ambio*, 39(3), May 2010, pp. 200–210.

18. Ibid.

19. E. Richard Atleo, *Principles of Tsawalk: An Indigenous Approach to Global Crisis*, UBC Press, 2012, p. 6.
20. Dara Kelly interview, 2018.
21. Ibid.
22. Beinhocker, *Evonomics*.
23. Ibid.

Chapter 16: A Seat at the Economic Table

1. Shannin Metatawabin interview.
2. Dara Kelly interview, 2018.

Index

About the Author

CAROL ANNE HILTON, MBA, is the CEO and Founder of The Indigenomics Institute and the Global Center of Indigenomics. Carol Anne is a dynamic national Indigenous business leader, author, speaker, and senior adviser with an international Masters Degree in Business Management (MBA) from the University of Hertfordshire, England. Carol Anne is of Nuu chah nulth descent from the Hesquiaht Nation on Vancouver Island.

Carol Anne has led the establishment of a line of thought called #indigenomics—growing from a single word to an entire movement which focuses on the re-building and strengthening of Indigenous economies. Carol Anne is an adjunct professor at Royal Roads University School of Business.

Carol Anne's work has been recognized with the 2020 BC Achievement Foundation's Award of Distinction in Indigenous Business as well as the national Excellence in Aboriginal Relations Award from the Canadian Council for Aboriginal Business. Carol Anne served on the BC Emerging Economy Taskforce, the BC Indigenous Business and Investment Council, and was the only Indigenous person appointed to the Canadian Economic Growth Council. Carol Anne currently serves as a Director on the McGill University Institute for the Study of Canada and the BC Digital Supercluster.

ABOUT NEW SOCIETY PUBLISHERS

New Society Publishers is an activist, solutions-oriented publisher focused on publishing books for a world of change. Our books offer tips, tools, and insights from leading experts in sustainable building, homesteading, climate change, environment, conscientious commerce, renewable energy, and more—positive solutions for troubled times.

We're proud to hold to the highest environmental and social standards of any publisher in North America. When you buy New Society books, you are part of the solution!

- We print all our books in North America, never overseas

- All our books are printed on **100% post-consumer recycled paper**, processed chlorine-free, with low-VOC vegetable-based inks (since 2002)

- Our corporate structure is an innovative employee shareholder agreement, so we're one-third employee-owned (since 2015)

- We're carbon-neutral (since 2006)

- We're certified as a B Corporation (since 2016)

At New Society Publishers, we care deeply about *what* we publish—but also about *how* we do business.

Download our catalog at https://newsociety.com/Our-Catalog or for a printed copy please email info@newsocietypub.com or call 1-800-567-6772 ext 111.

ENVIRONMENTAL BENEFITS STATEMENT

New Society Publishers saved the following resources by printing the pages of this book on chlorine free paper made with 100% post-consumer waste.

TREES	WATER	ENERGY	SOLID WASTE	GREENHOUSE GASES
44	**3,500**	**18**	**150**	**18,800**
FULLY GROWN	GALLONS	MILLION BTUs	POUNDS	POUNDS

Environmental impact estimates were made using the Environmental Paper Network Paper Calculator 4.0. For more information visit www.papercalculator.org.

MIX
Paper from responsible sources
FSC® C016245

new society
PUBLISHERS
www.newsociety.com